# HOLD THE FORT - OVERCOMING TEMPTATIONS

# HOLD THE FORT - OVERCOMING TEMPTATIONS

JAMES FABIYI

authorHOUSE®

AuthorHouse™ LLC
1663 Liberty Drive
Bloomington, IN 47403
www.authorhouse.com
Phone: 1-800-839-8640

Published by AuthorHouse  11/05/2013

ISBN: 978-1-4918-3374-2 (sc)
ISBN: 978-1-4918-3376-6 (hc)
ISBN: 978-1-4918-3375-9 (e)

Library of Congress Control Number: 2013919882

# Table of Contents

# Preface

More than a decade ago, I read a story about a young Austrian woman. She was married to one of the soldiers who fought for their country during the failed invasion of Russia in 1812 by Napoleon, King of France. At the end of that war, the surviving soldiers went back to their respective home countries and to their loved ones. The Austrian lady, excited to see her husband again, decided to wear her wedding dress in order to welcome him. After all these years of separation and probably silence, she wanted to make herself beautiful for him. She wanted to be ready for his return and give him the love that she guessed he had been starving for. She wanted to make him feel good at home. But, she waited and waited and waited for that husband who seemed lost in the war fields only to learn a few days later that he would never return to her again. He had been swallowed by the cold hands of death in a war that had proven to be futile. After such a long wait and silence, she would never see her beloved again. It is sad that our young Austrian lady had spent so much time and energy of remaining faithful to a man who ended up dying on the battlefield. All that effort seemed to be in vain. Or was it really vain?

A woman's wedding dress is a thing of pride; it helps her recall the sweet memories of the outset of her marriage. If this young lady had messed up her body with another man, she would not have been bold enough to put on her wedding dress to welcome her beloved. If she had jettisoned him in pursuit of another man, probably a rich man like King Solomon, she would have not cared to wait for him. She would have shunned that idea. Had she behaved like Demas who because of the love for this present

*James Fabiyi*

evil world forsook Apostle Paul, she probably would have been in the arms of another man or she would have pretended to love her husband and devised cunning plans to get away from him.

If this lady can be this patient, making herself ready for her beloved though not sure he would ever come back home alive, then why do we, Christians, find it so difficult to wait for the King of kings who promised that he was coming back to take us with Him? Jesus promised that He will come back. He promised that upon His return, we (true believers) would head back with him to the City that He has prepared for us, the New Jerusalem (John 14:1-3). The Holy Spirit through the Apostles confirmed that (1 Thessalonians 4:16-17; 2 Peter 3:1-4). So, we know it's true.

> "Let not your heart be troubled: ye believe in God, believe also in me. In my Father's house are many mansions: if it were not so, I would have told you. I go to prepare a place for you. And if I go and prepare a place for you, I will come again, and receive you unto myself; that where I am, there ye may be also" (John 14:1-3).

> "For the Lord himself shall descend from heaven with a shout, with the voice of the archangel, and with the trump of God: and the dead in Christ shall rise first: Then we which are alive and remain shall be caught up together with them in the clouds, to meet the Lord in the air: and so shall we ever be with the Lord. Wherefore comfort one another with these words" (1 Thessalonians 4:16-18).

> "This second epistle, beloved, I now write unto you; in both which I stir up your pure minds by way of remembrance: That ye may be mindful of the words which were spoken before by the holy prophets, and of the commandment of us the apostles of the Lord and Saviour: Knowing this first, that there shall come

*in the last days scoffers, walking after their own
lusts, And saying, Where is the promise of his coming?
for since the fathers fell asleep, all things continue
as they were from the beginning of the creation"* (2
Peter 3:1-4).

The Shulamite lady, in the Song of Solomon, remained hopeful
and faithful to her beloved Shepherd boy, knowing for sure that
one day, all the troubles and temptations would be over, and
she would be able to live a settled life and have a peaceful
home with whom her soul loved. She did not allow fund, fame,
and female in the palace of Solomon to lure her to go contrary
to her wish. The question is, will you be ready when the Lord
comes back?

The collection of messages in this book titled "Hold the Fort:
Overcoming Temptation" was the exposition on the book of *Song
of Solomon* delivered in eighteen series, during the Sunday Bible
Teaching, to the Congregation of the Revival Pioneers Ministry
International in the United States of America in 2009. However,
I first prepared and preached the sermons on this book to the
Revival Pioneers Ministry International members at Akure, Ondo
State, Nigeria in 2002. The difference between the messages
preached in these two places was that I had little access to
various Bible commentaries in 2002. During the preparation of
the messages in 2009, I consulted many commentaries, critically
examined various opinions, interpretations, and applications,
and took notice of where they differed from my understanding,
interpretation and application of the book of *Song of Solomon*. I
must confess that there are about two commentators who tried
their best to break away from the traditional (long-established,
conventional, popular) view. One of these, though totally not a
deviation presented a great and strong introductory explanation
on Song of Solomon. The presentations in this book in your hand
are basically in support of these two commentators.

# Chapter One

## Introduction to the Book of Song of Solomon

There are two main reasons for our consideration of this book. First, throughout the universal church, the Song of Solomon is the least referred book in the Bible. The most widely quoted verses are *Song of Solomon 1:5-6; 2:15; 3:1-2; and 8:6-7*. The second reason is that its traditional interpretation has been misleading countless number of people. Indeed, this book has been widely viewed as a book that reveals and signifies the relationship between Christ and the Church with King Solomon being portrayed as a type of Christ and the Shulamite lady as a type of the Church. This is the traditional view. However, a critical meditation and thorough consideration of the principals or individuals in this book reveals that Solomon is a type of Satan, the tempter of the Shulamite lady, trying to lure her into marrying him. He used words that a holy God would not and will not use because of their seductive connotations. The Shulamite lady can indeed be referred to as a type of the Church of Christ. The Shepherd boy, the sincere lover of the Shulamite lady can be taken as a type of Jesus Christ. The Court ladies can be referred to as the unbelievers who know not their right from the left. Initially, they were helping Solomon to persuade the Shulamite lady to succumb to his advances but were later convinced by the love she had for her Shepherd boy and agreed with her to help seek for her lover. Listen to this:

*"I charge you, O daughters of Jerusalem, if ye find my beloved, that ye tell him, that I am sick of love. What is thy beloved more than another beloved, O thou fairest among women? what is thy beloved more than another beloved, that thou dost so charge us? My beloved is white and ruddy, the chiefest among ten thousand. His head is as the most fine gold, his locks are bushy, and black as a raven. His eyes are as the eyes of doves by the rivers of waters, washed with milk, and fitly set. His cheeks are as a bed of spices, as sweet flowers: his lips like lilies, dropping sweet smelling myrrh. His hands are as gold rings set with the beryl: his belly is as bright ivory overlaid with sapphires. His legs are as pillars of marble, set upon sockets of fine gold: his countenance is as Lebanon, excellent as the cedars. His mouth is most sweet: yea, he is altogether lovely. This is my beloved, and this is my friend, O daughters of Jerusalem. Whither is thy beloved gone, O thou fairest among women? whither is thy beloved turned aside? that we may seek him with thee." (Song of Solomon 5:8-16; 6:1).*

The brethren of the Shulamite lady are in this text likened to be the caring and heavenly minded ministers and Christians who are trying their best to set various boundaries and limitations for us so that we do not derail from our racing track. The watch men are the preachers or overseers who watch over the flock of Christ (Ezekiel 3:17; 33:7-9; Acts 20:28). However, the watch men in the Song of Solomon seemed to be the wicked, unconcerned, self-centred people (Isaiah 56:10-11; Song of Solomon 5:7). More emphasis is laid on these essential points in the text that you are about to read.

The Song of Solomon is one of the smallest and seemingly most difficult to understand among the books of the Bible. The exact time that Solomon penned this sacred song is not known. Some think that he wrote it after his recovery from backsliding just like he did in the book of Ecclesiastes as a proof of his repentance from the strongholds of lust for women and worship of idols. He thereby testified about his deplorable and depraved conditions as a backslider.

The actions in the Song of Solomon are too interwoven but a careful analysis of it can help the readers to rightly divide it into acts and scenes. This book reveals two opposite acts which are love and lust displayed by the Shulamite lady and Solomon respectively. The Church's love for her Bridegroom is a central gem as declared in Matthew Chapter 22 verses 36-38:

> *"Then one of them, which was a lawyer, asked him a question, tempting him, and saying, Master, which is the great commandment in the law? Jesus said unto him, Thou shalt love the Lord thy God with all thy heart, and with all thy soul, and with all thy mind. This is the first and great commandment."*

Unfortunately, the unbelievers and careless so-called Christians do allow themselves to be dragged into the mud of the sin of immorality through the lust of the eyes. Lust of the eyes is a great weapon that Satan uses to enslave man into the grave of darkness. Solomon lamented in the book of Ecclesiastes 2:10-11 that ". . . *whatsoever mine eyes desired I kept not from them, I withheld not my heart from any joy; for my heart rejoiced in all my labour: and this was my portion of all my labour. Then I looked on all the works that my hands had wrought, and on the labour that I had laboured to do: and, behold, all was vanity and vexation of spirit, and there was no profit under the sun."* Job had solution to this problem; *"I made a covenant with mine eyes; why then should I think upon a maid?"* We are warned not to destroy ourselves with the lust of flesh and lust of the eyes. *"Love not the world, neither the things that are in the world. If any man loves the world, the love of the Father is not in him. For all that is in the world, the lust of the flesh, and the lust of the eyes, and the pride of life, is not of the Father, but is of the world."*

The lust of the flesh includes unchaste desires, thoughts, words, and actions, rape, fornication, adultery, incest, sodomy, and so on. The lust of the eyes implies unchaste and lascivious looks, eyes full of adultery. If you look at a woman with lustful eyes, then your eyes are evil and your whole body shall be full of darkness (Matthew 6:23).

In the light of what has been said about love and lust, it should not appear absurd to think that God gave us this book to help us not to follow the pernicious way of backslidden Solomon but pursue steadfastness and chastity in this adulterous generation like the Shulamite lady. We should not allow the Solomons of this world to despise our youth. *Keep yourself* pure. Consequently, we shall do well to consider the values of this book. It is a revelation of the characteristics of genuine love that must be exhibited between husband and wife. In his notes on Song of Solomon, Dr. Thomas L. Constable outlined that this book "reveals four things about human love: foundation of love, strength of love, how to love and fruits of love." I hereby shed more light on these points.

First of all, it reveals the foundation of love. The deeper and stronger the foundation of a building is, the longer the lifespan of such a building is. It must be recalled that the Bible says "If the foundations be destroyed, what can the righteous do?" (Psalm 11:3). In the book of Song of Solomon, it is clear that mutual satisfaction is the bedrock of love. The Shulamite lady and the Shepherd boy find perfect rest in each other; the lady refused to find her rest in Solomon's glory and gold. She has supreme affection for the one who satisfies her ultimately, which is the basis for long lasting marriage. In addition, the love that exists between the duo is exclusive. They saw each other as the only one that is enough for them. Someone once stated that the foundation of love is mutual satisfaction that is both complementary and exclusive.

Secondly, this book reveals the strength of love. It is the strongest glue that binds a man and a woman together in marriage for life.

> *"Set me as a seal upon thine heart, as a seal upon thine arm: for love is strong as death; jealousy is cruel as the grave: the coals thereof are coals of fire, which hath a most vehement flame. Many waters cannot quench love, neither can the floods drown it: if a man would give all the substance of his house for love, it would utterly be contemned."* (Song 8:6-7)

This type of love was found in Ruth towards her mother-in-law as written in the book of Ruth 1:1-18:

> *"Now it came to pass in the days when the judges ruled, that there was a famine in the land. And a certain man of Bethlehemjudah went to sojourn in the country of Moab, he, and his wife, and his two sons. And the name of the man was Elimelech, and the name of his wife Naomi, and the name of his two sons Mahlon and Chilion, Ephrathites of Bethlehemjudah. And they came into the country of Moab, and continued there. And Elimelech Naomi's husband died; and she was left, and her two sons. And they took them wives of the women of Moab; the name of the one was Orpah, and the name of the other Ruth: and they dwelled there about ten years. And Mahlon and Chilion died also both of them; and the woman was left of her two sons and her husband. Then she arose with her daughters in law, that she might return from the country of Moab: for she had heard in the country of Moab how that the LORD had visited his people in giving them bread. Wherefore she went forth out of the place where she was, and her two daughters in law with her; and they went on the way to return unto the land of Judah. And Naomi said unto her two daughters in law, Go, return each to her mother's*

house: the LORD deal kindly with you, as ye have dealt with the dead, and with me. The LORD grant you that ye may find rest, each of you in the house of her husband. Then she kissed them; and they lifted up their voice, and wept.

And they said unto her, surely we will return with thee unto thy people. And Naomi said, Turn again, my daughters: why will ye go with me? are there yet any more sons in my womb, that they may be your husbands? Turn again, my daughters, go your way; for I am too old to have an husband. If I should say, I have hope, if I should have an husband also to night, and should also bear sons;

Would ye tarry for them till they were grown? would ye stay for them from having husbands? nay, my daughters; for it grieveth me much for your sakes that the hand of the LORD is gone out against me. And they lifted up their voice, and wept again: and Orpah kissed her mother in law; but Ruth clave unto her.

And she said, Behold, thy sister in law is gone back unto her people, and unto her gods: return thou after thy sister in law. And Ruth said, Intreat me not to leave thee, or to return from following after thee: for whither thou goest, I will go; and where thou lodgest, I will lodge: thy people shall be my people, and thy God my God: Where thou diest, will I die, and there will I be buried: the LORD do so to me, and more also, if ought but death part thee and me. When she saw that she was stedfastly minded to go with her, then she left speaking unto her." (Ruth 1:1-18)

This satisfying and steadfast love will guide against intruders, breakdown in communication, lost of affection, and consequently against divorce.

Thirdly, this book shows how to love. Despite the fact that this young lady was kidnapped by Solomon and imprisoned in the palace of gold against her will, her song every moment centred on her beloved Shepherd boy. Love is not only in action, it is also in word. We are to communicate it to our spouse that we love and care much for him or her. When you travel, try and take time to call or send text message to your spouse expressing your love for him or her. Tell him or her that she is the most beautiful, virtuous, and caring person you have ever met. In addition, pledge your allegiance to loving him or her to the end in spite of various experiences and circumstances of life. Most married women kill their marriages because they refused to reach out their hand and voice of love to their husbands. They always expect the initiative to come from the husband; thinking that if they are the first to do that, it may connote that women are weaker vessels. Remember, the Shulamite lady took the initiative in reaching out to her beloved Shepherd boy with a passion. Likewise, the shepherd boy tried his best by risking his life to find his beloved Shulamite lady by coming to the house of her captor, Solomon. Both responded to each other by yielding and trusting. Indeed, this reveals the usual actions and reactions between male and female in love but should continue even after many years of their marriage.

Fourthly, this book reveals the fruits of love. In true love, there is a perfect rest and assurance which no boisterous storm outside or within can destroy. In true love there is an everlasting joy which no poverty, problem, predicament, disaster, disease, demon can turn sour. Also, in true love there is courage. The Shulamite lady and the shepherd boy gained strength from their love to face circumstances boldly and to recover from their separation caused by a powerful and influential king of Israel. In true love, there is no divorce or separation in the dictionary of both the husband and wife until death do them part.

The book of Song of Solomon is one of the poetical books of the Bible. Its subject is the deepest emotion of the soul.

King Solomon is known to be the author of the book (Song of Solomon 1:1; 1 Kings 4:32; Ecclesiastes 12:9). However, one critic urges that "it is psychologically impossible that Solomon would have satirized himself by writing a poem to show how his artful blandishments to seduce a virtuous woman utterly failed." Nevertheless, we must understand that the Scripture is a book to guide, correct, and reprove man (1 Corinthians 10:6, 11, 12; 1 Timothy 3:16-17).

The Song of Solomon was written in a dramatic style. However, this is a true story about a fair maiden who has developed a sexually pure relationship with a young shepherd. Then one day the king notices her beauty and desires to have her. The king can provide pleasure and luxury, but the shepherd is capable of building a relationship. The shepherd cares about her heart and soul, while the king cares only about her body. She must make her choice between a common labourer who offers her true love and a wealthy king who offers only sensual love. This poem is a romantic one in which Solomon had erotic love for the Shulamite lady. One of the greatest lessons that this book teaches us is about practical righteousness exemplified by a young maiden who was subjected to the strongest temptation by the one who occupied the highest position in the land of Israel.

## The Prelude to the Book of Song of Solomon

The book of Song of Solomon has some characters which need to be identified in order to enhance its proper interpretation and application; they are:

1. King Solomon
2. The Shulamite lady
3. Shepherd lover of the Shulamite lady
4. The court-ladies of Jerusalem
5. Brothers of the Shulamite lady
6. Queens and concubines
7. Villagers

8. Inhabitants of Jerusalem
9. The watchmen

There are many interpretations of this book. The literal interpretation maintains that the primary object of the poem is to present pure ideal human love and by means of this example give a lesson in practical righteousness. The allegorical interpretation embraces the idea that this story refers to Jehovah and Israel (The Jewish view), Christ and the church (the Protestant view) in the bond of love. Lastly, the spiritual and typical regards it as a type of Solomon's wedding, or as a type between Christ and the Gentiles or the church. Both the typical and allegorical bring Jehovah and Christ to the level of a seducer and put words of coarse, unrefined flattery on their lips. God said *"now when I passed by thee, and looked upon thee, behold, thy time was the time of love; and I spread my skirt over thee, and covered thy nakedness: yea, I sware unto thee, and entered into a covenant with thee, saith the Lord GOD, and thou becamest mine"* (Ezekiel 16:8); not describe the nakedness of a woman.

## The Purpose of the Book of Song of Solomon

1. To expose the weakness of Solomon and his disobedience to God's instruction of keeping the Law. Here, we see the fall of a preacher doing things that are contrary to his message. He forgot that God had used him to preach against lusting after women (Prov. 6:20-29: *My son, keep thy father's commandment, and forsake not the law of thy mother: Bind them continually upon thine heart, and tie them about thy neck. When thou goest, it shall lead thee; when thou sleepest, it shall keep thee; and when thou awakest, it shall talk with thee. For the commandment is a lamp; and the law is light; and reproofs of instruction are the way of life: To keep thee from the evil woman, from the flattery of the tongue of a strange woman. Lust not after her beauty in thine*

9

*heart; neither let her take thee with her eyelids. For by means of a whorish woman a man is brought to a piece of bread: and the adulteress will hunt for the precious life. Can a man take fire in his bosom, and his clothes not be burned? Can one go upon hot coals, and his feet not be burned? So he that goeth in to his neighbour's wife; whosoever toucheth her shall not be innocent).*

No wonder, the Spirit of God through the Apostle Paul declared: *"For if I build again the things which I destroyed, I make myself a transgressor"* (Galatians 2:20). For Solomon, it was easier preached than done; he became the defaulter of his ministry. It is a pity in our generation that most pastors who preach against immorality are also guilty of the same act just like Solomon. These pastors hide under the lie that the Holy Spirit is the one leading them to act in such a way. And after they might have raped (defiled) innocent souls, they use the Holy Spirit and the Bible to threaten their victims not to tell anyone. Another important lesson from Proverbs 6:20-29 is that the adulteress will hunt for the precious life. The satanic agents in our churches and communities will always hunt for the precious soul, wealthy men, political leaders, and highly respected pastors. Our pastors must be very careful not to fall into the trap of the adulterous women. Always remember that beauty is deceitful; most of the agents of darkness that are in our churches are not revealing themselves as ugly, dirty girls but beautiful, gorgeously dressed girls. Our Christian brothers in their offices must be very careful and not be carried away with the beauty or talking eyes of their secretaries. "Lust not after her beauty in thine heart; neither let her take thee with her eyelids" (Proverbs 6:25).

2. To give insight into the genuine love of a young lady (the Shulamite) to her espoused or betrothed man despite the allurement of a wealthy king to steal her love: Song

of Solomon 1:1-4 (the lady), Song of Solomon 1:9-11 (Solomon); Jeremiah 2:2; 31:34-4; Deuteronomy 7:6-8; Isaiah 54:5. Watch out for gold, guy (man) or girls, and glory which will always try to blindfold your eyes from making the right decision.

3.  To show how king Solomon tried to lure the young lady into forgetting her betrothed man and selling her love to him. This, he did with sweet and enticing words. For example, Solomon flattered her by saying *"Behold, thou art fair, my love; behold, thou art fair; thou hast doves' eyes within thy locks: thy hair is as a flock of goats, that appear from mount Gilead. Thy teeth are like a flock of sheep that are even shorn, which came up from the washing; whereof every one bear twins, and none is barren among them. Thy lips are like a thread of scarlet, and thy speech is comely: thy temples are like a piece of a pomegranate within thy locks. Thy neck is like the tower of David builded for an armoury, whereon there hang a thousand bucklers, all shields of mighty men. Thy two breasts are like two young roes that are twins, which feed among the lilies"* (Song of Solomon 4:1-5). *"Return, return, O Shulamite; return, return, that we may look upon thee. What will ye see in the Shulamite* [said by King Solomon]*? As it were the company of two armies"* (Song of Solomon 6:13). However, she responded *"I am my beloved's, and his desire is toward me"* (Song of Solomon 7:10).

4.  To help us understand that troubles and inconveniences will be parts of our experiences as we seek to identify with our bridegroom. This is revealed in the lady's dreams.

# The Parts of Each Character in the Book

## Part One:

- ➤ **Scene One**
- ❖ The Shulamite lady:
    - ✓ Her imagination of the shepherd lover: Song of Solomon 1:2-4a
    - ✓ Her answers to the Court ladies: Song of Solomon 1:5-6
    - ✓ Court ladies interjected her conversation: Song of Solomon 1:5b
    - ✓ Her dialogue to the Shepherd lover: Song of Solomon 1:7
- ❖ The Court ladies: they speak to the Shulamite lady: Song of Solomon 1:5b, 8

- ➤ **Scene Two**:
- ❖ Solomon admired the beauty of the Shulamite lady: Song of Solomon 1:9-10; 15; 2:2
- ❖ The Court ladies: they speak to the Shulamite lady: Song of Solomon 1:11
- ❖ The Shulamite lady:
    - ✓ Her imagination of the Shepherd lover: Song of Solomon 1:12-14
    - ✓ Her imagination of her future with the Shepherd lover: Song of Solomon 1:16-17
    - ✓ The Shulamite lady to the king: Song of Solomon 2:1
    - ✓ The Shulamite lady, thinking of the Shepherd lover: Song of Solomon 2:3-6

- ➤ **Scene Three**:
After dinner, the Shulamite lady is prepared for bed by her attendants. She has wisely chosen to sleep alone.
- ❖ The Shulamite lady: the Shulamite lady to the maidens of Jerusalem: Song of Solomon 2:7-17

➤ **Scene Four**:
During the Shulamite lady sleep, she dreams.

❖ The Shulamite lady:
   ✓ Her dream: Song of Solomon 3:1-4
   ✓ The Shulamite lady to the maidens of Jerusalem: Song of Solomon 3:5

## Part Two

➤ **Scene One: Jerusalem**
The detail account on how King Solomon brought the Shulamite lady into his palace. It happened that as the king and his entourage are returning to Jerusalem, they pass by the side of the Shulamite lady where she cares for the sheep in the wilderness. Solomon exercised his power as king to force the Shulamite lady into marriage.

❖ Shulamite lady ask about the entourage that is drawing closer to her: Song of Solomon 3:6
❖ One of the inhabitants of Jerusalem answer her question: Song of Solomon 3:7-11

➤ **Scene Two**:
The king is back in his palace. Though he has an opportunity to have a conversation with the Shulamite lady, he again expresses his desire for her because of her physical appearance.

❖ The king to the Shulamite lady: Song of Solomon 4:1-5,7
❖ The Shulamite lady to the king: Song of Solomon 4:16

## Scene Three: Garden
The Shulamite lady was likened to the natural beauty of a garden or park just to flatter her. It is surely tempting for her to choose a life full of pleasure in the palace rather than to deal with the hard work that a marriage to the shepherd could bring.

❖ The Shulamite lady, remembering the shepherd: Song of Solomon 4:8-5:1a

### Scene Four: Shulamite's Palace Bedchamber
The Shulamite has returned to the palace where she is having a restless night.
❖ The Shulamite lady's dream: Song of Solomon 5:2-7

## Part Three

➢ **Scene One: Shulamite's Palace Room**
The Shulamite awakens without having seen her beloved in her dream.
❖ The Shulamite lady speaks to the court ladies: Song of Solomon 5:8, 10-16; 6:2-3
❖ The Court ladies: speak to the Shulamite lady: Song of Solomon 5:9; 6:1

### Scene Two: Palace Hall
❖ Solomon:
  ✓ The king to the Shulamite lady: Song of Solomon 6:4-9; 7:6-9a
  ✓ The king to the queens and concubines: Song of Solomon 6:11-12
  ✓ The king, his queens and concubines to the exiting Shulamite lady: Song of Solomon 6:13a
  ✓ King Solomon talking to the Shulamite: Song of Solomon 7:1-9
❖ The Court ladies: the queens and concubines to the king: Song of Solomon 6:10;
❖ The Shulamite lady:
  ✓ The Shulamite lady: Song of Solomon 6:13b the Shulamite to the king: Song of Solomon 7:9b-10
  ✓ The Shulamite to the entering shepherd: Song of Solomon 7:11-8:2
  ✓ The Shulamite to the maidens of Jerusalem: Song of Solomon 8:3-4

**Scene Three: Shepherd's Village**

The Shulamite returns to her village and enjoys her wedding procession.

❖ Villagers: to the Shulamite lady: Song of Solomon 8:5a

❖ The Shepherd boy: the Shepherd to the Shulamite: 8: Song of Solomon 5b-7

**Scene Four: Wedding Banquet**

This is surely a similar scene to the first one in the play, but the king's tents have been replaced with a feast among the vineyards and orchards.

❖ As the family and friends gather, the Shulamite lady speaks to her brothers and guests: 8:8-10

❖ The Shulamite lady sends a message to King Solomon: 8:11-12

❖ The Shepherd to the Shulamite lady: 8:13

❖ The Shulamite lady and the Shepherd finally tie the knot: 8:14

# Chapter Two

## Panting for Stronger Relationship

*"Let him kiss me with the kisses of his mouth: for thy love is better than wine. Because of the savour of thy good ointments thy name is as ointment poured forth, therefore do the virgins love thee. Draw me, we will run after thee: the king hath brought me into his chambers: we will be glad and rejoice in thee, we will remember thy love more than wine: the upright love thee."* (Song of Solomon 1:2-4)

Our study is centred on the drama (scene one) that took place on the first day of the Shulamite lady in the court of Solomon in Jerusalem. She was separated from her shepherd lover by Solomon. However, her passion and pleasure were to be rescued by her lover (the shepherd lover) from the hand of her kidnapper (Solomon). At this point, she refused to be won by the glory of Solomon's mansion and comfort of the palace.

The first scene starts with the Shulamite lady being taken into the apartments of the king. As she is being carried, she cries and expresses her deep love for her lover, the shepherd boy. From this study, we shall see an expression of sincere desires, loves, and affections for only one man—her truly espoused shepherd lover. Remember, the church is the espoused wife of the bridegroom.

*"And there came unto me one of the seven angels which had the seven vials full of the seven last plagues, and talked with me, saying, Come hither, I will shew thee the bride, the Lamb's wife. (Rev 21:9).*

*For I am jealous over you with godly jealousy: for I have espoused you to one husband, that I may present you as a chaste virgin to Christ."* (2 Corinthians 11:2)

We will do well in this present, pernicious, polluted time never to forget and forsake our Shepherd Lover—Jesus Christ because of the love for the things of this world (2 Timothy 4:10).

## Expression of Sincere Love

Desire to be kissed by the Shepherd lover: Song 1:2a

As a tired traveller in a burning desert is longing for water to soothe his dried soul, the Shulamite lady longs to be kissed by her lover. That longing represents the love that she feels for the shepherd. Indeed, kissing is the physical expression of love between two people but it can also have different meanings.

1.  Kissing is a symbol of love between married people. Mouth to mouth kissing is a token of love that only exists between two mutually and sexually attracted lovers. During kissing, there is a chemical in the saliva that is passed from man to a woman that causes sexual sensation, so the woman would always be attracted to the man who always kisses her.

    In my culture, we believe that when children born by the same parents eat from the same plate especially sharing meat by one cutting it with teeth while the other picks and eats it they tend to have filial love for one another. This could be scientifically explained based on the chemical that they exchange through saliva.

The types of kisses that exist between the non-sexually attracted people include mouth to feet: *"Thou gavest me no kiss: but this woman since the time I came in hath not ceased to kiss my feet."* (Luke 7:45), mouth to cheek, and mouth to hand. Originally, these different types of kisses were practiced by individuals who were not in wed locks. Unfortunately, kissing has been abused in our society whereby mouth to mouth has become the predominant type of kissing among same sex and opposite sex humans. Individuals who are not married will kiss each other on the mouth thus sharing their saliva, thereby experiencing an intimacy that was only reserved to married people. No wonder, sexual immorality prevails in our modern age.

> *"For at the window of my house I looked through my casement, And beheld among the simple ones, I discerned among the youths, a young man void of understanding, Passing through the street near her corner; and he went the way to her house, In the twilight, in the evening, in the black and dark night: And, behold, <u>there met him a woman with the attire of an harlot</u>, and subtil of heart.*
>
> *(She is loud and stubborn; her feet abide not in her house: Now is she without, now in the streets, and lieth in wait at every corner.) <u>So she caught him, and kissed him, and with an impudent face said unto him</u>, I have peace offerings with me; this day have I payed my vows. Therefore came I forth to meet thee, diligently to seek thy face, and I have found thee. I have decked my bed with coverings of tapestry, with carved works, with fine linen of Egypt. I have perfumed my bed with myrrh, aloes, and cinnamon. <u>Come, let us take our fill of love until the morning: let us solace ourselves</u>*

*with loves. For the goodman is not at home, he is gone a long journey: He hath taken a bag of money with him, and will come home at the day appointed. With her much fair speech she caused him to yield, with the flattering of her lips she forced him. He goeth after her straightway, as an ox goeth to the slaughter, or as a fool to the correction of the stocks; Till a dart strike through his liver; as a bird hasteth to the snare, and knoweth not that it is for his life. Hearken unto me now therefore, O ye children, and attend to the words of my mouth. Let not thine heart decline to her ways, go not astray in her paths. <u>For she hath cast down many wounded: yea, many strong men have been slain by her. Her house is the way to hell, going down to the chambers of death</u>.*" (Proverbs 7:6-27)

Most men are seeking sexual sensation caused by the chemical released in the mouth of the woman through the kissing act. Our streets are filled with boys and girls who throw their arms around the opposite sex necks, and embracing such individuals, kissing them so as to stir up wanton affections and impure desires in them. BEWARE OF THEM. The bible says that such women have cast down many strong men wounded and slain physically and spiritually. Joshua Harris in his book titled "I kissed Dating Good-bye" commented that *"By doing this, they are awakening love at the wrong time and most often with the wrong person, causing untold damages in their life and the life of their partners. Even among Christians, there is a great number of dating relationships in which the pair who is dating will exchange mouth to mouth kissing, preventing them to see clearly whether their partner is the right mate for them. Wrong*

> *kisses have the power, most of the time to bring confusion in relationships because when two people who are in courtship start kissing, they lose focus on their characters or getting to know each other but start focusing on intimacy and passion."*

2. Kissing is a symbol of friendship. The Christians in Rome were commanded to *"Salute one another with a holy kiss."* (Roman 16:16). Such a holy kiss is a token of sincere affection and friendship for one another in the Christians' assembly. It is called "holy", to differentiate it from an unchaste kiss.

3. Kissing is used at the meeting places for the purpose of salutation/homage: Exodus 4:27; 18:7; 1 Thessalonians 5:26. Moses had gone for many years so when he met his brother Aaron, they kissed each other. The kiss that is exchanged by people during normal, casual greeting is usually not mouth to mouth but either mouth to cheek or mouth to back of the hand.

4. Kissing is a sign of favour and reconciliation. For example, Absalom, the son of king David killed one of his brothers for a sin he committed. After the murder, he fled the country but was brought back years later. Unfortunately, his father refused to see his face and was left to still stay in exile. He was frustrated and requested that the commander in chief of the armies of David, Joab should help him appease his father. Listen to his word in 2 Sam 14:32-33:

> *"And Absalom answered Joab, Behold, I sent unto thee, saying, Come hither, that I may send thee to the king, to say, Wherefore am I come from Geshur? it had been good for me to have been there still: now therefore let me see the king's face; and if there be any iniquity in me, let him kill me. So Joab came to the king, and told him: and when he had called for Absalom,*

*he came to the king, and bowed himself on his*
*face to the ground before the king: and the king*
*kissed Absalom."*

The kiss that David gave to his son here is a sign of acceptance and reconciliation. In addition to that, when the father of the prodigal son saw him, he kissed his son for returning home; a sign of reconciliation. So, the significance of the request of the Shulamite lady is that she is seeking to be reconciled to her lover from whom she was kidnapped. She wants him to show her that she still found favour in his sight. She desired the love of her heart (shepherd boy) to know that the fact that she had been kidnapped by Solomon did not mean that she loved, agreed or succumbed to him.

5. Kissing is a sign of subjection
   In honour of their idols and as a token of respect and subjection, idol worshippers always kissed their hand after they might have touched their idols. *"Yet I have left me seven thousand in Israel, all the knees which have not bowed unto Baal, and every mouth which hath not kissed him."* (1 Kings 19:18)

When a woman kisses a man, what she is doing is that she is voluntarily or involuntarily, consciously or unconsciously subjecting and submitting herself to the man. Our exchange of kiss with Jesus Christ is a symbol of our love and absolute submission unto Him and obedience to His commandments. Jesus Christ kisses us in love and kindness by teaching and applying the grace of the gospel unto us. The kiss of His mouth symbolizes His lovely and gracious doctrines.

Moreover, the Shulamite lady clearly compared her love for the shepherd boy with wine: *"for thy love is better than wine."* The greatest effect of wine is to gladden the heart. Unadulterated wine invigorates the spirit, exhilarates the heart, and brightens the countenance by strengthening the muscles and bracing the nerves of man (Psalm 104:15). This tells us that the love of the Shulamite lady for her shepherd is a love that has the power to make her merry and happy. It gives her the greatest joy and warm up her heart. She is lost of love for this ruddy man who tends for sheep. This love gives her strength and unspeakable joy. This is the type of love we, Christians, should have for our Saviour who is actually our Shepherd and our Lord.

Despite the cheerfulness that the wine brings to the heart of man, genuine, gracious, godly love is better than it. The effect of wine is but for a short period of time; love lasts forever, it never fails (1 Corinthians 13:8). Christ's love for the church is free from all sediments of dissimulation and deceit. It is preferable to drink wine in that it not only revives and cheers heavy hearts, but quickens dead sinners, and comforts distressed saints. Christ's love sanctifies and cleanses us with the washing of water by the word of life which wine cannot do. The tokens of the affection of Christ are more desired than any other delights.

A careful analytical study of the Bible reveals that the priests were instructed not to drink wine only when they were about to minister in the tabernacle. Nazarites were not to drink it at all. *"And the LORD spake unto Aaron (the priest), saying, Do not drink wine nor strong drink, thou, nor thy sons with thee, when ye go into the tabernacle of the congregation, lest ye die: it shall be a statute for ever throughout your generations"* (Leviticus 10:8-9). But to the Nazarites, God commanded that *"Speak unto the children of Israel, and say unto them, When either man or woman shall separate themselves to vow a vow of a Nazarite, to separate themselves unto the LORD: He shall separate himself from wine and strong drink, and shall drink no vinegar of wine, or vinegar of strong drink, neither shall he drink any liquor of grapes, nor eat moist grapes, or dried. All the days of his separation shall he eat nothing that is made of the vine tree, from the kernels even to the husk."* (Numbers 6:2-4)

Christians like the Nazarites are called to higher spiritual ground; we are to be spiritual mountaineers. We are to chorus our commitment and consecration with Apostle Paul as he stated:

> *"But what things were gain to me, those I counted loss for Christ. Yea doubtless, and I count all things but loss for the excellency of the knowledge of Christ Jesus my Lord: for whom I have suffered the loss of all things, and do count them but dung, that I may win Christ, And be found in him, not having mine own righteousness, which is of the law, but that which is through the faith of Christ, the righteousness which is of God by faith: That I may know him, and the power of his resurrection, and the fellowship of his sufferings, being made conformable unto his death; If by any means I might attain unto the resurrection of the dead. Not as though I had already attained, either were already perfect: but I follow after, if that I may apprehend that for which also I am apprehended of Christ Jesus. Brethren, I count not myself to have apprehended: but this one thing I do, forgetting those things which are behind, and reaching forth unto those things which are before, I press toward the mark for the prize of the high calling of God in Christ Jesus. Let us therefore, as many as be perfect, be thus minded: and if in any thing ye be otherwise minded, God shall reveal even this unto you."* (Philippians 3:7-15)

Therefore, Christians should seek Christ's love more than pleasure. They should drink the water of life instead of wine, panting after righteousness daily. They are to separate themselves unto the Lord, to honour his name by devoting themselves to Him, and to set apart their time to serve Him in a stricter and purer manner than others. They are to seek His love more than the goodies of this life. Christian women are to seek Christ's love and shun the selling of their bodies for worldly gain. Remember, Esau sold his birthright just for a morsel of pottage. Please, do not exchange your relationship with God, your salvation, your holiness for fund and fame.

The call or personal decision to be a Nazarite unto the Lord by the Christians strongly connote separation from all forms of worldly pleasure and worldly amusements that stand on our way to the pursuit of loving God with all our heart, might, strength, soul, spirit, and body. Indeed, Jesus turned water to wine for consumption by people that attended the wedding in Galilee and also touched the dead but did not give to Himself the pleasure of it. There is a difference between touching the dead to bring it back to life and touching the dead during burial and ceremonial events. Christ and the Christians are to touch the spiritually dead through morals and messages in order to regenerate them to God through genuine repentance and faith in Christ. They are also to touch the physically dead as to bring them back to life through the manifestation of the miracle of power. However, touching the dead for ceremonial sake like wasting time and money in celebration of the dead is hereby condemned. A perfect example can be found in Luke 9:57-61 as He made known the cost of discipleship to the would-be disciples.

> *"And it came to pass, that, as they went in the way, a certain man said unto him, Lord, I will follow thee whithersoever thou goest. And Jesus said unto him, Foxes have holes, and birds of the air have nests; but the Son of man hath not where to lay his head. And he said unto another, Follow me. But he said, Lord, suffer me first to go and bury my father. Jesus said unto him, Let the dead bury their dead: but go thou and preach the kingdom of God. And another also said, Lord, I will follow thee; but let me first go bid them farewell, which are at home at my house. And Jesus said unto him, No man, having put his hand to the plough, and looking back, is fit for the kingdom of God."*

The explanation on touching the dead may seem to be a digression from the topic of our consideration; however, I decided to discuss it because of the critics who may want to tell us that majoring on wine while touching the dead was also forbidden then.

All loves for pleasure at expense of building strong relationship with Christ are to be forsaken in the pursuit of Christ's love. In the days of the prophet Isaiah and in our generation too, it is sad to see that priests and prophets sips wine or strong drink as seen Isaiah 28:7, *"But they also have erred through wine, and through strong drink are out of the way; the priest and the prophet have erred through strong drink, they are swallowed up of wine, they are out of the way through strong drink; they err in vision, they stumble in judgment."*

The Bible did not only warn the Nazarites from drinking wine but also the kings. *"It is not for kings, O Lemuel, it is not for kings to drink wine; nor for princes strong drink: Lest they drink, and forget the law, and pervert the judgment of any of the afflicted. Give strong drink unto him that is ready to perish, and wine unto those that be of heavy hearts. Let him drink, and forget his poverty, and remember his misery no more"* (Proverbs 31:4-7). The kings ought to be grave and sober; they are to maintain the grandeur and dignity of their office. However, Solomon did contrary to this advice by giving himself unto wine and women (Ecclesiastes 2:3). The love of most people who were once fervent in the spirit, waiting patiently for the coming of Christ, and living above reproach are in time like this waxing cold or lukewarm because of tribulation, distress, persecution, poverty, famine, joblessness, nakedness, peril, problem of delays in marriage even when over-aged, delay in child bearing, spiritual affliction. If you are already falling from grace to grass because of these things, you need to awake unto righteousness. *"Sow to yourselves in righteousness, reap in mercy; break up your fallow ground: for it is time to seek the LORD, till he come and rain righteousness upon you."* (Hosea 10:12). Make up your mind that none of these things will move you from your steadfastness in seeking the love of Christ. Do not allow anything whatsoever to remove your affection from Christ.

> *"Who shall separate us from the love of Christ? shall tribulation, or distress, or persecution, or famine, or nakedness, or peril, or sword? As it is written, For thy sake we are killed all the day long; we are accounted as sheep for the slaughter. Nay, in all these things we are more than conquerors through him that loved us. For I am persuaded, that neither death, nor life, nor angels, nor principalities, nor powers, nor things present, nor things to come, Nor height, nor depth, nor any other creature, shall be able to separate us from the love of God, which is in Christ Jesus our Lord."* (Romans 8:35-38)

Remember that the pleasure and prosperity of this world cannot be compared at all with the love of Christ that compelled Him to suffer, go to the cross and died for our sins. This is where most preachers of the word of God miss the mark. They major on worldly possession and prosperity but dwell little on what matters most, the salvation of the souls. The Bible says, *"He that loveth pleasure shall be a poor man: he that loveth wine and oil shall not be rich"* (Proverbs 21:17). *"But she that liveth in pleasure is dead while she liveth"* (1 Timothy 5:6). We are warned against indulgence in good eating and drinking, pampering our bodies at the expense of our sound relationship with God or the safe-guarding of our salvation with trembling and fear. There is no excuse to exonerate yourself from the penalty and punishment of living in pleasure at the expense of your soul. Your pastor may not teach you the whole counsel of the word of God. He or she may be feeding you with the mundane things of this world and neglecting the weightier matter—holiness without which no man shall see the Lord, but it's still not reason enough to neglect the word of God. Let it be known unto you that every man shall stand before the throne of judgement and give account of how he or she lived his life.

Summarily, in comparison to the effects of wine on man, the grace of Christ and comfort of His Spirit exceed all worldly pleasures and destroy the root of afflictions, poverty, and miseries unlike wine that mask the sorrow of afflictions, poverty, and miseries for a moment.

## Exaltation of the Shepherd Lover

> <u>Embracing the sweetness of the odour of the lover</u>: Song 1:3a *". . . The odour of your ointments is fragrant . . ."*

What she is saying is that she knows him, she understands his affection for her, she enjoys his presence at all times; so she cannot because of the pleasure and position that the king Solomon presented to her, forget the Lover of her soul. *"For the which cause I also suffer these things: nevertheless I am not ashamed: for I know whom I have believed, and am persuaded that he is able to keep that which I have committed unto him against that day"* (2 Timothy 1:12). This is contrary to the lives of most Christians who *"professed that they know God; but in works they deny Him, being abominable, and disobedient, and unto every good work reprobate"* (Titus 1:16). Sound doctrine and dynamic preaching open the closed box of ointment thereby enhancing the diffusion of a fragrant smell. *"Now thanks be unto God, which always causeth us to triumph in Christ, and maketh manifest the savour of his knowledge by us in every place. For we are unto God a sweet savour of Christ . . ."* (2 Corinthians 2:14-15). The word of Christ to His disciples toward the end of His earthly ministry was: *"Let these sayings sink down into your ears: for the Son of man shall be delivered into the hands of men"* (Luke 9:44). We need to allow the word of God to sink down into our ears and be imprinted on the table of our hearts so that we can employ it to fight against the temptation to sin and the troubles of life that come to distract us from the Lord. Satan's tactic to lure men into the sin of disobedience and denying the Lord is still the same as of old: the misinterpreting of Scriptures to confuse man. He deceived Eve by alluding to the instruction that God had given her and her husband in Genesis 3:1-3. He tempted Jesus Christ, our Master and Saviour, by using the same approach in Matthew 4:1-11. Jesus used the word of God to defeat Satan but Eve did not. So, we need to know and understand Him and His word to stand against every temptation that the "backslidden Solomon" of this world may bring our way. *"Having their understanding darkened because of the blindness of their heart can alienate men from the life God promised to those who would follow Him"* (Ephesians 4:18).

➤ <u>Emphasis of the good name</u>: Song of Solomon 1:3 *". . . your name is like perfume poured out . . ."*

A Good name is better than gold and silver or wealth (Ecclesiastes 7:1). Money can make somebody popular but a good name will make people trust him and honour him. And what's the benefit of being famous if you cannot be trusted? Christians must therefore know and understand the importance of keeping a good reputation. It is indeed like a perfume poured out around one's community or nation. People will usually talk about your deeds whether good or bad. Someone once said that an act of kindness and good works can make you become famous but a bad behaviour can have the same effect. Mother Theresa will always be known for her generosity towards poor people and lepers while the famous American John Dillinger will always be known for his bank robberies and the murders his activities caused him to commit during the Great Depression era. Mother Theresa is honoured up to today for her works in India while Dillinger was jailed twice, killed by the police at the age of 31 and is remembered today for the pain he caused to an entire nation. These are two famous people with two different legacies. Two famous names, two different perfumes poured out of them. God has anointed Jesus Christ with the oil of gladness above His fellows (Psalm 45:6-11; Hebrew 1:9; Luke 4:18; Acts 10:38). A Good name added to a sinless life makes Christ honoured above all the religious leaders of old and our present time. He can be trusted because he lived a sinless life and he remains true to His word. Every Christian knows him as the deliverer because he has delivered them. Therefore, they trust him to do everything he says he will do. Because of his trustworthiness, Satan Himself fears Jesus. He tempted him and tried him but Jesus never gave in.

## Engaging the Saviour's Love

> *"Draw me, we will run after thee: the king hath brought me into his chambers: we will be glad and rejoice in thee, we will remember thy love more than wine: the upright love thee."* (Song 1:4)

Many Christians are contented staying in the palace of pleasure where Solomon dwells. Thank God, there was still a faithful few during the Bible days and there is still a faithful few in our contemporary time who would not and will not defile themselves with the portion of the king's polluted meat. Daniel and his three Hebrew companions were among such people as recorded in Daniel 1:3-8:

> *"And the king spake unto Ashpenaz the master of his eunuchs, that he should bring certain of the children of Israel, and of the king's seed, and of the princes; Children in whom was no blemish, but well favoured, and skilful in all wisdom, and cunning in knowledge, and understanding science, and such as had ability in them to stand in the king's palace, and whom they might teach the learning and the tongue of the Chaldeans.*

29

*And the king appointed them a daily provision of the king's meat, and of the wine which he drank: so nourishing them three years, that at the end thereof they might stand before the king. Now among these were of the children of Judah, Daniel, Hananiah, Mishael, and Azariah: Unto whom the prince of the eunuchs gave names: for he gave unto Daniel the name of Belteshazzar; and to Hananiah, of Shadrach; and to Mishael, of Meshach; and to Azariah, of Abednego. But Daniel purposed in his heart that he would not defile himself with the portion of the king's meat, nor with the wine which he drank: therefore he requested of the prince of the eunuchs that he might not defile himself."*

The eating of the king's meat or the drinking of his wine might not have been unlawful in themselves for them but since they did not know whether the meat was from swine's flesh or from an idol's sacrifice, they could not partake of it. Jewish law expressly forbids the eating of pork's meat or meat that had been sacrificed to idols. Despite the fact that they were in a strange land as slaves, they decided to distinguish themselves from other nations and keep up the honour of their God.

Solomon succeeded in bringing the Shulamite lady from her dwelling place to the palace in Jerusalem, the city of gold during his reign but she took special care not to partake in any form of sin. She could not give herself to Solomon because of the strong love she felt for the shepherd. How wonderful it would be for us Christians, especially our young people, to be dead to the lust of the flesh and lust of the eyes. We should be more afraid of defiling ourselves with the pollution of sin than of any outward trouble. Every Christian brother and sister must act like Daniel, his three Hebrew companions, and the Shulamite lady by resolving it in their mind, weighing it, and considering it within themselves never to defile themselves with the mundane things of this world.

1.  *Request for deliverance from the camp of the kidnapper for intimate relationship with the lover: "Draw me . . ."* (Song 1:4a)

Because she was determined not to enjoy the pleasure of sin for a season, she prayed for her lover boy to come to her rescue—*"Draw me"*. This is exactly what Jesus Christ came to do.

*"When Israel was a child, then I loved him, and called my son out of Egypt. As they called them, so they went from them: they sacrificed unto Baalim, and burned incense to graven images. I taught Ephraim also to go, taking them by their arms; but they knew not that I healed them. I drew them with cords of a man, with bands of love: and I was to them as they that take off the yoke on their jaws, and I laid meat unto them."* (Hosea 11:1-4)

When we were weak, helpless, depressed, oppressed, and bound by the chains of Satan, God extended His love towards us by rescuing us from all our predicaments. Our Lord Jesus publicly declared *"The Spirit of the Lord is upon me, because he hath anointed me to preach the gospel to the poor; he hath sent me to heal the broken-hearted, to preach deliverance to the captives, and recovering of sight to the blind, to set at liberty them that are bruised,"* (Luke 4:18). He came to set the captives free. No matter the type of captivity you are presently experiencing, He is ready to set you free. Are you in a tight hole of immorality with a strange woman or man? This woman or man may be your boss, or breadwinner, it does not matter, if you would cry aloud unto Jesus, He will come, save you and set you free. Are you in a palace of corruption or an office where bribery is legalized? *"Depart ye, depart ye, go ye out from thence, touch no unclean thing; go ye out of the midst of her; be ye clean, that bear the vessels of the LORD."* (Isaiah 52:11). I realized that the problem may not be that you do not want to come out of this evil act, but that the power to break away from it is not within you. Then, just cry out to Jesus, He will come to your rescue.

*"For that which I do I allow not: for what I would, that do I not; but what I hate, that do I. If then I do that which I would not, I consent unto the law that it is good. Now then it is no more I that do it, but sin that dwelleth in me. For I know that in me (that is, in my flesh,) dwelleth no good thing: for to will is present with me; but how to perform that which is good I find not. For the good that I would I do not: but the evil which I would not, that I do. Now if I do that I would not, it is no more I that do it, but sin that dwelleth in me. I find then a law, that, when I would do good, evil is present with me. For I delight in the law of God after the inward man: But I see another law in my members, warring against the law of my mind, and bringing me into captivity to the law of sin which is in my members. O wretched man that I am! who shall deliver me from the body of this death? I thank God through Jesus Christ our Lord. So then with the mind I myself serve the law of God; but with the flesh the law of sin."* (Romans 7:15-25)

2. *Readiness to do the will of the Shepherd lover*
   *"We will run after thee."* (Song 1:4b).

Running indeed signifies readiness of affection, speedy performance in action as stated in Psalm 119:32: *"I will run the way of thy commandments, when thou shalt enlarge my heart."* We are to make haste, press toward the mark of our high calling—doing the will of God—by laying aside every weight and sin that easily beset us (Heb 12:1-2).

*"Hast thou not known? Hast thou not heard, that the everlasting God, the LORD, the Creator of the ends of the earth, fainteth not, neither is weary? There is no*

*searching of his understanding. He giveth power to the faint; and to them that have no might he increaseth strength. Even the youths shall faint and be weary, and the young men shall utterly fall: But they that wait upon the LORD shall renew their strength; they shall mount up with wings as eagles; they shall run, and not be weary; and they shall walk, and not faint."* (Isaiah 40:28-31)

She and those that listened to her were ready to follow every instruction or will of the Shepherd lover. She was not ready to do the will of her kidnapper but the will of the lover of her soul. Dear reader, are you not dancing to the tune of your boss in the office just because you do not want him or her to dismiss you from your office? Just because you want promotion, are you not shunning the will of God by submitting your body to your boss? Are you among those who because they met a new person who is richer or more influential in the society than their God-given spouse end their relationship with the spouse for the pursuit of good luck or greener pasture? The trees that God instructed Adam and Eve to eat from in the Garden of Eden were good enough to nourish them forever but Eve saw the forbidden trees with lustful eyes and decided to go for that; so she ate it and gave it to her husband. The consequence of it was death. Most people who marry their spouses because of money or worldly possessions and satisfactions end up in divorce or patched up homes.

Following Jesus entails keeping away from sin.

*"These are they which were not defiled with women; for they are virgins. These are they which follow the Lamb whithersoever he goeth. These were redeemed from among men, being the first fruits unto God and to the Lamb. And in their mouth was found no guile: for they are without fault before the throne of God."* Revelation 14:4-5

33

The groups of people mentioned in this reference are described by their chastity and purity: *They are virgins.* They are described by their loyalty and steadfast adherence to Christ: *They follow the Lamb wherever he goes* as the sheep follow the shepherd of the flock (John 10:4). They accepted and followed Him as their Lord and master, leaving it to him to lead them wherever He pleases rather than embracing the prosperity, position and power promised by Satan. Despite the whoredom of our generation, a remnant that is free from such pollutions and sex perversion is needed. We need such people for their beauty and comeliness in Christ, chastity, sincerity of their love, discipline in doctrine and worship, and for the uprightness of conversation. Heavenly-minded brides of Christ should be able to declare their allegiance to follow the Bridegroom, Jesus Christ like the words of the song written in 1868 by <u>John E. Bode</u>:

1.  O Jesus, I have promised to serve Thee to the end;
    Be Thou forever near me, my Master and my Friend;
    I shall not fear the battle if Thou art by my side,
    Nor wander from the pathway if Thou wilt be my Guide.

2.  O let me feel Thee near me! The world is ever near;
    I see the sights that dazzle, the tempting sounds I hear;
    My foes are ever near me, around me and within;
    But Jesus, draw Thou nearer, and shield my soul from sin.

3.  O let me hear Thee speaking in accents clear and still,
    Above the storms of passion, the murmurs of self will.
    O speak to reassure me, to hasten or control;
    O speak, and make me listen, Thou Guardian of my soul.

4. O Jesus, Thou hast promised to all who follow Thee
   That where Thou art in glory there shall Thy
   servant be.
   And Jesus, I have promised to serve Thee to the end;
   O give me grace to follow, my Master and my Friend.

5. O let me see Thy footprints, and in them plant mine
   own;
   My hope to follow duly is in Thy strength alone.
   O guide me, call me, draw me, uphold me to the end;
   And then in Heaven receive me, my Saviour and my
   Friend.

Most pastors and Bible teachers did run well when they first set out to work in God's vineyard. They embraced it and held fast to it, and were zealously attached to the truths of the Gospel; they were in the lively exercise of grace on its proper object, and very diligent in the discharge of duty; they made great proficiency in the knowledge of divine things, and ran with cheerfulness and without weariness in the ways of Christ, and in the paths of truth and holiness. However, when Satan presented to them one or more of the three major sources of temptation which are women, wealth and worship, they began to shift grounds from the true gospel to a refined, adulterated brand, preaching—what-people-want-to-hear. They now major on prosperity, preaching without a mention of righteousness and holiness. They are now numbered among those that hide the truth but preach for gain. It is a pity that many pastors in our nations are making merchandise of the gospel of Christ and selling the gifts that were given to them to bless God's people. This is a grievous sin in the sight of God. *"The heads thereof judge for reward, and the priests thereof teach for hire, and the prophets thereof divine for money: yet will they lean upon the LORD, and say, Is not the LORD among us? none evil can come upon us. Therefore shall Zion for your sake be plowed as a field, and Jerusalem shall become heaps, and the mountain of the house as the high places of the forest"* (Micah 3:11-12). They engage in preaching doctrines that are most pleasing to carnal men, encouraging them to indulge in their lusts, presumption, and vain confidence. Preachers *"Which have forsaken the right way, and are gone astray, following the way of Balaam the son of Bosor, who loved the wages of unrighteousness"* (2 Peter 2:15).

3. *Restating her frustration and displeasure in the camp of the kidnapper: "the king hath brought me into his chambers" (Song of Solomon 1:4b).*

Whenever you find yourself in the camp of the enemy, a place where sin dwells, please, do not keep quiet. Cry out for help, let your Saviour, Jesus Christ, your pastor or mentor, your prayer partner or spouse know what you are passing through. If you keep quiet, your problem will remain with you. A problem shared is a problem half solved. Do not be an actor or an actress, that is, do not pretend to be who you are not in your spiritual life. If you are working in an office as a secretary and your male boss is always trying to sexually abuse you—either verbally or through touch,—you need not to manage it. CRY aloud to stop such proposal. If your cry will not do, run for your life like Joseph in the hand of Potiphar's wife.

*"And it came to pass from the time that he had made him overseer in his house, and over all that he had, that the LORD blessed the Egyptian's house for Joseph's sake; and the blessing of the LORD was upon all that he had in the house, and in the field. And he left all that he had in Joseph's hand; and he knew not ought he had, save the bread which he did eat. And Joseph was a goodly person, and well favoured. And it came to pass after these things, that his master's wife cast her eyes upon Joseph;*

*and she said, lie with me. But he refused, and said unto his master's wife, Behold, my master wotteth not what is with me in the house, and he hath committed all that he hath to my hand; There is none greater in this house than I; neither hath he kept back any thing from me but thee, because thou art his wife: how then can I do this great wickedness, and sin against God? And it came to pass, as she spake to Joseph day by day, that he hearkened not unto her, to lie by her, or to be with her. And it came to pass about this time, that Joseph went into the house to do his business; and there was none of the men of the house there within. And she caught him by his garment, saying, lie with me: and he left his garment in her hand, and fled, and got him out. And it came to pass, when she saw that he had left his garment in her hand, and was fled forth" (Genesis 39:7-13).*

Please, *"deliver thyself as a roe from the hand of the hunter, and as a bird from the hand of the fowler."* (Proverbs 6:5) *"Give not sleep to thy eyes* till thou hast *delivered thyself.* Strive and struggle to the utmost, and hasten with all speed, *as a roe* or a *bird* delivers herself out of this snare of *the fowler* or hunter. Delays are dangerous, and feeble efforts will not serve."

4. *Renouncing the enticing glory of the kidnapper:*
   *". . . the king hath brought me into his chambers: we will be glad and rejoice in thee . . ."* (Song 1:4c)

We are to renounce every form of enticement from Satan. Eve did not renounce the promise of becoming wiser than God that Satan presented to her, so she fell into the sin of disobedience unto God's commandment. It is the responsibility of every Christian to walk in the footstep of Jesus. When the tempter, Satan, came unto Him at the beginning of His earthly ministry, He resisted him with the Word of God. His responses can be found in Matthew 4:8-10:

*"Again, the devil taketh him up into an exceeding high mountain, and sheweth him all the kingdoms of the world, and the glory of them; And saith unto him, All these things will I give thee, if thou wilt fall down and worship me. Then saith Jesus unto him, get thee hence, Satan: for it is written, Thou shalt worship the Lord thy God, and him only shalt thou serve."*

Like Jesus, most ministers of the gospel had been tempted but they could not withstand it and fell. Satan brought before them the kingdoms of the world with their glory, their riches, pomp, pleasure, power, and grandeur and they could not withstand the temptations. Most pastors were doing fine in their ministry when it came to preparing souls for the kingdom of heaven. Yet, when they visited a mega-church pastor, envying his success, they would seek to copy his methods. So when they would go back to their church to apply those new methods, things would begin to take a snow dive: they would align themselves with the pastor's reward on the earth. They, like Demas, forsook the preaching of the true gospel, having loved this present world. There are many Levites or ministers of God who because of the gain that they will acquire refuse to reprove the works of darkness. Instead of this, like a base and degenerated branch of that sacred tribe in Judges 17, they will go to offer their service unto the gods of this world.

They solicit for jobs from the ungodly, "have you any work for a Levite or pastor? For I am out of business."

All they aim at is to get bread, not to work for God. They are not ready to be Voices in the wilderness preparing the way of the Lord but Noises in the world raising up church members that form gangs and armed bandits who steal public funds and forge companies' accounts to build large structures as places of worship. May God have mercy on such pastors, opening their eyes to see that not everything that glitters is gold. Now, read the account of a Levite that I already alluded to in Judges 17:1-13:

*"And there was a man of mount Ephraim, whose name was Micah. And he said unto his mother, the eleven hundred shekels of silver that were taken from thee, about which thou cursedst, and spakest of also in mine ears, behold, the silver is with me; I took it. And his mother said, blessed be thou of the LORD, my son. And when he had restored the eleven hundred shekels of silver to his mother, his mother said, I had wholly dedicated the silver unto the LORD from my hand for my son, to make a graven image and a molten image: now therefore I will restore it unto thee. Yet he restored the money unto his mother; and his mother took two hundred shekels of silver, and gave them to the founder, who made thereof a graven image and a molten image: and they were in the house of Micah. And the man Micah had an house of gods, and made an ephod, and teraphim, and consecrated one of his sons, who became his priest. In those days there was no king in Israel, but every man did that which was right in his own eyes. And there was a young man out of Bethlehem of the family of Judah, who was a Levite, and he sojourned there. And the man departed out of the city of Bethlehem to sojourn where he could find a place: and he came to mount Ephraim to the house of Micah, as he journeyed. And Micah said unto him, Whence comest thou? And he said unto him, I am a Levite of Bethlehem, and I go to sojourn where I may find a place. And Micah said unto him, dwell with me, and be unto me a father and a priest, and I will give thee ten shekels of silver by the year, and a suit of apparel, and thy victuals. So the Levite went in. And the Levite was content to dwell with the man; and the young man was unto him as one of his sons. And Micah consecrated the Levite; and the young man became his priest, and was in the house of Micah.*

*Then said Micah, Now know I that the LORD will do me good, seeing I have a Levite to my priest."*

Dear reader, please, do not be contented in the camp of enemy, renounce the enticing glory of your captor.

5.  *Remembering the love of her true lover:*
    *". . . we will remember thy love more than wine . . ."*
    (Song 1:4d).

As Christians, we must always remember the love of our Lord Jesus Christ. We are to remember how wretched we were in sin and how He came to die for us and save us from the power, penalty and punishment of sin. There is always the need to record, rehearse, and relay how the love of our Bridegroom is more than wine (Isaiah 12:3-6; 63:7; Psalm 71:16).

There is a popular song we loved to sing in the old days which goes like this:

*when I remember what the Lord has done,*
*I will never go back anymore; when I remember what the Lord has done,*
*I will never go back anymore;*
*No, no, no, no, no, I will never go back anymore; when I remember what the Lord has done,*
*I will never go back anymore.*

Remember, when you were a sinner, Jesus Christ died for you.

6.  *Resounding her position with the Shepherd lover:*
    *". . . the upright love thee . . ."* (Song 1:4e)

*"Who shall separate us from the love of Christ? shall tribulation, or distress, or persecution, or famine, or nakedness, or peril, or sword? As it is written, For thy*

*sake we are killed all the daylong; we are accounted as sheep for the slaughter. Nay, in all these things we are more than conquerors through him that loved us. For I am persuaded, that neither death, nor life, nor angels, nor principalities, nor powers, nor things present, nor things to come, Nor height, nor depth, nor any other creature, shall be able to separate us from the love of God, which is in Christ Jesus our Lord"* (Romans 8:35-38).

Sickness, suffering, suppression, scarcity of jobs and food, scary experiences of delay in child bearing and in marriage may come but we must not sell our affection for Christ to another. We must have our submissive love for Christ. Fanny Crosby wrote a song in 1883; resounding her submissive love for Christ.

1.  I am Thine, O Lord, I have heard Thy voice,
    And it told Thy love to me;
    But I long to rise in the arms of faith
    And be closer drawn to Thee.

    *Chorus*
    *Draw me nearer, nearer blessed Lord,*
    *To the cross where Thou hast died.*
    *Draw me nearer, nearer, nearer blessed Lord,*
    *To Thy precious, bleeding side.*

2.  Consecrate me now to Thy service, Lord,
    By the power of grace divine;
    Let my soul look up with a steadfast hope,
    And my will be lost in Thine.

3.  The pure delight of a single hour
    That before Thy throne I spend,
    When I kneel in prayer, and with Thee, my God
    I commune as friend with friend!

4. There are depths of love that I cannot know
Till I cross the narrow sea;
There are heights of joy that I may not reach
Till I rest in peace with Thee.

# Chapter Three

## Danger of Busy Life

*"I am black, but* [you are] *comely* [the court ladies assured her], *O ye daughters of Jerusalem, as the tents of Kedar, as the curtains of Solomon. Look not upon me, because I am black, because the sun hath looked upon me: my mother's children were angry with me; they made me the keeper of the vineyards; but mine own vineyard have I not kept."* (Song of Solomon 1:5-6)

The theme of this chapter is centred on the private life of the Shulamite lady which she made known publicly in the court of Solomon at Jerusalem. She expressed her feelings of disappointment and frustration at having to obey her brothers who made her not to take care of herself but worn her out with their assignments. Being busy to the point of neglecting one's spiritual nourishment and life causes spiritual dryness. The signs of spiritual dryness are almost the same for all who pass through such stage. These signs include:

1. **Bible reading and study no longer enliven our spirit.** Normally, when a Christian reads the Bible, he/she begins to see himself or herself in the mirror of the word of God. The Spirit of God rebukes and reproves us whenever we read the Scripture; our spirits are ignited and enlightened through it.

*"And all the people gathered themselves together as one man into the street that was before the water gate; and they spake unto Ezra the scribe to bring the book of the law of Moses, which the LORD had commanded to Israel. And Ezra the priest brought the law before the congregation both of men and women, and all that could hear with understanding, upon the first day of the seventh month. And he read therein before the street that was before the water gate from the morning until midday, before the men and the women, and those that could understand; and the ears of all the people were attentive unto the book of the law. And Ezra the scribe stood upon a pulpit of wood, which they had made for the purpose; . . . And Ezra opened the book in the sight of all the people; (for he was above all the people) and when he opened it, all the people stood up: And Ezra blessed the LORD, the great God. And all the people answered, Amen, Amen, with lifting up their hands: and they bowed their heads, and worshipped the LORD with their faces to the ground . . . and the Levites, caused the people to understand the law: and the people stood in their place. So they read in the book in the law of God distinctly, and gave the sense, and caused them to understand the reading. And Nehemiah, which is the Tirshatha, and Ezra the priest the scribe, and the Levites that taught the people, said unto all the people, This day is holy unto the LORD your God; mourn not, nor weep. For all the people wept, when they heard the words of the law."* (Nehemiah 8:1-9)

However, when the Bible reading no longer enlightens and enlivens our spirits, it is signalled that we are treading the downward movement of our Christian life. When powerful messages from an anointed man of God no longer moves us or have meaning to us, that is a red card pointing to our spiritual dryness. At a certain time during the period when Elijah and other prophets were messengers of God in Israel, the Israelites were spiritually dried to the point that no challenge from the word of God has any meaning to them: *"And Elijah came unto all the people, and said, How long halt ye between two opinions? if the LORD be God, follow him: but if Baal, then follow him. And the people answered him not a word"* (1 Kings 18:21). *"To whom shall I speak, and give warning, that they may hear? behold, their ear is uncircumcised, and they cannot hearken: behold, the word of the LORD is unto them a reproach; they have no delight in it"* (Jeremiah 6:10).

There is no way we can worship the living God and at the same time worship Baal (corruption or immorality); these will definitely result in spiritual dryness.

2. **Prayer becomes pointless and undesirable**
   Spiritual dryness gives way to slumber in prayer. Instead of praying to the Creator of heaven and earth, a spiritually dried person will start seeking for answers where there is no solution like King Saul seeking for the Witch of Endor. Instead of praying all night, the victims sleep all night. Such people lack prayer points. Prayer becomes mechanical and methodical. No wonder, our churches are filled with many organizers of programs while there are few or no agonizers in prayer. When people begin to give one flimsy excuse or the other for their absence at the prayer meetings, this should tell you that such people's spiritual lives are in shambles or dangers.

3. **Obedience to God wanes, and what remains is very mechanical**
   It is generally agreed that Christians are to promptly and completely obey the words of God; however, spiritual dryness usually erodes this obedience. Most roads that are constructed without drainage system normally end up being eroded by floods. So also is a Christian who

45

does not check-guard his or her heart against the spirit of disobedience.

"And Samuel said, When thou wast little in thine own sight, wast thou not made the head of the tribes of Israel, and the LORD anointed thee king over Israel? And the LORD sent thee on a journey, and said, Go and utterly destroy the sinners the Amalekites, and fight against them until they be consumed. Wherefore then didst thou not obey the voice of the LORD, but didst fly upon the spoil, and didst evil in the sight of the LORD? And Saul said unto Samuel, Yea, I have obeyed the voice of the LORD, and have gone the way which the LORD sent me, and have brought Agag the king of Amalek, and have utterly destroyed the Amalekites. But the people took of the spoil, sheep and oxen, the chief of the things which should have been utterly destroyed, to sacrifice unto the LORD thy God in Gilgal. And Samuel said, Hath the LORD as great delight in burnt offerings and sacrifices, as in obeying the voice of the LORD? Behold, to obey is better than sacrifice, and to hearken than the fat of rams. For rebellion is as the sin of witchcraft, and stubbornness is as iniquity and idolatry. Because thou hast rejected the word of the LORD, he hath also rejected thee from being king. And Saul said unto Samuel, I have sinned: for I have transgressed the commandment of the LORD, and thy words: because I feared the people, and obeyed their voice." (1 Samuel 15:17-24)

Partial obedience is no obedience; it is a sign of spiritual dryness. However, this is not so when we are spiritually sound; we obey God's word hundred percent.

4. **Service once motivated by love for our Lord steadfastly dwindles down to duty done just because it has to be done**

   Spiritual vibrancy brings motivation to doing services like evangelism, follow-up, intercessory prayer, preaching, and serving as a choir member. However, spiritual dryness may not necessarily take away these activities from you but the zeal and passion for them fade away like the stars in the dark sky seem to disappear when the sun rises. Doing them, if you do them at all, becomes a burden. You do them because people or the pastor will ask you the reason why you are not doing them. The love that lubricates the service in the time past is no longer there. It is like you are just an empty barrel that makes a loud noise. Sometimes, you like to rise up as at other times but the ointment of grace and the spiritual strength both to will and do are already dried up like that of Samson after Delilah had shaved off the secret of his strength.

5. **Fellowshipping with God becomes terribly monotonous and boring.**
   The desire to fellowship with God at all times is no longer in your dictionary. 2 hours church programs like Bible study meetings, prayer meetings, and Sunday services become so boring to you. It is like you are wasting your precious time. All these are evidences that you are spiritually dry. At the start of your Christian life, you longed to fellowship with God and the brethren, but spiritual dryness will cause you to hide yourself from it. Counting mid-week church programs as non-essential is a sign of spiritual dryness.

## Causes of Spiritual Dryness

1. **Engaging in too many activities**
   *"Look not upon me, because I am black, because the sun hath looked upon me: my mother's children were angry with me; they made me the keeper of the vineyards; but mine own vineyard have I not kept."*
   (Song of Solomon 1:5-6)

The Shulamite lady was black, which can be likened to as being in a state of spiritual darkness because she engaged in too many activities at the neglect of her working towards her personal spiritual growth and building stronger relationship with God. Her case is so similar to that of Moses if not for his father-in-law who counselled him to practice delegation of authority by shedding out some of his activities with able and trustworthy men among his brethren.

*"And it came to pass on the morrow, that Moses sat to judge the people: and the people stood by Moses from the morning unto the evening. And when Moses' father in law saw all that he did to the people, he said, What is this thing that thou doest to the people? why sittest thou thyself alone, and all the people stand by thee from morning unto even? And Moses said unto his father in law, because the people come unto me to enquire of God: When they have a matter, they come unto me; and I judge between one and another, and I do make them know the statutes of God, and his laws. And Moses' father in law said unto him, The thing that thou doest is not good. Thou wilt surely wear away, both thou, and this people that is with thee: for this thing is too heavy for thee; thou art not able to perform it thyself alone."*
(Exodus 18:13-18).

There are many brethren who are so busy with too many activities in the church at the neglect of nourishing their spiritual life. After leaving their office work around 4:00 or 5:00 PM as the case may be, they run immediately to church and start jumping from one thing to the other. They may start with choir practice, then jump to counselling program, from there to visitation and follow up of first timers or young converts; the next activity waiting on the line for them would be building committee meetings, then leadership meeting, and so on. It would be around 10:30 or 11:00 PM before they get back home. At such time they are already so worn out that they just find little time to eat their dinner and as they are eating, they are drowsing. The next day, they have to rise up early and get ready for secular work with little or no time to fellowship with God before they jump out. Some pastors, engage in so much church activities that people who want prayers or counselling will knock on their door as early as 5:00 AM. To make the matter worse, they will not be able to go back to a private life until around 12:00 or 1:00 AM. At such time, they are completely exhausted. When this experience becomes a daily routine, the danger will be that they will burn out their spiritual life and will have no time to replenish it by having a good time with God through personal Bible study and prayer. Too many activities always lead to worn out and finally cause burn-outs. Our spiritual leaders must understand that garbage in equals garbage out. When you pour out all the water in a jar but fail to refill it, the problem is that you will not have means of refreshing your soul when needed. Carelessness will always make church activities to siphon all your spiritual energy and leave you as an empty barrel. Remember, an empty barrel rolling on the ground makes more noise than a liquid-filled barrel. No wonder we have many **Noises** in our churches and communities today, whereas God wants our churches and communities to be filled with **Voices** for Him. The Bible says, *"The voice of one crying in the wilderness, Prepare ye the way of the Lord, make his paths straight."* Let us remind ourselves of a fact that cannot be ignored. It is not all the churches or pastors that are springing up that are intentionally raised to make money or set up churches as business enterprises. Most have genuine minds of preparing the way of the Lord but allowing themselves to be engulfed with too many activities. By so doing, they drain their spiritual life and they eventually become extremely dried.

Some pastors or elders are so busy that they have no time for their spiritual life and children. No wonder most pastors' children are like Hophni and Phinehas, the sons of the Prophet Eli—they were wayward, arrogant, immoral, and rotten. Unfortunately, the children of the first seer in Israel, our dear Prophet Samuel, were not well taken care of by their father because of his busy life. He was always moving from one town to another and did not take the time needed to properly raise his kids. His children could not be relied upon by the Israelites, so they were forced to request for a king. Note that jack of all trades does not profit any man. Indeed, Satan is much more interested in you as a Christian being too busy with mere church activities to debar you from preparing for your own spiritual and family life. This reminds us of the account of Jacob's life in the house of Laban as recorded in Genesis 30:25-30:

*"And it came to pass, when Rachel had born Joseph, that Jacob said unto Laban, Send me away, that I may go unto mine own place, and to my country. Give me my wives and my children, for whom I have served thee, and let me go: for thou knowest my service which I have done thee. And Laban said unto him, I pray thee, if I have found favour in thine eyes, tarry: for I have learned by experience that the LORD hath blessed me for thy sake. And he said, Appoint me thy wages, and I will give it. And he said unto him, Thou knowest how I have served thee, and how thy cattle was with me. For it*

*was little which thou hadst before I came, and it is now increased unto a multitude; and the LORD hath blessed thee since my coming: and now when shall I provide for mine own house also?"*

Dear beloved reader, let us quickly go over the scenario of Jacob's life. He had served Laban for many years, growing Laban's business to a high level of great achievement. However, he did not think about his own at all. Laban had been preying on the star of Jacob: *for I have learned by experience that the LORD hath blessed me for thy sake.* Thank God for the spiritual enlightenment and the light that shone into the heart of Jacob at a point in his servitude: *"For it was little which thou hadst before I came, and it is now increased unto a multitude; and the LORD hath blessed thee since my coming: and now when shall I provide for mine own house also?"* As an individual or an employee of a one man's business, have you ever thought about it that your employer is just preying on your star or talent? Truly they nicknamed you as a reliable, faithful, hardworking and humble worker. What a good quality they ascribed to you! Is it not because you are just everywhere? This department where you are helping out, that section where you are so good at, this customer service you are super excellent at, this sales representative you are so great at, it is not surprising that you are the backbone of your company. The question is when are you going to prepare for your own house? When are you going to become an employer of labour instead of remaining as an employee? I am not trying to say that all the readers of this book are meant to become employers but most likely, many can be, if they sit back, pray through and think through. Unfortunately, the too many activities in your company would not allow you to think beyond your horizon. The most energy-siphoning work is working for a one man business.

The case of Jacob is also true for the ministers of God. They toil all their lives to bless people, counsel people and even raise godly congregations but ruining their lives because they have little or no time to prepare *for their own house also.* They are jacks of all trades and become masters of nothing; there is nothing to write home about concerning their spiritual life. Their spiritual oil is dried upto the point that there is nothing left to kindle their light: their eyes are waxing dim that they cannot see. What a pity. The lamp of God is burning out in the temple of the LORD.

2. **Exposing oneself to harsh condition/atmosphere**
   *"Look not upon me, because I am black, because the sun hath looked upon me"* (Song 1:6b)

In the early 1990s, I used to have night prayers (vigil) with two pastors in a village. These pastors volunteered to stay in that village after their headquarter church came to that place for an evangelistic outreach. Unfortunately, it seemed that the headquarter church was not taking care of them financially as expected. So, these pastors did their best to engage in farming to meet their family needs. As you know, manual farming is labour intensive and energy demanding. Anytime we gathered for vigil, about 30 minutes or 1 hour into the prayer, they would be sleeping and even snoring heavily. Initially, I used to wonder why such pastors, who were well aware of the powerful demons' operations in their village, could be so prayer-less and love to sleep like that. Then, I quickly realised that it was not because they did not love to pray or because they were lazy or visionless, but it was because they had worked so much during the day on the farm that they were extremely tired by the time the vigil would start. Their situation is what I likened to engaging or exposing oneself to a harsh condition or atmosphere. How can you expect a pastor who sustains his living by engaging in a stone-breaking job or any hard labour during the day to be effective in prayer and the study of the word of God in the night? That would be too demanding for him. It's a hard task! The Shulamite lady cried out of her frustration, *"Look not upon me, because I am black, because the sun hath looked upon me."* What a sympathetic situation! If you want to be a dynamic pastor, having the power of God, there is no way you can earn your livelihood by engaging in an energy-sapping job. It is not good for pastors or Christian workers that want to be on fire for God to involve themselves in such activities. It is better to look for a labour that is less intensive or a job that does not require too much energy or to simply do business. The Apostle Paul could not have involved himself in such activities, so he settled for tent-making.

Another dimension to this issue is that, pastors should not occupy themselves with any time-consuming business or else they will not have time to fellowship effectively and efficiently with God. No wonder our churches are filled with pastors of passion but powerless. There is no way we can do the work successfully in the flesh. It is a spiritual work which needs spiritual strength to accomplish great things for the Master. Most pastors who spend much time and energy in secular jobs may be able to present a well-organized and fluent sermon on Sundays but that will not benefit the spiritual life of the hearers because it lacks power. May be this is the reason why in most churches today, the church members always shout: "ride on pastor!" with lots of laughing which they now regard as laughing in the spirit. The word of God is supposed to be sinking deep down into their hearts at such a time, transforming them, causing them to pray for hours after the church service without anybody forcing them to pray. Let me tell you that such a prayer will not be mechanical or methodical but led by the Holy Spirit just like it happened the day that Jonathan Edward preached on <u>Sinners in the Hand of an Angry God</u> and when people prayed all night after Charles G. Finney preached at a crusade in a community.

Dear readers, please refuse the sun to look upon you by refusing to take up a job or appointment that will take away your time of fellowshipping with God. Remember, "little is much when God is in it, labour not for wealth and fame for there is a crown and you can win it, if you decide to go in Jesus' name."

Another way to expose self to harsh conditions is by not minding one's business. King Saul was busy pursuing David and wanting to kill him just because of envy. For days, he searched for David, from the mountains to the valleys, all to no avail. He and his armies were so tired that they all slept in a trench. *"So David took the spear and the cruse of water from Saul's bolster; and they gat them away, and no man saw it, nor knew it, neither awaked: for they were all asleep; because a deep sleep from the LORD was fallen upon them"* (1 Samuel 26:12). When you engage in deceit, destruction and demotion of others, you are bound to experience spiritual dryness.

3. **Experiencing hatred from the brethren or close relatives**
   *"my mother's children were angry with me; they made me the keeper of the vineyards"* (Song 1:6c)

Another cause of spiritual dryness occurs when people are experiencing hatred from their brethren or close relatives. Unfortunately this ought not to be so. Persecutions, afflictions, trials and hatred should draw us closer to God knowing for sure that He alone is the only one who cannot let us down. There are reasons why we suffer hatred from our brethren or close relatives. One is envy, which was the reason that made the brothers of Joseph to hate him.

*"Now Israel loved Joseph more than all his children, because he was the son of his old age: and he made him a coat of many colours. And when his brethren saw that their father loved him more than all his brethren, they hated him, and could not speak peaceably unto him. And Joseph dreamed a dream, and he told it his brethren: and they hated him yet the more. And he said unto them, Hear, I pray you, this dream which I have dreamed: For, behold, we were binding sheaves in the field, and, lo, my sheaf arose, and also stood upright; and, behold, your sheaves stood round about, and made obeisance to my sheaf. And his brethren said to him, Shalt thou indeed reign over us? or shalt thou indeed have dominion over us? And they hated him yet the more for his dreams, and for his words. And he dreamed yet another dream, and told it his brethren, and said, Behold, I have dreamed a dream more; and, behold, the sun and the moon and the eleven stars made obeisance to me. And he told it to his father, and to his brethren: and his father rebuked him, and said unto him, What is this dream that thou hast dreamed? Shall I and thy mother and thy brethren indeed come to bow down ourselves to thee to the earth? And his brethren envied him; but his father observed the saying. And when they saw him afar off, even before he came near unto them, they conspired against him to slay him. And they said one to another, Behold, this dreamer cometh. Come now therefore, and let us slay him, and cast him into some pit, and we will say, some evil beast hath devoured him: and we shall see what will become of his dreams."*
(Genesis 37:3-11, 19-20)

The hatred of Joseph's brothers emanated from two main things: their father *made him a coat of many colours* and he also got God-given visions and dreams for his future headship. He was going to rule over them, so they hated him. How can he rule over his elder brothers? They were ready to either debar or destroy him so that such dreams never see the light of the day. They might have thought that casting him into a solitary pit of sorrow and suffering would cause his soul to wear out and would consequently break his relationship with the Giver of his dream. Or selling him into slavery would be more severe than casting him into the pit because slaves are always made to engage in hard labour! There, his spiritual connection to the Giver of his dreams was supposed to break because he would not have time to commune with God at all, they might think.

Is this not the same thing that we suffer from today? Many of the hatred that we suffer from the church brethren and even close relatives, are they not because of the God-given visions or dreams that they see us possessing? They see us becoming their leaders in the church despite the fact that they were our trainers when we newly joined the church. To them, they could not understand why we, that do not have many years of experience in the same church now become great Apostle of power with God and man just like Apostle Paul, the least but the greatest of all the apostles. Hence, they are ready to grind us into pulp.

In the same vein, people suffer hatred from their co-workers at their workplace and students from their classmates or course-mates at schools. Unfortunately, most people who suffer from such hatred are so dejected and depressed to the point that they cannot understand why these are befalling them and even query God for allowing such. Some become so weary that their Bible reading loses its meaning and prayer becomes a no-go area to them. Before long, the ointment of grace in their lives begins to leak and later dry up. Some may be so disappointed to the level of quitting on God, thereby making a shipwreck of their faith. Thinking that if this can happen in the church then there is no more use of being a Christian on earth. Before leaving this point, I would like to share with you the case of one of my close friends who pastored a church in Lagos State, Nigeria.

My friend pastored a church under another pastor who oversaw a part of the ministry-at-large. It came to a time when the pastor over him disciplined him by removing him as the pastor of the church where he had been appointed and left him without any portfolio. The sins of my friend were two: his church was growing numerically and financially and a genuine revival was happening there. One day, the senior pastor called my friend and asked him the secret of his financial blessings. He replied that apart from the monthly salary that he earned from his normal duty at his working place, he also won contract jobs in a telecommunication company. So the senior pastor got interested and my friend introduced him to a Christian brother who linked him up with the telecommunication company. Unfortunately, none of the senior pastor's project proposals and quotes was accepted. Probably in his mind, he saw my friend as the devil behind his failures, thinking that this brother was the one blocking him up there. So envy and hatred entered into a satanic matrimony in the heart of the senior pastor. The fruit of the womb of that wedded couple (envy and hatred) was the dismissal of my friend from being the pastor in that local church. My friend told me that if not because of God, he would have left the whole ministry (church). When his wife called me, she told me that my friend was no longer interested in attending the workers' meeting because of that event. Can you guess what was happening to the spiritual life of my dear friend? That is spiritual dryness. Thank God that his wife opened up to me what the family was passing through. So, I counselled my friend and prayed with him. Today, he is more spiritually dynamic than before this dismissal from pastoring that local church. He did not pastor any church from 2008 till the time of writing this book

4. **Excusing self from the services that count**
   *"but mine own vineyard have I not kept"* (Song 1:6d)

We have seen that engaging in too many activities, exposing oneself to harsh conditions or jobs, and hatred from the brethren and close relatives are sources of spiritual dryness. These are genuine reasons for spiritual dryness but they are genuine excuses for exonerating ourselves from finding time to carry out services that count—cultivation of our spiritual life. During the earthly ministry of Jesus, we read that he also experienced tiredness, yet he still found time to pray to his heavenly Father. He would retreat into a solitary place, fellowship with God and refill His anointing in order to advance his ministry. A Christian who has no option than to take up a job that is labour intensive and energy-sapping can decide to cultivate the habit of taking off weekends or few days in a month to consecrate himself or herself to prayer, study of the word, and fellowship with God. The important thing is that you remain faithful to God in finding time to fellowship with Him. The problem of most people is that they lack time management and cannot set their priorities right. When they choose laziness over diligence, this can often lead to spiritual dryness: *"they made me the keeper of the vineyards; but mine own vineyard have I not kept."*

5. **Love for pleasure**
   **Enjoying too much bodily exercise while doing little or no spiritual exercise:**
   *"but mine own vineyard have I not kept"* (Song 1:6d).

Truly, Satan may not succeed in keeping the true Christians from going to church but he can steal away their time, thereby keeping them away from reading their Bibles and knowing the truth. David was supposed to be on the battle field but because he probably wanted to relax, stay away from the horror of the battlefield, he saw what he ought not to see. And because he did not make covenant with his eyes that he would not think upon a maid, he fell into the sin of immorality, adultery with Uriah's wife.

*"And it came to pass, after the year was expired, at the time when kings go forth to battle, that David sent Joab, and his servants with him, and all Israel; and they destroyed the children of Ammon, and besieged Rabbah. But David tarried still at Jerusalem. And it came to pass in an eveningtide, that David arose from off his bed, and walked upon the roof of the king's house: and from the roof he saw a woman washing herself; and the woman was very beautiful to look upon. And David sent and enquired after the woman. And one said, Is not this Bathsheba, the daughter of Eliam, the wife of Uriah the Hittite? And David sent messengers, and took her; and she came in unto him, and he lay with her; for she was purified from her uncleanness: and she returned unto her house. And the woman conceived, and sent and told David, and said, I am with child."* (2 Samuel 11:1-5)

What a great disgrace! It is not good for a king to give his strength unto women or his ways to that which destroys kings (Proverbs 31:4) but King David did. Most Christians today give up themselves to spiritual dryness because they love pleasure. She that gives herself to pleasure is dead while she lives. *"He that loveth pleasure shall be a poor man: he that loveth wine and oil shall not be rich."* Frivolity will drain your spiritual life. Spending too much time in watching television and playing games will definitely eat up your devotional time. Giving yourself to partying at all time will consume your fellowshipping time with God. Laziness and love for sleep are very destructive to our spiritual life.

*"Love not sleep, lest thou come to poverty; open thine eyes, and thou shalt be satisfied with bread."* (Proverbs 20:13)

*"Go to the ant, thou sluggard; consider her ways, and be wise: Which having no guide, overseer, or ruler, Provideth her meat in the summer, and gathereth her food in the harvest. How long wilt thou sleep, O sluggard? when wilt thou arise out of thy sleep? Yet a little sleep, a little slumber, a little folding of the hands to sleep: So shall thy poverty come as one that travelleth, and thy want as an armed man."* (Proverbs 6:6-11)

6. **Evil association**

Evil communication or association corrupts good manner. He that walks with the wise shall be wise but a companion of fools shall be destroyed. Our dear friend Dinah, the daughter of Leah, which she bare unto Jacob, made friendship with the ungodly daughters of Shechem and was probably set up and raped. She lost her glory, her virginity to Shechem the son of Hamor the Hivite, prince of the country (Genesis 34:1-2). What a tragedy! Do you ever think that the ungodly friends that you are keeping now may eventually set you up and land you in rape, fornication, adultery, smoking, drinking alcohol or even taking hard drugs? The ungodly counsel that the young people gave to Rehoboam, the son of King Solomon, robbed him of his rulership over the whole tribe of Israel. The ungodly counsel that your ungodly friends are giving you may rob you of your relationship with God and even your heaven or eternal life with God. Beware!

## Consequences of Spiritual Dryness

1. **Guilt: Song 1:5-6**

   The Shulamite lady was not happy with herself seeing that the colour of her skin was different from that of the court ladies. They were light in complexion while the Shulamite was black. She felt ashamed of her skin compared to the other ladies' skin. The high degree of culpability she experienced made her try to justify herself, explaining why she had such a skin.

   Guilt of soul is caused by spiritual dryness. The same problem of guilt fills the heart of people whose spiritual cups are empty. Adam and Eve had committed the sin of disobedience unto the instruction of God. They became uncomfortable in the presence of God, eaten away with guilt. Their culpability made them quickly sought for solutions which were to cover their nakedness and also hid themselves from God. Spiritually dried people always try to avoid the brethren. If you are looking for a man that carries a bag with a hole that is containing ash, it would not be difficult to trace him. This is because the ash will be leaking and tracing a white line on the path of the man. So also is a spiritually dried man or woman. The guilt of spiritual dryness will be following him or her wherever he or she goes. Call such a person to come and pray for the sick, the shame will shine on his face. He may try to use bold face and do the job but in his heart, the problem of guilt looms.

2. **Spiritual darkness**

   At the moment of a spiritual dryness, there is a spiritual darkness. Vision becomes blurring. The way of the wicked is as darkness: they know not at what they stumble. They cannot receive direction and guidance from God at such a time. These people look so confused. There is no more enlightenment or illumination from the Bible study.

*"Now Samuel was dead, and all Israel had lamented him, and buried him in Ramah, even in his own city. And Saul had put away those that had familiar spirits, and the wizards, out of the land. And the Philistines gathered themselves together, and came and pitched in Shunem: and Saul gathered all Israel together, and they pitched in Gilboa. And when Saul saw the host of the Philistines, he was afraid, and his heart greatly trembled. And when Saul enquired of the LORD, the LORD answered him not, neither by dreams, nor by Urim, nor by prophets. Then said Saul unto his servants, Seek me a woman that hath a familiar spirit, that I may go to her, and enquire of her. And his servants said to him, Behold, there is a woman that hath a familiar spirit at Endor."* (1 Samuel 28:3-7)

The spiritual drought of King Saul caused a lot of havoc in his life and kingdom. All his efforts to gain God's attention failed as *the LORD answered him not, neither by dreams, nor by Urim, nor by prophets.* Unfortunately, most pastors, prophets, or people who suffer from this problem do use carnal wisdom to still say: "thus saith the Lord . . ." when God has not said anything. They still prophesy, but not through the Holy Spirit, through their own spirit. What they are saying is "I am black but comely; I am spiritually dried but can still prophecy or see vision." What a great deception.

*"And Jehoshaphat said unto the king of Israel, Enquire, I pray thee, at the word of the LORD today. Then the king of Israel gathered the prophets together, about four hundred men, and said unto them, Shall I go against Ramothgilead to battle, or shall I forbear? And they said, Go up; for the Lord shall deliver it into the hand of the king. And Jehoshaphat said, Is there not here a prophet of the LORD besides, that we might enquire of him? And the king of Israel said unto Jehoshaphat, There is yet one man, Micaiah the son of Imlah, by whom we may enquire of the LORD: but I hate him; for he doth not prophesy*

good concerning me, but evil. And Jehoshaphat said, Let not the king say so. Then the king of Israel called an officer, and said, Hasten hither Micaiah the son of Imlah. And Zedekiah the son of Chenaanah made him horns of iron: and he said, Thus saith the LORD, With these shalt thou push the Syrians, until thou have consumed them. And all the prophets prophesied so, saying, Go up to Ramothgilead, and prosper: for the LORD shall deliver it into the king's hand. And Micaiah said, As the LORD liveth, what the LORD saith unto me, that will I speak. And he said, I saw all Israel scattered upon the hills, as sheep that have not a shepherd: and the LORD said, These have no master: let them return every man to his house in peace. And there came forth a spirit, and stood before the LORD, and said, I will persuade him. And the LORD said unto him, Wherewith? And he said, I will go forth, and I will be a lying spirit in the mouth of all his prophets. And he said, Thou shalt persuade him, and prevail also: go forth, and do so. Now therefore, behold, the LORD hath put a lying spirit in the mouth of all these thy prophets, and the LORD hath spoken evil concerning thee. But Zedekiah the son of Chenaanah went near, and smote Micaiah on the cheek, and said, Which way went the Spirit of the LORD from me to speak unto thee?
(1 Kings 22:5-9, 11-12, 14, 17, 21-24)

There are lots of Zedekiahs today who are spiritually empty but still stand on the church altars to declare and prophesy falsely. They are blind and their inner mind is darkened. The glory of the Lord has departed from many so called prophets of our age but they still prophecy; some even by a spirit of divination.

You may say that you are not a pastor or prophet, so there is no difference if you are dried in your spiritual life too. The question is: when did you receive inspiration, illumination, and enlightenment from your personal bible study time for the last time? Is it not

good concerning me, but evil. And Jehoshaphat said, Let not the king say so. Then the king of Israel called an officer, and said, Hasten hither Micaiah the son of Imlah. And Zedekiah the son of Chenaanah made him horns of iron: and he said, Thus saith the LORD, With these shalt thou push the Syrians, until thou have consumed them. 

because you were just patching it up? You know that things are not going well with you. Before this period, you always had a clear mind to pursue a project but now confusion of whether you should take a step or not clouds your spirit. Is this not because you are drained up by these spiritual killers that we have considered in the causes of spiritual dryness?

3. **Wear out and burn out:** Exodus 18:13-18.
   Another consequence of spiritual dryness is burn outs. Involvement in too many activities will cause stress and fatigue. The danger of this is that you look older than your age. Spiritual dryness will make you so empty within and without. You look so miserable.

## Cure for Spiritual Dryness

There is a common saying in a tribe that states that the day when a mentally sick man knows that he is mad marks the beginning of his healing. Therefore, for a spiritually dried Christian to receive cure, he or she must first know and accept that he is spiritually off-balance. Then, he/she should identify the cause(s) of his/her dryness and be ready to work on it.

1. *Take time to cultivate your spiritual life.*
   God created Adam, put him in the Garden of Eden, and saddled him with the responsibility of dressing and keeping it. Man was created not to live an idle life but to be industrious. Our salvation experience could be likened to us being placed in the Garden of Eden just like the first man on the earth. We are then saddled with the task of tending, dressing, nourishing, fertilizing, weeding, and protecting the garden of our soul. We are not to neglect it in such a way that it grows up to be bushy or filled with tares.

   We all know the purpose of weed removal on our farm. It is to avoid competition for nutrients between weeds (unwanted plants or grass) and our crops. Competition between the two will definitely affect the growth of the crops because the available nutrients are just enough to make the plants strive well. Weeding also helps keep the farm free from an outbreak of diseases and an attack by insects. Therefore, we need to carry out this operation to keep our farm clean. A weeding operation requires time and energy. So, we need to take time to pulverize the soil of our heart, break up its fallow ground. Remember, stony and thorny hearts would not permit the proper growth and development of our spiritual life. All the stones need to be gathered and removed from it so that nothing from without might damage it and nothing within might obstruct its fruitfulness. The stones that do hinder our tap roots to go deeper into the soil, which wrestle with the downward growth of our roots and upward development of our Christian experiences, are trials, afflictions, persecutions, and hatred from the brethren, close relatives and friends. Every thorn on the farm must be cut down or uprooted and removed. These thorns are the care of this world and the deceitfulness of riches which do choke the word of God in our hearts, thereby causing it to become unfruitful.

It is our responsibility to draw near to God through faith by the grace He has provided, asking for grace and mercy to help us remove the stones and thorns that are contending with our spiritual life and pilgrim journey. We must draw near to God in prayer with true and genuine hearts. The heart that has rebelled must be brought to the foot of God. The spirit that was distant and estranged from a life of communion and conversation with God must become acquainted with him. We can never hope for his favour, mercy, and strength while we remain at a distance from Him. William D. Longstaff in 1882 wrote a hymn emphasizing the importance of spending quantity of time in prayer, seeking the face of God:

1. Take time to be holy **(or behold Him)**, speak oft with thy Lord;
   Abide in Him always, and feed on His Word.
   Make friends of God's children, help those who are weak,
   Forgetting in nothing His blessing to seek.

2. Take time to be holy **(or behold Him)**, the world rushes on;
   Spend much time in secret, with Jesus alone.
   By looking to Jesus, like Him thou shalt be;
   Thy friends in thy conduct His likeness shall see.

3. Take time to be holy **(or behold Him)**, let Him be thy Guide;
   And run not before Him, whatever betide.
   In joy or in sorrow, still follow the Lord,
   And, looking to Jesus, still trust in His Word.

4. Take time to be holy **(or behold Him)**, be calm in thy soul,
   Each thought and each motive beneath His control.
   Thus led by His Spirit to fountains of love,
   Thou soon shalt be fitted for service above.

We are to take time to be holy and to also behold Him because the more time we spend beholding Him, the more of Him we know and the more like Him we become. There is an adage in Nigeria that says that if a leaf stays long inside a local soap, it will eventually become soap itself. Prayer is a tool that helps us to behold Him as we come to Him with a humble heart. William Walford in 1845 wrote a hymn titled sweet hour of prayer:

Sweet hour of prayer! Sweet hour of prayer!
That calls me from a world of care,
And bids me at my Father's throne.
Make all my wants and wishes known.

In seasons of distress and grief,
My soul has often found relief.
And oft escaped the tempter's snare by thy return,
Sweet hour of prayer!

The LORD will be with you while you remain with him; and if you seek him, he will be found by you. But if ye forsake him, he will forsake you. Seeking and remaining with Him will afford us of seeing his face, and enjoying his favour, and having his presence. It will also benefit us by receiving help from him in every time of need. A constant seeking of his face will guide us against a spiritual aridity. Instead, it will bring spiritual refreshment. We must seek him by the studying of His word. We must delight ourselves in the law of the LORD and in his law we should meditate day and night. Then, shall we be like a tree planted by the rivers of water, that brings forth its fruits in its season; its leaves also shall not wither; and whatsoever we doeth shall prosper.

Every Christian must invest precious and quantity time to fellowship with God through prayer and personal Bible study because garbage in equals garbage out. *"Be not deceived; God is not mocked: for whatsoever a man soweth, that shall he also reap. For he that soweth to his flesh shall of the flesh reap corruption; but he that soweth to the Spirit shall of the Spirit reap life everlasting."* (Galatians 6:7-8)

2. ***Do not subject yourself to unnecessary stress and activities that steal away your time of fellowship with God and the brethren.***

One of the ways to curb spiritual deterioration and dryness is to avoid any job that can cause us unnecessary stress. Do not involve yourself in any activity that steals away your time of fellowship with God and the brethren. This is not a license for you to stay idle in your fellowship or church, folding your hands doing nothing. It is just a caution to cherish your spiritual nourishment and freshness. You should avoid an involvement in too many activities that will destroy your vine. You are the one to judge which activities to carry out in such a way that you still have quantity and quality time with God in prayer and personal bible study. Jesus is much more concerned about your spiritual life than your service life; life first before service.

3. **Manage your time effectively to accommodate your spiritual exercise (Prov. 6:3-11).**

Time management is a missing tool in the hand of most Christians. Without engaging in effective time management, we cannot live a dynamic balanced Christian life. We are to learn how to *redeem the time, because the days are evil.* We are to recover our time from waste, utilize it effectively and efficiently.

*"Give not sleep to thine eyes, nor slumber to thine eyelids. Deliver thyself as a roe from the hand of the hunter, and as a bird from the hand of the fowler. Go to the ant, thou sluggard; consider her ways, and be wise: Which having no guide, overseer, or ruler, Provideth her meat in the summer, and gathereth her food in the harvest. How long wilt thou sleep, O sluggard? when wilt thou arise out of thy sleep? Yet a little sleep, a little slumber, a little folding of the hands to sleep: So shall thy poverty come as one that travelleth, and thy want as an armed man"* (Proverbs 6:4-11).

In order to effectively manage your time, you need to set your priorities right. Which assignment needs urgency or carries heavy weight or is more beneficial? Arrange them in order of priority to the last. Learn to use a calendar or a diary whereby you can arrange different assignments according to dates and times. Let everything be done decently and in order. Ants are remarkable insects; they have foresight, industry, and economy. They gather food when there is the need for it; they are very economic with their time and resources. Spend your time wisely by orientating yourself and by assigning time to fellowship with God every day.

4. ***Learn to delegate authority: Let there be division of labour in whatever work you engage yourself.***

Most pastors may be thinking that they are the only one who know how to do everything best. This may be far from the reality; there are many talented and gifted brothers and sisters in your church that can even do better than you. Or if they cannot do the job as perfect as you, remember, Rome was not built in a day. Thus, they can improve through on-the-job training. Realise that nobody would ever expect Jephthah, a bastard, to become the deliverer and head of the Gileadites. *He was the son of an harlot. "And Gilead's wife bare him sons; and his wife's sons grew up, and they thrust out Jephthah, and said unto him, Thou shalt not inherit in our father's house; for thou art the son of a strange woman."* There are lots of Jephthahs, the outcasts in your congregation that you should allow to serve. They can be mighty weapons in the hands of God. So, do not kill your spiritual life, do not burry yourself alive because of involvement in too many activities.

With the great vision and passion that Nehemiah had, he did not allow himself to be fooled by this caterpillar of spiritual lives—involvement in too many activities. He believed in his people and divided the works of building the broken wall of Jerusalem among them. What you need to do is to share your work with your church workers. Let them see the importance of the task ahead, and call them to join you in doing it together.

# Chapter Four

## Setting Spiritual Boundary— Safeguarding the Christians

*"I am black, but comely, O ye daughters of Jerusalem, as the tents of Kedar, as the curtains of Solomon. Look not upon me, because I am black, because the sun hath looked upon me: my mother's children were angry with me; they made me the keeper of the vineyards; but mine own vineyard have I not kept."* (Song of Solomon 1:5-6, KJV)

*"We have a little sister, and she hath no breasts: what shall we do for our sister in the day when she shall be spoken for? If she be a wall, we will build upon her a palace of silver: and if she be a door, we will inclose her with boards of cedar. I am a wall, and my breasts like towers: then was I in his eyes as one that found favour."* (Song of Solomon 8:8-10, KJV)

Amplified Bible helps us to comprehend the meaning of Song of Solomon 8:8-9 better:

*8[Gathered with her family and the wedding guests in her mother's cottage, the bride said to her stepbrothers, When I was a little girl, you said] We have a little sister and she has no breasts. What shall we do for our sister on the day when she is spoken for*

*in marriage? ⁹If she is a wall [discreet and womanly],*
*we will build upon her a turret [a dowry] of silver; but*
*if she is a door [bold and flirtatious], we will enclose*
*her with boards of cedar.*

Boundary is something that indicates bounds or limits. It is a border line while limitation implies restrain, restriction and check. Boundaries and limitations are set to maintain checks and balances. Heavenly-minded Christians must set boundaries and limitations to help them stay in the faith and the race. One of the main reasons for the fall of most people, especially Christian leaders like prophets, pastors, evangelists and others, is their failure to set proper boundaries and proper limits for themselves.

Although we have considered Song of Solomon 1:5-6 as the dangers of a busy life, another perspective reveals that the actions of the siblings of the Shulamite were not without a purpose. We can clearly see the reason in Song of Solomon 8:8-10: it was to help her maintain her purity and virginity. They even promised her that if she remained a virgin till her wedding day, they would give her gifts. Therefore, they might have intentionally made the Shulamite keep their vineyards instead of hers as a way of setting boundaries or limitations. These restrictions were to prevent her from living a life of worldly pleasures, frivolity, and wantonness. Church members often complain that their pastors set too many boundaries and limitations for them but they do not understand that it's for their own good and protection. They even quote the Bible in order to affirm that they are no longer under the law but under grace, forgetting that our grace liberty is not a license to sin. Naturally, no man wants to operate under a restriction or a border line. No man wants monitoring. Man craves for liberty and freedom. Listen to this Bible reference:

*"For whom the Lord loveth he chasteneth, and*
*scourgeth every son whom he receiveth. If ye endure*
*chastening, God dealeth with you as with sons;*

*for what son is he whom the father chasteneth not? But if ye be without chastisement, whereof all are partakers, then are ye bastards, and not sons. Furthermore we have had fathers of our flesh which corrected us, and we gave them reverence: shall we not much rather be in subjection unto the Father of spirits, and live? For they verily for a few days chastened us after their own pleasure; but he for our profit, that we might be partakers of his holiness. Now no chastening for the present seemeth to be joyous, but grievous: nevertheless afterward it yieldeth the peaceable fruit of righteousness unto them which are exercised thereby."* (Hebrew 12:6-11)

## Causes of boundaries and limitations

I know a church (name withheld) that has set a lot of boundaries and limitations which are being preached from time to time, as a reminder to their members. Unfortunately, many other churches do criticise this church's set boundaries. The critics forget that the Bible is filled with lots of set boundaries and limitations for both the Old and New Testament believers. The Apostle Paul instructed a young minister, Timothy thus *"O Timothy, keep that which is committed to thy trust, <u>avoiding profane and vain babblings</u>, and oppositions of science falsely so called: Which some professing have erred concerning the faith. Grace be with thee. Amen."* (1Timothy 6:20-21) The word "avoid" means "do not go there, there is a border line."

The Shulamite lady might have felt bad when the children of her mother did prevent her from messing herself around their village, not allowing her to mingle with the worldly system and amusements around her. But what pushed her brothers to react in such a manner? It is the drive to keep their sister pure till her wedding day. Those boundaries and limitations, with the grace of God, helped her remain a virgin (a wall, Song of Solomon 8:8-10) until she was wedded. All the set boundaries and limitations become a norm through life's experiences and circumstances. Keeping yourself within these barriers will enhance your spiritual growth and help you make heaven on the last day. The Apostle Paul emphasized the idea of Christian brethren setting spiritual boundaries and watching over each other's soul when he said, *"For I am jealous over you with godly jealousy: for I have espoused you to one husband, that I may present you as a chaste virgin to Christ. But I fear, lest by any means, as the serpent beguiled Eve through his subtilty, so your minds should be corrupted from the simplicity that is in Christ"* (2 Corinthians 11:2-3).

There are various reasons it would be advisable to set boundaries and limitations, especially by Bible believers. Few of these reasons are:

1. **To avoid sin**
   An unguarded man is very susceptible to failure and sin. So a perfect walk with God requires us to set appropriate, meaningful and practicable boundaries and limitations to avoid failures.

   One of the powerful and effective ways to avoid falling into sin, especially sexual immorality, is to abstain from all appearance of evil like watching pornographic pictures. Matthew Henry, a great Bible commentator wrote: *"We should therefore abstain from evil, and all appearances of evil, from sin, and that which looks like sin, leads to it, and borders upon it. He who is not shy of the appearances of sin, who shuns not the occasions of sin, and who avoids not the temptations and approaches to sin, will not long abstain from the actual commission of sin."* King David failed to abstain from the initial appearance of evil, the naked woman. He took pleasure in watching the pornographic movie of Bathsheba (while she took her bath) from the top of his building. He did not run away from the enticing nakedness and beautiful body structure of Bathsheba. The beauty of Uriah's wife had captured him like a bird in the hands of the fowler. He failed to make a covenant with his eyes never to think upon a maid unlike Job (Job 31:1). It is easy to cast all the blame on King David but who knows whether Bathsheba herself had not been longing for such an opportunity, to hunt down the king of Israel. The Bible says that the harlot hunts for precious life. Why was she taking her shower herself there, knowing full well that her husband had gone to the battlefield while king David tarried in the palace? Probably the pool filled with water was not her normal place of showering. The point is, there are many ladies, office secretaries, personnel assistants, office cleaners, and co-workers who hunt for their boss' life by dressing in a sexy manner, wearing transparent clothes, decking their faces with powder and lip sticks like Jezebel in the Bible, or wearing half-naked dresses. Everything that they do is targeted to trap you into their net just like Tamar did to Judah (Genesis 38:13-16). Nevertheless, whosoever is deceived by such acts is not wise. Dear bosses, you have no excuse for falling into such trap because you are commanded to abstain from all appearance of evil. I know of a University Dean, whenever his Secretary (a woman) is in his office with him, he always makes sure that the door is widely opened for other staff to see what is going on inside the office. That is setting a limitation for himself to avoid falling into sin.

The author of the letters to Corinth stated *"but I keep under my body, and bring it into subjection: lest that by any means, when I have preached to others, I myself should be a castaway."* (1 Corinthians 9:27). Removal of every passion that corrupts our soul and manifests carnal inclination demand subjecting ourselves to self-mortification or self-denial in order to separate us from carnal living. God set boundaries for the Israelites and Christians concerning marriages with unbelieving persons in Deuteronomy 7:1-4 and 2 Corinthians 6:14-18, respectively.

To the Israelites He said: *"When the LORD thy God shall bring thee into the land whither thou goest to possess it, and hath cast out many nations before thee, the Hittites, and the Girgashites, and the Amorites, and the Canaanites, and the Perizzites, and the Hivites, and the Jebusites, seven nations greater and mightier than thou; . . . thou shalt make no covenant with them, . . . : Neither shalt thou make marriages with them; thy daughter thou shalt not give unto his son, nor his daughter shalt thou take unto thy son. For they will turn away thy son from following me, that they may serve other gods: so will the anger of the LORD be kindled against you, and destroy thee suddenly."*

And to the Christians: *"Be ye not unequally yoked together with unbelievers: for what fellowship hath righteousness with unrighteousness? and what communion hath light with darkness? And what concord hath Christ with Belial? or what part hath he that believeth with an infidel? And what agreement hath the temple of God with idols? for ye are the temple of the living God; as God hath said, I will dwell in them, and walk in them; and I will be their God, and they shall be my people. Wherefore come out from among them, and be ye separate, saith the Lord, and touch not the unclean thing; and I will receive you, And will be a Father unto you, and ye shall be my sons and daughters, saith the Lord Almighty."*

The reason for such boundaries and limitations is that the children of God could be easily swayed from following God, which would therefore make them serve other gods. Solomon failed to observe this commandment and so he removed the ancient landmark by marrying many strange women. So, he faced the music. He or she who becomes an in-law to Satan must be ready for daily attacks and troubles. So is he or she who marries any unbeliever.

2. ***To set a good example and to protect your brother***
Sometimes we do not have to set boundaries just to avoid falling into sin but for the sake of those brethren around us. Also for leaders, they have to set boundaries and limitations in order to set a good example to the people under them.

*"But meat commendeth us not to God: for neither, if we eat, are we the better; neither, if we eat not, are we the worse. But take heed lest by any means this liberty of yours become a stumblingblock to them that are weak. For if any man see thee which hast knowledge sit at meat in the idol's temple, shall not the conscience of him which is weak be emboldened to eat those things which are offered to idols; And through thy knowledge shall the weak brother perish, for whom Christ died? But when ye sin so against the brethren, and wound their weak conscience, ye sin against Christ. Wherefore, if meat make my brother to offend, I will eat no flesh while the world standeth, lest I make my brother to offend."* (1 Corinthians 8:8-13)

Apostle Paul, here, talked about setting restrictions concerning the eating of meat. He would not eat meat for life if eating it would cause the falling away of some brethren. Can you place restrictions on most of your lifestyle just for the sake of letting your brother or sister in the Lord remain in the faith?

The writing of Dr. Whitby on 1 Corinthians 8:13 (an excerpt from Matthew Henry commentary) is full of details that every Christians ought to know.

1. The greater our reputation for knowledge and sanctity, the greater mischief we shall do by our influence and example if we turn aside from the holy commandment delivered unto us. Every man should walk so as either to light or lead his brother to heaven.

2. It is the duty of every Christian to watch against apostasy in his own case, and to prevent it as much as possible in that of others. That a person for whom Christ died may finally perish is strongly argued, by thus offending, saith the apostle, "ye sin against Christ; viz. by sinning against him whom he has purchased by his blood; and destroying them for whose salvation he has suffered." If this intent of Christ's death be denied, how can we show how Christ has demonstrated his great love to them that perish? Is it possible that they can sin against redeeming love? And how, by thus offending them who neither do nor can belong to him as members of his mystical body, are we injurious to Christ?

3. Persons of an over tender and scrupulous conscience may be very troublesome in a Christian society; but as this excessive scrupulosity comes from a want of more light, more experience, or more judgment, we should bear with them. Though such should often run into ridiculous extremes, yet we must take care that we do not attempt to cure them either with ridicule or wrath. Extremes generally beget extremes; and such persons require the most judicious treatment, else they will soon stumble and turn out of the way. We should be very careful lest in using what is called Christian liberty we occasion their fall; and for our own sake, we must take heed that we do not denominate sinful indulgences, Christian liberties.

When we talk about Christian dressing for the sake of preserving purity, safeguarding against the evil of lust—immoral desire among our brethren—most modern day preachers will frown at it.

Most Christian women that are deeply influenced by the wind of civilisation would argue in support of dressing that reveals their body structure and nakedness. "If a brother falls because of the way I dress that is his problem, not mine," they say.

They forget or decide not to care about the fact that we are to be our brothers' keepers. Do not wonder why the sin of immorality and divorce are rampant in our churches and the world! Is it not because of the accommodations of these Jezebel types of dressing?

After the fall of man in Genesis 3, it is really difficult to pin-point the exact date in the history of man when resurgence of naked dressing began. What is clear though is that it came to a time when artists began to produce naked women images. Women became sex objects. Can't we, Christian leaders, discern that Satan is into the church to defile and destroy us with this wind of doctrine on civilised Christian dressing—the attire of harlots? Why is it that we still allow this thing to seduce our brethren to commit immorality?

*"And of the children of Issachar, which were men that had understanding of the times, to know what Israel ought to do; the heads of them were two hundred; and all their brethren were at their commandment."* (1 Chronicles 12:32)

The church needs men and women who have understanding of the times, to know what we ought to do. Satan is not resting; he is busy going to and fro, wanting to defile and destroy Christianity and renders it to rubble. Sadly, we are like the daughters of Zion who are at ease. Satan is destroying the work of God in our hands and we care not about it. To him that knows how to do good but does it not, it is a sin.

*"And unto the angel of the church in Thyatira write; These things saith the Son of God, who hath his eyes like unto a flame of fire, and his feet are like fine brass; I know thy works, and charity, and service, and faith, and thy patience, and thy works; and the last to be more than the first. Notwithstanding I have a few things against thee, because thou sufferest that woman Jezebel, which calleth herself a prophetess, to teach and to seduce my servants to commit fornication, and to eat things sacrificed unto idols."* (Revelation 2:18-20)

Pastors, the accommodation of half-naked women in the church because we want a large population and popularity will send many of our older and young brothers under your watch to hell.

My dear sisters in the Lord, please, if your pastors refuse to tell you the truth, the unadulterated word of God, I believe that you have your Bible and common sense. Do not you read your Bible and pray to live a holy, blameless, unblemished life? Why do you want to continue to put on the dress of a harlot? Do not you know that there are weak brothers who cannot stand seeing the nakedness of a woman without lusting in their hearts? Do not you pity them? They are vexing their righteous soul every Sunday and mid-week days of Church programs because of your dressing style. The Bible talked about Lot that dwelt in Sodom *"that righteous man dwelling among them, in seeing and hearing, vexed his righteous soul from day to day with their unlawful deeds;"* (2 Peter 2:8). The Apostle Paul said that if eating meat, which is very good for our health, would make just a brother to sin or be offended, he would stop eating it as long as he lives. For the sake of your Christian brothers, please learn to dress to cover your nakedness properly and decently.

Two among the qualifications to be a Christian leader refers to the character of a bishop. The bishop then must be blameless, must have a good report of them which are without lest he falls into reproach and the snare of Satan. He should be a man of irreproachable character for truth, honesty, chastity, and general uprightness. He must not live a shady life. How will you think that other brethren will view it if they begin to see you with a particular lady who is not your wife at all times, especially, when your family is not around? There was a case of a brother and a sister in my church who lived not above reproach a few years ago. This brother was very spiritual and became one of our leaders when I travelled to another place, far from them. He noticed that the sister needed assistance like accommodation and food, so he decided to help by allowing the sister to come and live with him in a room of about six feet by eight feet. They were not married and were not siblings. Actually, they were from different States. They ate whatever the sister cooked and slept in the same room. Then, the brethren began to complain and murmur about it. When I heard it, I called the brother and he told me that he was doing that because the sister needed help. When he would not let the sister go to a separate place, I decided to discipline him, relieving him of pastoring the church. Then, he decided to leave our church. I did not discipline him because he helped the sister, nor because I alleged him of committing fornication but because he was not showing a good example by living with the sister in a room! They were not even married! I disciplined him because I knew that he was not living above reproach. Allowing him to continue leading the church would amount to I condoning sin, and the people in their community would always refer to them as bad Christian leaders. Allowing him would have laid a bad legacy for the generation of the church members to come. We need to set boundaries and limitations that will help us to live an exemplary life for our followers. Boundaries and limitations on what to eat, what to wear, what to say, where to go, not because doing or not doing such is condemnable but just to accord ourselves courtesy and honour. Listen again to the Apostle Paul in his epistle to the Church at Thessalonica:

*Ye are witnesses, and God also, how holily and justly and unblameably we behaved ourselves among you that believe:"* (1 Thessalonians 2:10). To the Church at Philippi he wrote: *"Finally, brethren, whatsoever things are true, whatsoever things are honest, whatsoever things are just, whatsoever things are pure, whatsoever things are lovely, whatsoever things are of good report; if there be any virtue, and if there be any praise, think on these things."* (Philippians 4:8)

Some things in themselves might not be out rightly wrong but because a fellow brother might be struggling with these things, we ought to refrain from such things for their sake. I pray the very God of peace may grant you understanding.

## Setting appropriate boundaries and limitations

As we have considered, there is a need to set appropriate borderlines and restrictions. By our carnal reasoning, we cannot set these but with the help of God, we can do it.

1. **Knowledge of the Word of God. *Joshua 1:8, John 5:39; Psalms 119:11.***
   *"And it shall be, when he sitteth upon the throne of his kingdom, that he shall write him a copy of this law in a book out of that which is before the priests the Levites: And it shall be with him, and he shall read therein all*

*the days of his life: that he may learn to fear the LORD his God, to keep all the words of this law and these statutes, to do them: That his heart be not lifted up above his brethren, and that he turn not aside from the commandment, to the right hand, or to the left: to the end that he may prolong his days in his kingdom, he, and his children, in the midst of Israel."* (Deuteronomy 17:18-20)

The word of God directs us. It is a lamp to our feet. The studying and understanding of the Bible will help us know what we ought to and not to do, thereby enhancing our judgement and decision making on what and where to set our boundaries. If a child knows that his mummy commands him not to break anything in the living room, then he can better set his limits when it comes to running around in the house. In setting such limits, he can serve as an example to his younger ones as to where they should set their limits as well.

2. **Ask God to reveal your faults to you**
   Setting boundaries and limitations are very sensitive issues of life, so we need to earnestly seek the face of God through prayer as we go through the word of God. When we pray, especially with fasting, what we are doing is, mortifying the flesh and submitting to the will of God. He is the only one that can give us the blueprint of the boundaries and limitations to set.

*"O LORD, thou hast searched me, and known me. Thou knowest my downsitting and mine uprising, thou understandest my thought afar off . . . Search me, O God, and know my heart: try me, and know my thoughts: And see if there be any wicked way in me, and lead me in the way everlasting."* (Psalm 139:1-2, 23-24)

No man knows himself well. I hold the hypothesis that the best a person can ever get to know himself on a scale of 1-10 where 10 is perfection is 6. A person might think he is inherently quiet and calm until someone really steps on his toes, then he blows up like a volcano and is surprised at his behaviour. More often than not, different situations dictate our reactions, because man had become reactive and not proactive. Going to God for self revelation would help us in setting boundaries for ourselves.

3.  **Seek the help of self revelation from your brothers**
    We do not know ourselves (that is why we regret); many times we do things and later on, wish that we did not do them. There is not a man who can claim to know himself perfectly well. Your brother is a mirror to you. Through him, you can see your faults and weaknesses. The Bible says in Proverbs 27:17 *"Iron sharpeneth iron."* There are many things that we do and we do not realise that we did them, especially things that we are passionate about. In doing such things, you might get too passionate and do the wrong thing or say things that are not good, or think evil thoughts. In such situations, it would be helpful to look at yourself in the mirror that is your brother or sister. Apostle Peter would not have identified his mistake if not for Apostle Paul who became his mirror and cautioned him into correction. We need men and women of God to draw the line of no-go area before us so that we do not fall into the trap of Satan. For the king of Israel, Elisha helped in this regard when the king of Syria warred against him.

    *"Then the king of Syria warred against Israel, and took counsel with his servants, saying, in such and such a place shall be my camp. And the man of God sent unto the king of Israel, saying, Beware that thou pass not such a place; for thither the Syrians are come down. And the king of Israel sent to the place which the man of God told him and warned him of, and saved himself there, not once nor twice."* (2 Kings 6:8-10)

4. **Be attentive to the Holy Spirit**
   *"Howbeit when he, the Spirit of truth, is come, he will guide you into all truth: for he shall not speak of himself; but whatsoever he shall hear, that shall he speak: and he will shew you things to come."* (John 16:13)

   In setting boundaries for ourselves, we have to be attentive to the Holy Spirit, and seek His direction as well. Because we are very unaware of the future, it is important that we seek the guidance of the Holy Spirit who knows all things and is aware of everything, especially when we are tempted by Satan. We need to listen to the Holy Spirit who will help us set up and respect strong boundaries.

5. **Avoid compromises**
   Compromises are deadly. The road to compromise is often steep and slippery. Once a Christian begins to compromise, it is all downhill for such a person. Compromise is a very dangerous thing and if we fill ourselves with the unadulterated Word of God and steer clear of compromise, we will set our boundaries and limitations better.

## Consequences of misplaced priorities and lack of boundaries and limitations

For every misplaced priority and lack of boundary or limitation in our daily living, we are exposed to grievous consequences.

1. **Openness to attacks of Satan**
   *"These six cities shall be a refuge, both for the children of Israel, and for the stranger, and for the sojourner among them: that every one that killeth any person unawares may flee thither. But if the slayer shall at any time come without the border of the city of his refuge,*

*whither he was fled; And the revenger of blood find him without the borders of the city of his refuge, and the revenger of blood kill the slayer; he shall not be guilty of blood: Because he should have remained in the city of his refuge until the death of the high priest: but after the death of the high priest the slayer shall return into the land of his possession."* (Numbers 35:15, 26-28)

*"He that diggeth a pit shall fall into it; and whoso breaketh an hedge, a serpent shall bite him."* (Ecclesiastes 10:8)

In ancient Israel, any man who mistakenly killed another man was granted grace if he escaped to one of the six cities of refuge already provided. However, there was a limitation to that grace; he or she was to remain within the border line of the city. Sitting or crossing the border line would incur his or her capture by the avenger of blood and would be made to face the music. In the same way, Christians who were once sinners are condemned to death but through the grace provided by God in Christ Jesus, such persons can escape into the city of Refuge—Jesus Christ—in order to live again. We are therefore commanded to remain in Christ or else we will be destroyed by Satan.

When we do not set boundaries for ourselves, we lower our guard and it becomes easy for Satan to entice us with his deceit, and snatch us from the kingdom of light to the kingdom of darkness. No wonder, when the wall of Jerusalem broke down, Nehemiah could not but pray and act quickly to rebuild it, lest his people became exposed to the attacks of their enemies. The boundary that God set about the marriages of Israelites against the ungodly nations was removed by Solomon, and he suffered for it.

## 2. Openness to the evils in this world.

i. *Immorality*

Many Christians have been seduced by the adulterous women and men because of their failure to set boundaries or by breaking through the boundaries. Inability to set boundaries concerning lust for mundane things has sent so many people to hell. When your wife or husband travels, how far and deep is the relationship between you and her friend or his friend? Set a boundary, a no-go area for him or her. Has your housemaid become your second or even primary wife in terms of taking care of you because of the tight schedule of your wife? Watch out! You need to set a boundary. Are you engaged to someone? Please, set the boundary so that your bed will be honourable and not defiled before the wedding day. As both of you travel to see parents, relatives and friends for the introduction and other activities, be very careful! Avoid sitting close to each other in a public commuter or sitting together in the front or back of a car if you own one. Do not stay in dark places or stay out late in each other's house. Please, refuse to be pressurised to stay overnight together irrespective of the circumstances. Remember, you are not a wood or a stone. Women are sensitive to touch and men are sensitive to sight. Avoid kissing or hugging each other before marriage or else you are inviting sex, which will damn your soul.

ii. *Pride*

*"And thou say in thine heart, My power and the might of mine hand hath gotten me this wealth. But thou shalt remember the LORD thy God: for it is he that giveth thee power to get wealth, that he may establish his covenant which he sware unto thy fathers, as it is this day."* (Deuteronomy 8:17-18).

We need to set boundaries to what will help us live above reproach and the pride of life. Many men and women have been overcome by pride and have fallen very low because of their failure to set boundaries. Pride comes before a fall (Proverbs 16:18). Pride always gives birth to self conceit. This can be a problem when we advance spiritually if we fail to set boundaries above our pride. We ought to always remain humble in all circumstances, setting boundaries even in our mind so as not to become conceited.

*"For I say, through the grace given unto me, to every man that is among you, not to think of himself more highly than he ought to think; but to think soberly, according as God hath dealt to every man the measure of faith."* (Romans 12:3).

# Chapter Five

## Seeking the Genuine Lover

"[Addressing her shepherd, she said] *Tell me, O thou whom my soul loveth, where thou feedest, where thou makest thy flock to rest at noon: for why should I be as one that turneth aside by the flocks of thy companions?* [The court ladies counsel] *If thou know not, O thou fairest among women, go thy way forth by the footsteps of the flock, and feed thy kids beside the shepherds' tents. I have compared thee, O my love* [he said as he saw her], *to a company of horses in Pharaoh's chariots. Thy cheeks are comely with rows of jewels, thy neck with chains of gold. We will make thee borders of gold with studs of silver. While the king sitteth at his table* [she said], *my spikenard* [my absent lover] *sendeth forth the smell thereof* [over me]. *A bundle of myrrh is my well beloved* [shepherd] *unto me; he shall lie all night betwixt my breasts. My beloved* [shepherd] *is unto me as a cluster of camphire in the vineyards of Engedi. Behold, thou art fair, my love; behold, thou art fair; thou hast doves' eyes.* [She cried] *Behold, thou art fair, my beloved* [shepherd], *yea, pleasant: also our bed is green. The beams of our house are cedar, and our rafters of fir.*" (Song of Solomon 1:7-17, KJV and AMP mixed)

"[She said] *I am the rose of Sharon, and the lily of the valleys* [that grows in deep and difficult places]. [But Solomon replied] *As the lily among thorns, so is my love among the daughters. As the apple tree among the trees of the wood, so is my beloved* [shepherd] *among the sons* [cried the girl]. *I sat down under his shadow with great delight, and his fruit was sweet to my taste. He brought me to the banqueting house, and his banner over me was love. Stay me with flagons, comfort me with apples: for I am sick of love. His left hand is under my head, and his right hand doth embrace me.*" (Song of Solomon 2:1-6, KJV and AMP mixed)

## Petition of the Sincere Seeker Song 1:7

The true picture of her soul: 'O thou whom my soul loveth.' This is a fervent and unfeigned love for her Lover with a longing desire for true fellowship. Her soul is a sweet and affectionate one. This type of affectionate and ravishing love is not found in the soul of an unregenerated person. It is an ardent and vehement love in her towards him, so she might say that her soul loved, honoured, desired, and esteemed him. Such soul has displeasure for every other thing besides the lover Shepherd. He is the only object of her affection. He alone possesses her heart, and is on its throne as chief of her affections. He hath no co-partner there.

As a Christian, is it Christ that your soul loves and has enthroned as your only lover? If you really love Jesus Christ, He alone will be your desire and to Him alone will you give your love and life. Supreme love for the Saviour entails loving Him with all your heart, and with all your soul. Only a sanctified (set apart) heart can possess such love: rooted and grounded in Christ. If Christ is the only desire of your heart, you will long to fellowship with Him at all times. Your heart will pant after Him as the deer pants after the water brook. You will not want to miss His presence for anything.

She calls on her beloved, the one whom her soul loves, to tell her where he is feeding his flocks, and where he takes his noonday rest. She does not want her sweetheart to be wandering around the different encampments of her sweetheart fellow-shepherds, veiled against their gaze while looking for him and being mistaken for a loose woman. This keen interest in the shepherd compelled her to make two sincere and powerful requests:

1. **Revelation of the source of provision** (Song 1:7c; Psalm 9-10; 61:1-2; 23:1-5). She asked her lover to show her where he feeds his sheep. This indicates that she did not want to feed in the wrong place or on poisonous food (John 6:30-40,47-51,60,66-69). There are lots of shepherds today who have poisonous food, contaminated food, and adulterated food for the sheep that comes to them. Likewise, the food or doctrine that some pastors have for their church members or audience is a false doctrine that destroys their soul. It is a pity that in our age, some pastors are taking advantage of people who are poverty stricken by telling them that they can become millionaires in a few days if they would donate all that they have in order to sow a seed. Many of our churches are now money-milking machines. These pastors, that I normally call Positive-Thinking Preachers, are not really Christ's Gospel Preachers. They are making merchandise of the gospel. Many are masquerading themselves as deliverance ministers, prosperity preachers, etc. *but their end is destruction, their God is their belly, and their glory is in their shame because they mind earthly things.*

If truly you belong to the flock of Christ, you should be able to clearly recognise His voice and follow Him. Most of the so-called sheep of The True Shepherd prefer to follow strangers: the thieves and robbers. How wonderful it will be for all Christians to pray like the Shulamite lady for divine revelation and guidance to the source of divine provision of the undiluted word of God? Whenever we pray sincerely from the depth of our hearts, the Holy Spirit will show us the deeper revelation of His word. *"But unto the place which the LORD your God shall choose out of all your tribes to put his name there, even unto his habitation shall ye seek, and thither thou shalt come: And there ye shall eat before the LORD your God, and ye shall rejoice in all that ye put your hand unto, ye and your households, wherein the LORD thy God hath blessed thee"* (Deuteronomy 12:5, 7). The place where He feeds his sheep is not always easily discerned and discovered. Why? This is because there are many dead churches where leaders are seeking their own self-interests, not caring about people's salvation. *"Lo, here is Christ; or, lo, he is there; believe him not: For false Christs and false prophets shall rise, and shall shew signs and wonders, to seduce, if it were possible, even the elect. But take ye heed: behold, I have foretold you all things."* (Mark 13:21-23)

Let us quickly consider an example of the prevalence of false prophets and deliverance ministers in our days. Lusting after the things of this world will cause you to be spiritually lost. About fifteen years ago, I was praying for a Christian sister (a church worker) when the Holy Spirit revealed to me that she had gone to another church's pastor to seek for prayer. In the course of that prayer, that pastor touched her private part and conducted an operation (which he called deliverance) there. I told the sister what the Lord had revealed to me concerning her. She did not deny it; she explained that she went to the pastor for deliverance from satanic influence. Then, the pastor told her that both of them would need to pray in the midnight hour. When they started praying, the pastor told her that the deliverance would be conducted in a special way and that it would be by cutting the hairs on her private part. The desperate need for deliverance made her believe in those lies. The repercussion of that deliverance was grievous. She became insane a few years after. But the God of mercy has set her free.

Jesus, the good Shepherd feeds His sheep with green pastures and, beside the still waters. *"He shall feed his flock like a shepherd: he shall gather the lambs with his arm, and carry them in his bosom, and shall gently lead those that are with young"* (Isaiah 40:11). Christ's word is the food that He feeds His flocks with. According to the Bible in Jeremiah 3:15, pastors who are preaching the word according to God's pattern will feed the flock with knowledge and understanding.

2. **Direction to the place of comfort and refreshment** (Song 1:7d; Psalm 23:1-5).

   *"Tell me, . . . where thou makest thy flock to rest at noon: for why should I be as one that turneth aside by the flocks of thy companions?*

The sincere desire of the Shulamite was that her Lover would give her the direction to the place where his flocks rested, and were refreshed. She wanted to partake in that rest too, not wanting anything to derail her from the congregation of her Lover's flocks. The pain of separation from her Lover, the temptations she was confronted with, the fear of rape or coerced marriage with an unwanted man, and the suffering from peer pressure—the court ladies—were so depressing that she needed to take a rest. She wanted to take a rest right in the camp of the righteous and holy flock of her Lover; not in the camp of the ungodly.

It will be wonderful if all Christians who suffer these kinds of afflictions and temptations will pray for comfort and rest of mind from the Holy Spirit in order to be free from anxiety and fear. It is only the Holy Spirit who can give us calmness of the spirit in such a time like this. He is the only one that can lead us beside the still waters to refresh our soul.

The Invitation of the Lover of our souls to direct us to a place of rest whenever we are passing through a boisterous storming sea will not only grant us great peace but will also afford us good rest and pleasure. By our own strength, we cannot make it out of the tempter's stronghold. Thanks to God for we have a consolation in Him. He already promised us that when we pass through the fire and the water of temptations, He will not leave us nor forsake us. Are you confused about who to marry? You may be confused because you are just coming out of a broken relationship and wonder if you should enter the dating scene again. It could be there is somebody in your life who wants to marry you but you are having difficulties discerning whether that person is the will of God for your life or not. Dear reader, what you need to do is to pray like the Shulamite lady for a restful spirit and guidance. It is not a time to panic; the Psalmist says that *"though I walk through the valley of the shadow of death"*—sentenced to imprisonment in the camp of the tempter, fell from grace to grace, from virginity to dis-virginity, from morality to immoral guilt, purity of soul, spirit and body to polluted house—*"I shall fear no evil."* This is because His rod and staff will guide and comfort me.

The important lessons from these two petitions:

i.   The relationship between Christ and the believers: He is the Shepherd, and the Christians represent the flock (Isaiah 40:11; Ezekiel 34:11,12; Psalm 23:1,2).
ii.  Christ's flock may be in danger of going astray and be afflicted but He will never leave nor forsake them. He will not let them be defiled (Isaiah 43:1-3).
iii. Christ is the place of comfort and refreshment for His flock at all times when they go through storms (John 10:11; Isaiah 40:11; Micah 5:4).

iv. Believers may not know how to either get out of temptations or be quiet while under crosses, till help comes from above with light and strength. They may not know the well (source of water) whence their supply and consolation come from, till it is discovered by them, as it was to Hagar.
v. Christ alone knows how to provide protection against sin and shadow us from suffering.
vi. Believers ought to seek Him for help and direction at all times.

The reason for her two-fold petitions: she was not willing to turn aside to follow those who presented themselves as lovers of her soul. Today, we can refer to such people as false christs or false prophets (Matthew 24:23,24; Galatians 1:6-9; Exodus 32:1-10).

## Problems Confronted by Sincere Seekers Song 1:8-11

1. **Counsel from uninformed and unregenerated people.** The counsel given in verse 8: *"If thou know not, O thou fairest among women, go thy way forth by the footsteps of the flock, and feed thy kids beside the shepherds' tents"* that comment was not given by the king but the court ladies. Barnes, a Bible commentator rightly said, "their meaning seems to be: If thy beloved be indeed a shepherd, then seek him yonder among other shepherds, but if a king, thou wilt find him here in his royal dwelling." Since they did not know the True Way, they seemed to sit on the fence in their counselling. Such challenge is to call one's attention to do the right thing. Elijah once challenged the Israelites before the contest on Mount Carmel. *"And Elijah came unto all the people, and said, How long halt ye between two opinions? if the LORD be God, follow him: but if Baal, then follow him."* (1 Kings 18:21). This called people, encouraged them to do the right thing.

There are two types of counsels: counsel from the regenerated and well-informed people and also from sinners. Counsels from the ungodly can be two-fold: wise and foolish. Let us be sincere to ourselves, there are times that unbelievers do give wise and reasonable advice to Christians. God is able to use anything in favour of His frustrated children. He, here, used the court ladies in the office of the Holy Spirit, the comforter and counsellor to give guidance, direction and instruction to a desperate lady (Isaiah 30:21; John 16:13). Jethro, on a visit, found his son-in-law, Moses, judging the Israelites from morning till evening. Seeing how tiresome the task was for Moses, he advised him to delegate authority to able and trustworthy men who can stand in for him. Indeed, this was very good for Moses who followed the counsel. In fact, this counsel is still very much useful to pastors today to avoid wearing themselves out. About a decade ago, a close friend of mine was so desperate to get married. He had prayed a lot but nothing was forthcoming. One day, out of frustration when he got to his workplace, he called one of his female staff (she was single then) and told her bluntly that he would like to marry her.

The lady looked at my friend, her eyes revealing a look of amusement, and said, "Sir, I know that you are of age to marry but my guess is that you are asking for my hand in marriage not because you feel led by God, but because of frustration. Sir, if I marry you, I will be a problem to you because you are a Christian, a member of a holiness-believing church," changing the tone of her voice, she continued. "You know as well as I that I am not as Christian as you are. Though I go to church, the church I attend does not restrain me from worldly amusements. So if we tie the knot together, you will regret it for your lifetime sir," she explained.

Her counsel for him was that he should pray very well and wait patiently for God's best. This advice was spoken through her by the Holy Spirit, I believe. So, sinners can give good, intelligent, and wise counsel to Christians.

Generally speaking, sinners are more likely to give foolish advice than Christians. The common advice from our new generation counsellors is that believers should sit on the fence: one leg in, one leg out instead of being too close to the True Shepherd. They advise us to feed among or near the deceptive shepherds. The sincere seekers of Christ, heavenly-minded people, have a mandate from the almighty God which states that:

*"My son, if sinners entice thee, consent thou not. If they say, Come with us, let us lay wait for blood, let us lurk privily for the innocent without cause: Let us swallow them up alive as the grave; and whole, as those that go down into the pit: We shall find all precious substance, we shall fill our houses with spoil: Cast in thy lot among us; let us all have one purse: My son, walk not thou in the way with them; refrain thy foot from their path: For their feet run to evil, and make haste to shed blood. Surely in vain the net is spread in the sight of any bird. And they lay wait for their own blood; they lurk privily for their own lives. So are the ways of every one that is greedy of gain; which taketh away the life of the owners thereof."* (Proverbs 1:10-19)

It is delightful and wonderful to seek God's guidance when confusion seem to blind our eyes from seeing the right path. We need to depend upon the Lord and listen to the Holy Spirit's counsel when temptation comes our way.

The people of this world do sometimes advise us to take life easy, mellow down, and blend with the system since it is too hard to be a true and trustworthy follower of

Christ in this era. On the second day I started writing this Chapter, a pastor friend told me the tragic story of a Christian family who were members of his church denomination in another town. The husband and his wife had been married for about five years but had no children. Both of them had been seeking God to open the woman's womb so she could conceive. Her friends counselled her to find an alternative way to solve the problem since prayer was not working. They counselled her to go to an herbalist but she initially refused, claiming that she and her husband were true believers of Christ. They told her that if she refused to go, after many years of barrenness, her husband would dump her for another woman. Therefore, with much persuasion, she succumbed to their ungodly counsel. She followed them to an herbalist (a wizard). The man told her that she would give birth to children but must first make a sacrifice and carry it to the river's side. She told him that she could not do such a thing because of her husband. The wizard insisted that it is even her husband who would carry the sacrifice. Again, after must persuasion, she agreed to inform her husband. When she told him, the man bluntly refused and told her not to mention that again. Remember, a little yeast will leaven the bread (swell up). When the woman started crying, begging her husband to perform the sacrifice, he agreed. They both went to the wizard and did the sacrifice. When they got to the river's side, the water spirit that the wizard had consulted refused to either come out of the water or answer them. Finally, an instruction came from the water that there was a fire around this Christian husband and that the fire must be quenched before the sacrifice could be accepted. The wizard then suggested that the only way to quench the fire was for the man to have sexual intercourse with another woman. So, the wife helped him to get a woman and the brother slept with her. So, when they came back to offer the sacrifice, the water spirit came out and took the sacrifice and the man to the bottom of the water. Unfortunately, the evil spirit refused to release the man and later they found his dead body floating on the river. You may want to say that his wife sent him to hell! Yes you are right! However, he also participated to his untimely death and he will remain in the lake of fire for eternity.

My brothers and sisters in the Lord, when a sinner entices you, consent not to it. I remember that a similar event almost happened to me when I got married and for five years we were, my wife and I, without a child. I have many friends that are pastors who were fasting and praying with me. So, one of my uncles connected me with a pastor. We started praying together through the phone because of the long distance between us. Both of us lived in two different countries then. One day, the said pastor instructed my wife and I to put a cup of water outside and allow it to stay there overnight. Then, on the following day, we should drink it and bathe with it after the second day.

I said "Sir, I have enjoyed the prayers that we have been having together and I believe only in the name of Jesus Christ, my Saviour, not in the use of water or other things. Sir, I cannot do that."

What was going on in my mind then was that if we did that, then we would get a mammy-water (evil spirit from the water, bottom to head with human body while bottom down is fish tail) child. That is a sacrifice unto Satan not unto God. Christ had offered Himself as a completed sacrifice for us; no need for another. Therefore, are you seeking for the solution to your delay in child-bearing, marriage, getting an employment or other things? Please, wait on God and do not fall into the trap of these so-called prophets, apostles, and pastors who are agents of darkness. Satan raised them to deceive, steal, destroy and kill your relationship with the almighty God, the Saviour of your soul.

Stop halting between two opinions: whether to get the miracle from the kingdom of darkness and later come and share the testimony in house of God or to simply wait on God. I have heard people say that after they are done committing this or that sin, they will come back to God in repentance. Of course if you do, God will not cast you away, but remember, you may not have the opportunity to repent before Satan kills you. Remember Lot's wife, she might have thought that there would be an opportunity to repent after looking back to Sodom, but she immediately became a pillar of salt—she was dead. Please, do not be a careless one.

*"Go to now, ye that say, To day or to morrow we will go into such a city, and continue there a year, and buy and sell, and get gain: Whereas ye know not what shall be on the morrow. For what is your life? It is even a vapour, that appeareth for a little time, and then vanisheth away."* (James 4:13-14)

Those who plan to give their lives to God at the twelfth hour usually die at the eleventh hour. No man has any means of ascertaining what would occur in the next few seconds; whether he or she would live or die. The Bible says *"Cease ye from man, whose breath is in his nostrils"* (Isaiah 2:22).

Therefore, it is the responsibility of the heavenly-minded ministers of God to give the right guidance to the sincere seekers. Be precise in your counsel, do not hide or hoard the truth. Call a spade a spade. A good shepherd will not take his sheep to the field or prepare both good and poisonous food before them and instruct them to choose which one to feed on. He will take away the poisonous and set the good food before them. There are many pastors and even General Overseers that do keep silent over the rudiments of Christian daily living facts. They do not preach it. Some, when asked how a Christian should dress or choose who to marry, always reply that their wives are examples of modest dressing. What a great truth but not a great way to lead souls to heaven. In Psalm 51:15, David cried out: *"O Lord, open thou my lips; and my mouth shall shew forth thy praise."* Our mouth must preach the word, not only our lives. Most pastors' wives are always behind the screen, so nobody can see them let alone them be an example to ladies. Your mouth must declare it loud and long. Here is the charge:

*"I charge thee therefore before God, and the Lord Jesus Christ, who shall judge the quick and the dead at his appearing and his kingdom; Preach the word; be instant in season, out of season; reprove, rebuke, exhort with all longsuffering and doctrine.*

*For the time will come when they will not endure sound doctrine; but after their own lusts shall they heap to themselves teachers, having itching ears; And they shall turn away their ears from the truth, and shall be turned unto fables."* (2 Timothy 4:1-4)

Preachers should preach the doctrine of Christ with all earnestness upon their hearers. Please, publicly proclaim the word of God with a loud voice without adding to it, or taking away from it; preach it with all courage and boldness. This will help in saving their souls and yours too. Our hearers need to be well-equipped. henceforth there will *"be no more children, tossed to and fro, and carried about with every wind of doctrine, by the sleight of men, and cunning craftiness, whereby they lie in wait to deceive"* (Ephesians 4:11-32).

2. **Enticement with flattery words from seducer (Solomon) of her soul** (Song of Solomon 1:9-11). Solomon spoke and expressed his admiration for her by comparing her to the beautiful decorated horses of Pharaoh's chariots, saying that her cheeks were lovely with rows of jewels and her neck with chains of gold, and promising to make her bead-rows of gold and points of silver.

Solomon's promise was to make ornaments of gold, silver, and jewels for the Shulamite lady which would replace the beads of her rural attire. There are many Christian women that are facing this same problem. The Solomons in their lives or workplaces may be their boss, employers, co-workers or senior colleague. Satan has stationed such Solomons to promise gold (prosperity, increment in salary, allowances, opportunity to claim some emoluments) and glory (promotion). Such promises come with a demand for a night of sin as a price for the demonic blessing. These Solomons' promises, such as gold and glory include prosperity, power, popularity, prestige, and population increment (church growth in term of numerical strength) are also hanging on some pastors' lintels of their ministry. Whosoever is deceived thereby is not wise. There are many pastors in our country today who have lost their virginity, purity and call to the Solomons of this world. Comparisons of their successes with other "men of God" and dancing to the counsels of the ungodly colleagues have ruined their life and ministry. It may not be exaggerating to state that a large percent of those who are pastors in this age are making covenant with the kingdom of darkness in exchange of goodies and love of pleasure. Most of them want to win the battle of poverty, powerlessness in ministry and perpetual numerical stagnancy in their churches. They are becoming witchcraft and mammy water spirit customers just like King Saul that sought a familiar spirit through the woman at Endor (1 Samuel

28:5-20). I heard the story of a pastor in the South-western Nigeria who sought the counsel of his friend concerning how to grow a mega-church. Based on the story, this man was the General Overseer of a church that was founded many years ago but noticed that churches that were started around the same time were growing faster than his and were "very successful". So, his friend told him that he was the problem. Indeed, he preached only messages of holiness and righteousness to people. He told him another mystery of growing a mega-church, which is making covenants with the kingdom of darkness. Unfortunately, he agreed to change base from his holiness stand to do whatever it would take to be prosperous in ministry. Both of them went to a river in Lagos state where they conjured the spirit of mammy water for help. Initially, the demon refused to give any answer because the power-seeker pastor had no defilement in him. Eventually, the demon instructed them that nothing can be done until the pastor defile himself. So, the pastor sought for a prostitute and committed immorality with her. Then he went back and the demon instructed him to release the bible that he brought while a new bible from the pit of hell (from inside the water) would be given to him. The story ended in a tragedy because as the newly-initiated and satanic-power endowed pastor travelled back to his town, he got involved in an accident and died. He started well but ended badly. He started his pilgrim journey from the cross of Calvary but ended in hell. Satan did not even give him a chance to repent. May be Satan knew he would repent later, so he killed him. I pray that Satan will not have his way in your life and ministry. It is only Jesus Christ that comes to give you life and to give it to you more abundantly.

Dear reader, beware of the many Solomons and Absaloms in our churches and communities today. They are there to steal away your gold in order to replace it with glittering moulded ashes. They are there to win your heart to join their caucus of dead ministers or church members. Sad enough, they even quote the Bible to win their argument just like their father, Satan, did with Jesus. The fact is that they always hunt for your precious life.

Let us learn a great lesson from the temptations that Christ overcame in the wilderness. *"Again, the devil taketh him up into an exceeding high mountain, and sheweth him all the kingdoms of the world, and the glory of them; And saith unto him, All these things will I give thee, if thou wilt fall down and worship me. Then saith Jesus unto him, Get thee hence, Satan: for it is written, Thou shalt worship the Lord thy God, and him only shalt thou serve."*

Please, do not fall down and worship Satan because of the love for the gold and glory of this perishable world. The promotion you get in your office because you slept with your boss will one day bring sorrow into your life and family. If you have fallen into it before reading this book, thank God there is a second chance for you. Repent unto God. He will show you mercy.

*"Have mercy upon me, O God, according to thy lovingkindness: according unto the multitude of thy tender mercies blot out my transgressions. Wash me thoroughly from mine iniquity, and cleanse me from my sin. For I acknowledge my transgressions: and my sin is ever before me. Against thee, thee only, have I sinned, and done this evil in thy sight: that thou mightest be justified when thou speakest, and be clear when thou judgest. Behold, I was shapen in iniquity; and in sin did my mother conceive me. Behold, thou desirest truth in the inward parts: and in the hidden part thou shalt make me to know wisdom. Purge me with hyssop, and I shall be clean: wash me, and I shall be whiter than*

*snow. Make me to hear joy and gladness; that the bones which thou hast broken may rejoice. Hide thy face from my sins, and blot out all mine iniquities. Create in me a clean heart, O God; and renew a right spirit within me. Cast me not away from thy presence; and take not thy holy spirit from me. Restore unto me the joy of thy salvation; and uphold me with thy free spirit. Then will I teach transgressors thy ways; and sinners shall be converted unto thee. Deliver me from bloodguiltiness, O God, thou God of my salvation: and my tongue shall sing aloud of thy righteousness. O Lord, open thou my lips; and my mouth shall shew forth thy praise. For thou desirest not sacrifice; else would I give it: thou delightest not in burnt offering. The sacrifices of God are a broken spirit: a broken and a contrite heart, O God, thou wilt not despise."* (Psalm 51:1-17)

We must realize that temptations come in a subtle and seemingly harmless way. It is the careless and unguarded souls that are always been captured unaware. Therefore, every brother and sister in the Lord must be watchful and vigilant, having eagle's eyes that are able to see angle 360 degree because we are living in the midst of a polluted, perverted, pornographic, corrupted and crooked world. Every form of sexual immoral enticement and compromise must be shunned. We must keep on looking unto Jesus, the author and finisher of our faith.

# Chapter Six

## Power of Reunion

*"While the king sitteth at his table, my spikenard sendeth forth the smell thereof. A bundle of myrrh is my well beloved unto me; he shall lie all night betwixt my breasts."* (Song of Solomon 1:12-13)

*"I am the rose of Sharon, and the lily of the valleys. As the lily among thorns, so is my love among the daughters. As the apple tree among the trees of the wood, so is my beloved among the sons. I sat down under his shadow with great delight, and his fruit was sweet to my taste. He brought me to the banqueting house, and his banner over me was love. Stay me with flagons, comfort me with apples: for I am sick of love. His left hand is under my head, and his right hand doth embrace me."* (Song of Solomon 2:1-6)

Read the following as presented by Amplified Bible:

*[12] While the king sits at his table [she said], my spikenard [my absent lover] sends forth [his] fragrance [over me]. [13] My beloved [shepherd] is to me like a [scent] bag of myrrh that lies in my bosom. (Song of Solomon 1: 12-13)*

*[She said] I am only a little rose or autumn crocus of the plain of Sharon, or a [humble] lily of the valleys [that grows in deep and difficult places].* ² *But Solomon replied, Like the lily among thorns, so are you, my love, among the daughters.* ³ *Like an apple tree among the trees of the wood, so is my beloved [shepherd] among the sons [cried the girl]! Under his shadow I delighted to sit, and his fruit was sweet to my taste.* ⁴ *He brought me to the banqueting house, and his banner over me was love [for love waved as a protecting and comforting banner over my head when I was near him].* ⁵ *Sustain me with raisins, refresh me with apples, for I am sick with love.* ⁶ *[I can feel]* [a]*his left hand under my head and his right hand embraces me! (Song of Solomon 2: 1-6)*

## Panting for Reunion among Sincere Lovers

Unity makes two people to walk together in harmony without strife (Amos 3:3; Genesis 13:1-8), stay together for better or worse (Ruth 1:16-17), not to deceive each other (1 Samuel 18:1-4; 19:1-7), follow the same rules and regulations (Jeremiah 35:2-5, 18), and live in peace, power, and progress (Acts 2:44-45).

1.  **Sweet-smelling, the aroma in Christian's life**. Fruits of repentance, faith, love, and thanksgiving are the aroma that reveal and reflect a person that has an encounter with Christ (Song 1:12). The aroma in the life of Elisha made the woman at Shunem called him a holy man of God (2 Kings 4:9). This is rare. It was his lifestyle, after a long scrutiny that earned him this title: holy man of God. Elijah, as powerful as he was, was only referred to as a man of God but Elisha as a holy man of God. Let your light so shine that others may see the light in you and leave their darkness.

    Spikenard is a tree that produces ointment (Matthew 14:3) while myrrh is an aromatic gum resin used to perfume beds and clothing (Psalm 45:8; Proverbs 7:17), and also for the anointing of the Priests (Exodus 30:33). Spikenard here signifies the graces of the Spirit wherewith the believer is furnished out of the treasure of the sweet spices that are in Christ (Psalm 141:2). Though the seducer (Solomon) was sitting at his table, the Shulamite lady refused to sell her love to the king but her affection and soul stayed connected to her beloved Shepherd boy (Roman 8:35-39). The daughters of Zion found themselves in the country of Babylon, so they felt uncomfortable and wept bitterly with total frustration but reiterating their decision never to forget Jerusalem. Listen to them:

*"By the rivers of Babylon, there we sat down, yea, we wept, when we remembered Zion. We hanged our harps upon the willows in the midst thereof. For there they that carried us away captive required of us a song; and they that wasted us required of us mirth, saying, Sing us one of the songs of Zion. How shall we sing the LORD'S song in a strange land? If I forget thee, O Jerusalem, let my right hand forget her cunning. If I do not remember thee, let my tongue cleave to the roof of my mouth; if I prefer not Jerusalem above my chief joy."* (Psalm 137:1-6)

In times of trials and temptations, the grace of God that we have received should be the lubricating oil (grease) that cushions our souls. People around us must see its radiant power shining forth through us. "To send forth the smell, is to be in lively exercise, and to be fresh and vigorous; grace without smell, or lively exercise, is like flowers somewhat withered, that savour not, or like an unbeaten spice, that sends not forth its savour. It is exceedingly refreshing to believers, to have their graces flowing and acting."

2. **We can also state that her expression**: "*my spikenard sendeth forth the smell*" connotes prayers offered unto God. "*Let my prayers be set forth as incense before You.*" (Psalm 141:2). The offering of incense should be continual, from morning till evening. We are to pray without ceasing whether when things are going fine or very bad. The Shulamite lady was faced with King Solomon who demanded for her hand in marriage. So, she cried out that her prayers will ascend unto God for her deliverance from the tempting zone. Where can she go but unto the Lord, seeking a refuge for her soul? Do you think that there is any help anywhere when faced with temptations and troubles? King Asa turned to the king of Assyrian for help against the king of Israel and God rebuked Asa for not seeking Him alone, the creator of all. The Bible says "woe unto him that goes to Egypt to seek for help. In time of distress and discouragement." the Psalmist cried:

"*I will lift up mine eyes unto the hills, from whence cometh my help. My help cometh from the LORD, which made heaven and earth. He will not suffer thy foot to be moved: he that keepeth thee will not slumber. Behold, he that keepeth Israel shall neither slumber nor sleep. The LORD is thy keeper: the LORD is thy shade upon thy right hand. The sun shall not smite thee by day, nor the moon by night. The LORD shall preserve thee from all evil: he shall preserve thy soul. The LORD shall preserve thy going out and thy coming in from this time forth, and even for evermore.*" (Psalm 121:1-8)

Most Christians, when faced with temptations, trials, and troubles, look up to pastors, friends and family members, forgetting that their help can only come from God.

"*And there was a great famine in Samaria: and, behold, they besieged it, until an ass's head was sold for fourscore pieces of silver, and the fourth part of a cab* *of dove's dung for five pieces of silver. <u>And as the king of Israel was passing by upon the wall, there cried a woman unto him, saying, Help, my lord, O king. And he said, If the LORD do not help thee, whence shall I help thee? Out of the barnfloor, or out of the winepress?</u>"* (2 Kings 6:25-27)

Looking for help from mortal men will only bring failure, disappointment, depression, and frustration. So, our prayers for help should only go to God. He already promised us that if we can call Him in times of trouble, He will answer us.

3.  **Supernatural comfort and blessings in togetherness (Song 1:13).**

Fellowship brings admiration, refreshment, and power. If truly we love Jesus, the dark and bright times of our lives cannot sever us from Him. Most people who depart from the faith because of troubles, temptations, trials and turmoil that they experienced in life are not taking the right decision. Let us remain with Christ at all times, for we are not part of them that draw back unto perdition. Sun shine or rain, whatever it may be, let Jesus Christ be your all in all. This world has nothing to offer to us. Let us cleave to Jesus to the end.

In fact, there are many things that constantly press us to deny Christ and quit the Christian race. For Job, it was his sickness and tribulations that made his own wife to counsel him to curse God and die (Job 2:9). We must know that it is always the second class sufferer of a problem that feels the pain more. Those that are sick know how they feel and probably prepare their mind so that in case death comes, they will be ready to meet God. However, the people (second class sufferers) who care for the first class sufferers feel the pain much more because it might have cost them their job, peace, sleep, time, and even their lives. Nevertheless, like Job we must make our stand known that we cannot sin against Jehovah because of things that are not eternal. For Elisha who was persistently seeking for God's power in the life of his master, Elijah, it was discouragement he faced, caused by his school mates (the sons of prophets) and Elijah himself. They tried to persuade him from following Elijah (2 Kings 2:1-11). Elisha shunned all counsels to turn away from his master up to the point Elijah went up by a whirlwind into heaven. He looked steadfastly to heaven for his double portion anointing as his master was ascending to the heavens.

Our song and anthem should be:

"dwelling together, how happy we shall be, throughout eternity for we shall d-w-e-l-l together, my Lord and I."

The Shulamite lady felt satisfied in her beloved Shepherd boy. She characterised him as "a bundle of myrrh . . . unto her." Myrrh was a precious and savoury spice, used in the production of the 'anointing oil,' (Exodus 30:23). A bundle of it, signifies abundance of it; not a lesser quantity. Dwelling with our Lover and Good Shepherd fills our hearts with ointment of grace in abundance and with oil of gladness like a flowing river that never dries.

Our love and togetherness with Christ will compel us to have the same relationship with our brothers and sisters in the Lord. The dwelling together of Christians in unity and love helps to easily identify a going astray brother or sister and cause an immediate rescue.

*"Behold, how good and how pleasant it is for brethren to dwell together in unity! It is like the precious ointment upon the head, that ran down upon the beard, even Aaron's beard: that went down to the skirts of his*

garments; *As the dew of Hermon, and as the dew that descended upon the mountains of Zion: for there the LORD commanded the blessing, even life for evermore."* (Psalm 133:1-3)

*"And let us consider one another to provoke unto love and to good works: Not forsaking the assembling of ourselves together, as the manner of some is; but exhorting one another: and so much the more, as ye see the day approaching."* (Hebrew 10:24-25)

*"A man that hath friends must shew himself friendly: and there is a friend that sticketh closer than a brother."* (Proverbs 18:24)

In addition, the Shulamite affirmatively stated that *"he shall lie all night betwixt my breasts."* This implies that her Lover would have a dwelling place in her heart and she would be satisfied with him alone staying there. She would embrace and accommodate only her Lover in her heart. She would give him all-night hugs and refuse to let him go. Not just to allow him there once or twice but all night. I pray that we will accommodate and retain Christ in our hearts all our day till we close our eyes in death. Brethren, let Christ dwell in your heart. He says *"Behold, I stand at the door, and knock: if any man hear my voice, and open the door, I will come in to him, and will sup with him, and he with me."* (Revelation 3:20) If Christ and His word dwell richly in your heart, it will be difficult for you to quickly succumb to the tempter's enticing words. When temptation comes, you will be able to reply the evil thoughts or suggestions by a "Thus saith the Lord."

## 4. Satisfaction in Christ's fellowship

The Shulamite lady found a complete and perfect satisfaction in her relationship with her Lover, not Solomon.

*"My beloved is unto me as a cluster of camphire in the vineyards of Engedi. As the apple tree among the trees of the wood, so is my beloved among the sons. I sat down under his shadow with great delight, and his fruit was sweet to my taste. He brought me to the banqueting house, and his banner over me was love."* (Song 1:14; 2:3-4).

She likened her Lover to an apple tree which usually provides abundant shade and fruits. This makes it an outstanding tree among others. This connotes that she compared her Lover, the Shepherd boy to other men and rated him far above ruby. She was satisfied staying under his shade or roof and feeding on only that which he provided. Whosoever dwells in the secret place of the most High, shall abide under the shadow of the Almighty.

*"One thing have I desired of the LORD, that will I seek after; that I may dwell in the house of the LORD all the days of my life, to behold the beauty of the LORD, and to enquire in his temple. For in the time of trouble he shall hide me in his pavilion: in the secret of his tabernacle shall he hide me; he shall set me up upon a rock."* (Psalm 27:4-5)

*"Thou art my hiding place; thou shalt preserve me from trouble; thou shalt compass me about with songs of deliverance."* (Psalm 32:7)

She was very comfortable with her Shepherd boy, longing to abide in his home which was delightful, refreshing and reviving; she longed to abide under his protection where she would be preserved from all troubles of life.

What a wonderful picture we have here of our Lord Jesus Christ and His love for us. He is a shadow unto us all as Christians. *"For thou hast been a strength to the poor, a strength to the needy in his distress, a refuge from the storm, a shadow from the heat, when the blast of the terrible ones is as a storm against the wall."* (Isaiah 25:4)

He is also our provider, the supplier of all our needs, and feeds us with the bread of life and fruits of delight. He says, *"He who comes to Me will never hunger, and he who believes in Me will never thirst"* (John 6:35). He has brought us to his banquet to drink of his wine. *"And he said unto them, With desire I have desired to eat this passover with you before I suffer: And he took the cup, and gave thanks, and said, Take this, and divide it among yourselves: For I say unto you, I will not drink of the fruit of the vine, until the kingdom of God shall come."* (Luke 22.18). The wine is not only a symbol of joy and plenty but also of the blood that He shed for us as He gave Himself for our salvation, bearing on Himself the sins of the world (1 John 2:1-2), and through which He brings us into His new covenant (Matthew 26:27-28). Understanding length, breadth, depth and height of His love for us, which passes all knowledge will bring satisfaction (Ephesians 3:17-19). Whenever we think of His goodness and mercy and love for us, our souls cannot but shout halleluiah unto the Lord.

Her expressions in verses 13 and 14 show us: 1) her great love for the shepherd, 2) a satisfying spiritual senses of him, 3) a tenaciousness in holding on to him at all times, never to part from him, 4) giving him the right seat and place of residence; the bosom and heart is Christ's room and bed, and 5) a determination never to provoke him to depart but 'he shall lie all night.' These are good evidences of our affection to Christ.

## The Perfect Lover of Our Soul

The Shepherd boy congratulated his spouse that she was beautiful, lovely, and having dove-like eyes which meant that she was innocent, meek, and loving. Can Christ commend our lives like that?

1.  The Shepherd boy must have been a very loving and kind husband. He was a godly pattern to all husbands.

    *"Husbands, love your wives, even as Christ also loved the church, and gave himself for it; That he might sanctify and cleanse it with the washing of water by the word, That he might present it to himself a glorious church, not having spot, or wrinkle, or any such thing; but that it should be holy and without blemish. So ought men to love their wives as their own bodies. He that loveth his wife loveth himself. For no man ever yet hated his own flesh; but nourisheth and cherisheth it, even as the Lord the church:"* (Ephesians 5:27).

    Jesus loves you, cares for you, provides for you, and cherishes you with everlasting love. His love for you will never fail. So ought Christian husbands to love their wives.

2.  Understand that love is reciprocal. The more we love God, the more of His love we enjoy. *"Because he hath set his love upon me, therefore will I deliver him: I will set him on high, because he hath known my name. He shall call upon me, and I will answer him: I will be with him in trouble; I will deliver him, and honour him. With long life will I satisfy him, and shew him my salvation."* (Psalm 91:14-16). Our God is not a task-master. He will not forget

your labour of love towards Him and His children, even to unbelievers. He will reward you far better than you can imagine.

3. The Perfect lover knows the state of his bride's heart and declares her innocent (hast doves' eyes) despite the condemnation from the accuser of the brethren. After we might have remained faithful unto the Lord, Satan may come to bring condemnation into our heart for even suffering from temptations and trials. However, our focus should be to please Him who saved us. We are to live above reproach in all areas of our lives to the point that God would be able to bear witness that we are pure and innocent of Satan's allegations like that of Job.

   *"Now there was a day when the sons of God came to present themselves before the LORD, and Satan came also among them. And the LORD said unto Satan, Whence comest thou? Then Satan answered the LORD, and said, From going to and fro in the earth, and from walking up and down in it. And the LORD said unto Satan, Hast thou considered my servant Job, that there is none like him in the earth, a perfect and an upright man, one that feareth God, and escheweth evil?"* (Job 1:6-8)

4. He commended his spouse for having "doves' eyes. Doves cannot move their eyes from side to side but only look straight. They have a tunnel vision which cannot detect the peripheral movements. So, all happenings around the dove cannot enter into her field of vision (Prov. 4:25-26; 2 Kings 2:1-11). We are not to allow any distractions to take our eyes off the Author and Finisher of our faith. The dove spends much of her time sitting on water, so that if it sees the shadow of a hawk that is flying overhead, it can avoid it by fleeing. The Church protects itself with the scriptures, in order to escape the deceits of Satan. Therefore, Christians must be of singleness of purpose and vision.

A Someone wrote:

> "turn your eyes upon Jesus,
> look full into His wonderful face;
> And the things of earth will grow strangely dim
> in the light of His glory and praise."

5.  The Shepherd lover was happy because the Shulamite lady excelled in the midst of the thorns in which she grew (Song 2:2). In tears, troubles, tribulations, temptations to sin against God, we must hold fast to our faith in Christ, deciding that come what may, we will be faithful to our Saviour. Then, shall Christ be happy with us. For he that endures to the end shall be saved and be granted the opportunity to sit with Him on His throne (Revelations 3: 21). *"His lord said unto him, Well done, thou good and faithful servant: thou hast been faithful over a few things, I will make thee ruler over many things: enter thou into the joy of thy Lord."* (Matthew 25:21) So, there is a reward for faithfulness, keeping ourselves from every form of filthiness.

## Prosperity through Reunion of Sincere Lovers

The Shulamite lady replied with similar compliments, and then spoke of her hopes to lie with her beloved on the green grass and herbs beneath the boughs of the great cedars and firs; that would be their house. This abode depicts:

1.  **Refreshment and fruitfulness**
    *"Behold, thou art fair, my beloved, yea, pleasant: also our bed is green."* (Song of Solomon 1:16). She expressed further that their bed was green, which implies that it's simply a portion of a grass field—open, refreshing, endless, and flourishing (Psalm 23:1-2)—and that their house was built upon a solid foundation with good and strong pillars and rafters. Therefore, no storm could blow it off.

*"For he shall be as a tree planted by the waters, and that spreadeth out her roots by the river, and shall not see when heat cometh, but her leaf shall be green; and shall not be careful in the year of drought, neither shall cease from yielding fruit."* (Jeremiah 17:8)

When we unite with Christ, we begin to receive refreshment and fruitfulness as compliments. Dear beloved, you who have gone astray because of your falling into sin through temptations, if you come back unto Him, He will not cast you away. But you must come now, for tomorrow may be too late. When the prodigal son came back to his senses, he returned home to his father, and the father accepted him back to his inheritance. Do not let Satan deceive you that your sin is so grievous that God cannot forgive you. He will! *"Come now, and let us reason together, saith the LORD: though your sins be as scarlet, they shall be as white as snow; though they be red like crimson, they shall be as wool. If ye be willing and obedient, ye shall eat the good of the land:"* (Isaiah 1:18-19)

2.  **Everlasting shelter is secured**
    *"The beams of our house are cedar, and our rafters of fir."* (Song of Solomon 1:17a). Cedar is a durable wood. So our coming to be reunited with God through Christ brings us to a safe and everlasting secure place. Once we become reunited with God, we are no longer aliens to the full security that is Christ alone.

    *"Now therefore ye are no more strangers and foreigners, but fellow citizens with the saints, and of the household of God; And are built upon the foundation of the apostles and prophets, Jesus Christ himself being the chief corner stone; In whom all the building fitly framed together groweth unto an holy temple in the Lord: In whom ye also are builded together for an habitation of God through the Spirit."* (Ephesians 2:19-22)

That eternal place of habitation is heaven where moths do not corrupt (John 14:1-3). Once we become born again, our names are written in the book of life, then that everlasting shelter—heaven—is secured.

## 3. Full security in Christ

The lady cried out, *"Stay me with flagons, comfort me with apples: for I am sick of love. His left hand is under my head, and his right hand doth embrace me."* (Song of Solomon 2:5-6)

There is no security in this world except in Christ only. The Shulamite lady might seem weak and feeble to defend herself in the presence of King Solomon but she was so sure that her full security was in the hand of her Lover. She was love-sick because of the separation occasioned by the tempter and kidnapper. So at this point, she was yearning of curdling and cares by her Lover. She needed to be hugged and embraced by beloved. She knew for sure that the hands of her lover were able to sustain and support her from crumbling in the palace that had become a prison to her in spite of its great beauty. One day in 1990, I happened to read Isaiah 41:10-20 and got an inspiration that was life-changing for me. I thought that all the temptations, trials and troubles I was passing through then were strong enough to make me deny God and quit the race. I would have done so if I was the one holding or hanging onto God but because God was the one holding my hands, I could remain steadfast in Him. The blow of the wind and the storm were so enormous that it could have caused me to lose my grip. However, since I was not the one holding Him but Him holding me, the storms could not succeed in snatching me from His hands. Read Isaiah 41:10-20:

*"Fear thou not; for I am with thee: be not dismayed; for I am thy God: I will strengthen thee; yea, I will help*

*thee; yea, I will uphold thee with the right hand of my righteousness. Behold, all they that were incensed against thee shall be ashamed and confounded: they shall be as nothing; and they that strive with thee shall perish. Thou shalt seek them, and shalt not find them, even them that contended with thee: they that war against thee shall be as nothing, and as a thing of nought. For I the LORD thy God will hold thy right hand, saying unto thee, Fear not; I will help thee. Fear not, thou worm Jacob, and ye men of Israel; I will help thee, saith the LORD, and thy redeemer, the Holy One of Israel. Behold, I will make thee a new sharp threshing instrument having teeth: thou shalt thresh the mountains, and beat them small, and shalt make the hills as chaff. Thou shalt fan them, and the wind shall carry them away, and the whirlwind shall scatter them: and thou shalt rejoice in the LORD, and shalt glory in the Holy One of Israel. When the poor and needy seek water, and there is none, and their tongue faileth for thirst, I the LORD will hear them, I the God of Israel will not forsake them. I will open rivers in high places, and fountains in the midst of the valleys: I will make the wilderness a pool of water, and the dry land springs of water. I will plant in the wilderness the cedar, the shittah tree, and the myrtle, and the oil tree; I will set in the desert the fir tree, and the pine, and the box tree together: That they may see, and know, and consider, and understand together, that the hand of the LORD hath done this, and the Holy One of Israel hath created it."*

If you are the one holding unto God using your physical strength and your might, then you will fall flat from grace to grass in the times of storms. For by strength shall no man prevail or overcome the storms of life. That is why we need to continually pray for sustaining grace. The part you have to play is to just cast your cares upon Him, fully surrendering everything to Him, and totally depending on Him for the grace to remain standing till the end. Do not think that there are some spiritual boundaries and limitations that you have to set to help you maintain your track. The horse is prepared for the battle but only the Lord can guarantee safety and victory. The question is, will your anchor hold in the storms of life?

Priscilla J. Owens wrote in 1882 that we have an anchor:

1. Will your anchor hold in the storms of life,
   When the clouds unfold their wings of strife?
   When the strong tides lift and the cables strain,
   Will your anchor drift, or firm remain?

   *Chorus*
   *We have an anchor that keeps the soul*
   *Steadfast and sure while the billows roll,*
   *Fastened to the Rock which cannot move,*
   *Grounded firm and deep in the Saviour's love.*

2. It is safely moored, 'twill the storm withstand,
   For 'tis well secured by the Saviour's hand;
   And the cables, passed from His heart to mine,
   Can defy that blast, thro' strength divine.

3. It will surely hold in the Straits of Fear-
   When the breakers have told that the r.eef is near;
   Though the tempest rave and the wild winds blow,
   Not an angry wave shall our bark o'erflow.

4. It will firmly hold in the Floods of Death—
   When the waters cold chill our latest breath,
   On the rising tide it can never fail,
   While our hopes abide within the Veil.

5. When our eyes behold through the gath'ring night
   The city of gold, our harbour bright,
   We shall anchor fast by the heav'nly shore,
   With the storms all past forevermore.

As long as you remain faithful to Him and continue fellowshipping with Him in your heart, He will be your refuge and your fortress.

*"Surely he shall deliver thee from the snare of the fowler, and from the noisome pestilence. He shall cover thee with his feathers, and under his wings shalt thou trust: his truth shall be thy shield and buckler. Thou shalt not be afraid for the terror by night; nor for the arrow that flieth by day; Nor for the pestilence that walketh in darkness; nor for the destruction that wasteth at noonday. A thousand shall fall at thy side, and ten thousand at thy right hand; but it shall not come nigh thee. Only with thine eyes shalt thou behold and see the reward of the wicked. Because thou hast made the LORD, which is my refuge, even the most High, thy habitation"* (Psalm 91:3-9).

# Chapter Seven

## Rose of Sharon and Lily of the Valleys

*"I am the rose of Sharon, and the lily of the valleys. As the lily among thorns, so is my love among the daughters."* (Song of Solomon 2:1-2, KJV)

*[1] [She said] I am only a little rose or autumn crocus of the plain of Sharon, or a [humble] lily of the valleys [that grows in deep and difficult places]. [2] But Solomon replied, Like the lily among thorns, so are you, my love, among the daughters.* (AMP)

The statement *"I am the rose of Sharon, and the lily of the valleys"* has been generally ascribed to Christ but a careful study reveals that they are words spoken by the Shulamite lady.

First of all, let us do a thorough study on some key words like rose, Sharon, lily, valleys, and thorns from our text.

**Rose:** There are two Bible references that mentioned "rose" as related to a flower (Song of Solomon 2:1-2; Isaiah 35:1).

*"The wilderness and the solitary place shall be glad for them; and the desert shall rejoice, and blossom as the rose."* (Isaiah 35:1)

Roses commonly known as flowers convey an image of beauty. Amongst flowers, roses are deemed the most glorious, beautiful and sweetest. It is delightful to the eye while its scent is pleasant and refreshing to human senses.

**Sharon:** Sharon or Saron is mentioned seven times in the Bible (1 Chronicles 5:16; 27:29; Song of Solomon 2:1; Isaiah 33:9; 35:2; 65:10; Acts 9:35). There were three places carrying that name: 1) a district in the country of Bashan beyond Jordan; 2) a district (a fertile plain) between Caesarea of Palestine and Joppa; and 3) another district between Mount Tabor and the Sea of Tiberias.

Sharon is famous for its extraordinary beauty and fertility—rich pasture for herds and flocks.

**Lily:** Lily is mentioned five times while lilies are mentioned ten times in the Bible. The common lily is white and consists of six leaves opening like bells. The royal lily grows to the height of three or four feet. According to Pliny, the lily is more productive than the other plants, one root often producing fifty bulbs. It is an emblem of the beauty and purity of the soul in grace.

**Valleys:** it is a low place probably between mountains or hills.

**Thorns:** they are pointed or sharp and harmful outgrowth of plants.

Now combining these together, we are well-equipped to understand the Shulamite lady's stand when she called herself as the rose of Sharon and the lily of the valleys. In addition to that, her beloved Shepherd also called her the lily among thorns. So, let us consider this topic under two sub-headings: commendation for righteous living and continuity through strong determination.

## Commendation for Righteous Living

The Shulamite lady referred to herself as a person resembling a beautiful flower in a plain but fertile and fruitful land. Roses thrive best in sunny places. She is the lily of the valleys and among the thorns. In the valleys where flood can easily carry away plants or stain plants with mud when it rains, she remains unshakable, unmoveable, and maintains her white beautiful colour. What a great quality! In the midst of thorns, sharp pressure that could make her succumb to temptation, she thrives. Therefore, Christians are expected to demonstrate their beautiful colour and sweet odour whenever exposed to hardships, temptations and trials of faith. Their colour must not fade away and no foul odour must be released in such times. Let everyone that is around you know that where sin abounds, grace much more abounds (Romans 5:20). Despite the temptations she faced in the palace of Solomon, the pressure from the court ladies, sexual sensation that she was exposed to, her life delightfully testified that she was still the rose of Sharon. Though she was a plant among the thorns, she refused to be choked by their piercing weapon (Matthew 13:7). Jesus Christ after talking in parable about the seeds that fell among the thorns and choked by their influence, He interpreted what the thorns represent by saying that *"He also that received seed among the thorns is he that heareth the word; and the care of this world, and the deceitfulness of riches, choke the word, and he becometh unfruitful."* (Matthew 13:7). In your office, school, church, and community, are you bold enough to refer to yourself as the rose of Sharon, a beautiful flower in a heat-tormented environment?

In Genesis 6:1-9, as the world grew old and the people multiplied the more the atrocities and evils they innovated and committed. Therefore God was not happy with the people He created. He purposed to carry out a revolution but He found a man named Noah, who was a just and perfect man in that wicked and demonic cross-breed generation.

*"And it came to pass, when men began to multiply on the face of the earth, and daughters were born unto them, That the sons of God saw the daughters of men that they were fair; and they took them wives of all which they chose. And the LORD said, My spirit shall not always strive with man, for that he also is flesh: yet his days shall be an hundred and twenty years. There were giants in the earth in those days; and also after that, when the sons of God came in unto the daughters of men, and they bare children to them, the same became mighty men which were of old, men of renown. And GOD saw that the wickedness of man was great in the earth, and that every imagination of the thoughts of his heart was only evil continually. And it repented the LORD that he had made man on the earth, and it grieved him at his heart. And the LORD said, I will destroy man whom I have created from the face of the earth; both man, and beast, and the creeping thing, and the fowls of the air; for it repenteth me that I have made them. But Noah found grace in the eyes of the LORD. These are the generations of Noah: Noah was a just man and perfect in his generations, and Noah walked with God."*

From this Bible reference, it is not surprising to deduce the reason why when our godly sisters fall into the hand of ungodly men in marriage, they give birth to ungodly, difficult to control children—*when the sons of God came in unto the daughters of men, and they bare children to them, the same became mighty men which were of old, men of renown.* Many so-called Christians are causing confusion in the spiritual realm by making God an in-law to Satan: a child of God marrying a child of Satan. Instead of God remaining an in-law to Satan, He will quickly withdraw His fatherhood from such confusionist child. In those days, though a majority of people was perverting and changing God's orders, Noah remained as the lily in the valley and the lily among thorns. He was a perfect and faithful man in the sight of God, like the Shulamite lady in the sight of her Lover Shepherd boy.

The Shulamite considered herself as the lily of the valleys because she did not desire the grandeur and fine palace of

Solomon; she was contented being with her beloved and enjoying him in their beautiful countryside and surroundings. You do not value what you have until you lose it. She only qualified herself as white, holy, undefiled, chaste young lady in an immoral and corrupted world. Ironically, Jesus latter made a statement that Solomon in all his glory was not arrayed like one of the lilies (Matthew 6.28-29).

What makes people fall into temptation today is poverty, problems of delay in child bearing and of getting a spouse to marry as well as worldly pleasures. They forget that godliness with contentment is a great gain, for we brought nothing into this world and we shall definitely take nothing out of it. If you are a Christian, you must have it at the back of your mind that you are special, spiritually rich, an heavenly-endowed person. You do not need to bow or worship Satan before you wear your crown. Though you may be suffering, you must carry the cross before you can be crowned. What a great price! Note that butterflies that mature without battle mature without beauty. When you experience the valley life, let your garment remain white as snow. Keep yourself pure in this polluted and crooked generation. Do not bow to pressure from peers or civilisation going on around you. As I continue to witness to people every day, I begin to realise that many ladies who wear provocative dresses only do that because they see others doing so. They are only trying to blend with the worldly system of fashion; thereby parading themselves as sex object in our community. It is not for Christ's representative, Oh dear Christian, it is neither for you to dress seductively; nor for you to dress in such a way that passersby will take you for an harlot.

As a female student, you must not give away the temple of the Holy Spirit, that is, your body, to a male lecturer in your school in order to get good grades. When other female students do that, you must not do it. Abstain from it. Keep yourself pure. Others may, but you cannot. As a store keeper, a sales representative, an accountant, or an auditor, you must not involve yourself in any shady deal. Let your light so shine before men, that they may see your good works, and glorify your Father which is in heaven. Let your holy life, your pure conduct and lifestyle show everywhere, in all societies, in all businesses, at home and abroad, and every time, in prosperity, poverty and adversity. Without opening your mouth to tell the world that you are a Christian, let it be seen through your lifestyle and living that you are a real Christian.

## Continuity through strong determination

Sincerely speaking, it takes a sincere decision and a strong determination to remain unspotted, white as a lily in the mire of this world. Brother Joseph was right in the valley of temptation to sleep with the wife of his boss, but he decided to remain undefiled before God. He said *"how then can I do this great wickedness, and sin against God?"* (Genesis 39:1-13). Apostle Paul said that he put his body or flesh under subjection in order to maintain his righteous living according to the purpose of God for his life and ministry (1 Corinthians 9:27). As a human being, there may come a time in your life when you have sexual desires. If you are married and your spouse is not there, all you need to do is to pray and purpose in your heart that you will not defile your bed. If you are not married, pray hard to mortify the deeds of the flesh, and then tell your body that stolen water is sweet but the consequence of it is eternal condemnation and damnation.

# Chapter Eight

# Hope of His Coming

*"I charge you, O ye daughters of Jerusalem, by the roes, and by the hinds of the field, that ye stir not up, nor awake my love, till he please. [She picture it] The voice of my beloved [shepherd]! behold, he cometh leaping upon the mountains, skipping upon the hills. My beloved is like a roe or a young hart: behold, he standeth behind our wall, he looketh forth at the windows, shewing himself through the lattice. My beloved spake, and said unto me, Rise up, my love, my fair one, and come away. For, lo, the winter is past, the rain is over and gone; The flowers appear on the earth; the time of the singing of birds is come, and the voice of the turtle is heard in our land; The fig tree putteth forth her green figs, and the vines with the tender grape give a good smell. Arise, my love, my fair one, and come away. O my dove, that art in the clefts of the rock, in the secret places of the stairs, let me see thy countenance, let me hear thy voice; for sweet is thy voice, and thy countenance is comely. Take us the foxes, the little foxes, that spoil the vines: for our vines have tender grapes. My beloved is mine, and I am his: he feedeth among the lilies. Until the day break, and the shadows flee away, turn, my beloved, and be thou like a roe or a young hart upon the mountains of Bether."* (Song of Solomon 2:7-17)

There was an American Civil War fought between the Union (Federal) and the Confederate soldiers under the leadership of Major General W. T. Sherman and Lieutenant General J. B. Hood, respectively. A great and fierce battle ensued between the Union and Confederate soldiers led by Brigadier General J. M. Corse and Major General S. G. French, respectively in October 5, 1864 at Allatoona Pass, Georgia. This happened because over one million rations were stored at Allatonna by the Federal guided by the Union soldiers and Maj. Gen. French demanded that the Union soldiers surrender it to them, but Brig. Gen. Corse refused with a great resistance. The battle claimed many lives from both camps, even Corse was wounded. As the battle was ongoing, one of the Union soldiers sighted a white flag flown on Kennesaw Mountain, some miles away, and the messages sent by Major General W. T. Sherman which read "Sherman is coming in force: Hold Out!" and "Hold fast: We are coming" brought a great encouragement and strength to them. Then cheer went up by the Union soldiers and became strengthened until Sherman's army arrived, which caused French's army to retreat.

Indeed, the coming of the Shepherd boy to the Shulamite lady described as *"The voice of my beloved! behold, he cometh leaping upon the mountains, skipping upon the* hills" (Song of Solomon 2:8) fit well the description of the coming of the Commander, W. T. Sherman in the heat of the battle. It also describes well the coming of our Lord Jesus Christ who knows what we are passing through (temptations, trials, and troubles). He is a very present help in the time of troubles (Psalm 46:1). He will strengthen our weaknesses by speedily supplying divine reinforcements. So the message of our Great Commander like that of Sherman is "Hold the Fort; I am coming to your aid." There was a Christian group meeting which took place in Rockford, Illinois, on April 28-29, 1870 and one of the speakers named Major D. W. Whittle told the story of the Union defence of Allatoona Pass and the message signalled by Gen. Sherman to his Union soldiers to hold out in order to encourage the believers in attendance. An evangelist and composer named

Philip Paul Bliss who was present in the meeting was so inspired that he composed an hymn on the story which he titled "Hold the fort."

1. Ho! my comrades, see the signal
   Waving in the sky!
   Reinforcements now appearing,
   Victory is nigh!

   *Chorus*
   *"Hold the fort, for I am coming,"*
   *Jesus signals still,*
   *Wave the answer back to Heaven,—*
   *"By Thy grace, we will."*

2. See the mighty host advancing,
   Satan leading on;
   Mighty ones around us falling,
   Courage almost gone.

3. See the glorious banner waving,
   Hear the bugle blow;
   In our Leader's name we'll triumph
   Over ev'ry foe.

4. Fierce and long the battle rages,
   But our Help is near;
   Onward comes our Great Commander,
   Cheer, my comrades, cheer!

There are different trials that Christians are facing that stand to challenge their allegiance to Christ. However, there is the need to hope and trust His promise of coming back.

## Pals Pressure Shun by the Shulamite Lady

*"I charge you, O ye daughters of Jerusalem, by the roes, and by the hinds of the field, that ye stir not up, nor awake my love, till he please"* (Song of Solomon 2:7).

The Shulamite lady shunned all the persuasions and pressures that other women like her were exerting on her. Many ladies (both Christians and non-Christians) have fallen flat into the sin of sexual immorality because of the influence of pals. When they see their room-mates living in luxury and enjoying the goodies of life, they tend to follow their pernicious ways of sexual immorality and perversion. As it happens to women so it does to men. Amnon, the son of King David, might have probably not thought of raping his sister Tamar if not for the counsel of Jonadab (his friend) to him (2 Samuel 13:1-14). Many youths forsake the counsel of God's word and obey the advice of their friends like Rehoboam, the son of King Solomon, who yielded to the counsel of the young men he grew up with (1 Kings 12:8-10). I remember that even when I was not a born-again believer, I had made up my mind not to defile myself with the sin of sexual immorality because I was scared of falling into the hands of demonic ladies, who may want to use my sperm for money rituals or spiritual power. So, I lived a disciplined life in that aspect. However, some of my friends were not happy with the life I lived. They helped me woo a beautify lady, a classmate, and she agreed to be my girlfriend (sinful partner). My friends told me about the steps that they had taken and that the lady had promised to come and see me. When the lady came to me, I was confused. I did not know what to tell her. Later, I summed up courage and I told her that if she desired to be my future partner, I would marry her when we were ripe for marriage. I told her that we could begin to prepare ourselves for the future by giving special attention to the reading of our books. Then, I promised her that if she succeeded academically, I would marry her. When she heard my conditions, she ran away from me. The point that I am trying to make is how pals can exert a big influence on us. So, I know that your friends can go any length to lure you into sin of any type, especially sexual immorality. Many students join cultic groups because of the pressure from their friends. They entered into it before they realized that they had got themselves into trouble. It is unfortunate to see that married people as well can negatively influence their friends to go out of their wed-locks in order to meet their daily needs in case their spouse will not be able to satisfy them. Madam Sarah, the wife of father Abraham was the one who pressurised him to lay with (commit sexual immorality) her maid named Hagar.

*"Now Sarai Abram's wife bare him no children: and she had an handmaid, an Egyptian, whose name was Hagar. And Sarai said unto Abram, Behold now, the LORD hath restrained me from bearing: I pray thee, go in unto my maid; it may be that I may obtain children by her. And Abram hearkened to the voice of Sarai. And Sarai Abram's wife took Hagar her maid the Egyptian, after Abram had dwelt ten years in the land of Canaan, and gave her to her husband Abram to be his wife. And he went in unto Hagar"* (Genesis 16:1-4).

Abraham's compromise to accept that cheap but ridiculous and destructive gift led to the birth of Ishmael. Many women are heart-wounded while some are dead because of yielding to sexual immoral pressures.

Priest Aaron yielded to the pressure mounted on him by the Israelites and the mix multitudes in the congregation to give them a god that they can physically touch and visibly see instead of waiting for Moses who had gone to receive God's word for them. They thought that Moses delayed, too slow to bring words from God, so they forcefully requested the high priest, Aaron, who was left with them to make a god for them. Truly, in Egypt, the people were used to seeing gods carved with wood or stone. Is it not the same pressure that Aaron bowed to that many ministers of God is bowing to in our days? I have heard many ministers saying that they allow the use of physical object during healing and miracle services because the people they are ministering to are used to collecting charms from the spiritualists or herbalists. They said that if you want to take the charms from them, you must give them something that they can see and hold. There is wisdom in that but a misleading act. Ministers of God are to point people to Christ alone and nothing else. Jesus only is our message.

Kindly read the account about the mistake that Aaron made. *"And when the people saw that Moses delayed to come down out of the mount, the people gathered themselves together unto Aaron, and said unto him, Up, make us gods, which shall go before us; for as for this Moses, the man that brought us up out of the land of Egypt, we wot not what is become of him. And Aaron said unto them, Break off the golden earrings, which are in the ears of your wives, of your sons, and of your daughters, and bring them unto me. And all the people brake off the golden earrings which were in their ears, and brought them unto Aaron. And he received them at their hand, and fashioned it with a graving tool, after he had made it a molten calf: and they said, These be thy gods, O Israel, which brought thee up out of the land of Egypt. And when Aaron saw it, he built an altar before it; and Aaron made proclamation, and said, To morrow is a feast to the LORD. And they rose up early on the morrow, and offered burnt offerings, and brought peace offerings; and the people sat down to eat and to drink, and rose up to play. And the LORD said unto Moses, Go, get thee down; for thy people, which thou broughtest out of the land of Egypt, have corrupted themselves: They have turned aside quickly out of the way which I commanded them: they have made them a molten calf, and have worshipped it, and have sacrificed thereunto, and said, These be thy gods, O Israel, which have brought thee up out of the land of Egypt . . . And Moses said unto Aaron, What did this people unto thee, that thou hast brought so great a sin upon them? And Aaron said, Let not the anger of my lord wax hot: thou knowest the people, that they are set on mischief. For they said unto me, Make us gods, which shall go before us: for as for this Moses, the man that brought us up out of the land of Egypt, we wot not what is become of* him. *And I said unto them, whosoever hath any gold, let them break it off. So they gave it me: then I cast it into the fire, and there came out this calf"* (Exodus 32:1-8, 21-24).

If there is any man that ever have a genuine excuse before God for disobeying the will of God, that man is Adam. He did not request for a woman (wife) but God thought it good to give him one. The same woman made him sinned against God as he said *"The woman whom thou gavest to be with me, she gave me of the tree, and I did eat"* (Genesis 3:12). Despite his genuine excuse, God did not exonerate him. He was punished for it.

The Bible says, *"O foolish Galatians, who hath bewitched you, that ye should not obey the truth, before whose eyes Jesus Christ hath been evidently set forth, crucified among you? This only would I learn of you, Received ye the Spirit by the works of the law, or by the hearing of faith? Are ye so foolish? having begun in the Spirit, are ye now made perfect by the flesh? Have ye suffered so many things in vain? if it be yet in vain. He therefore that ministereth to you the Spirit, and worketh miracles among you, doeth he it by the works of the law, or by the hearing of faith?"* (Galatians 3:1-5).

Ministers of God are to train people to put their trust in God only; not in anything else.

*"I marvel that ye are so soon removed from him that called you into the grace of Christ unto another gospel: Which is not another; but there be some that trouble you, and would pervert the gospel of Christ. But though we, or an angel from heaven, preach any other gospel unto you than that which we have preached unto you, let him be accursed. As we said before, so say I now again, If any man preach any other gospel unto you than that ye have received, let him be accursed. For do I now persuade men, or God? or do I seek to please men? for if I yet pleased men, I should not be the servant of Christ"* (Galatians 1:6-10).

We must all have drawn a line that everyone around us must know. They should not cross for it is unpleasant and not tolerated by you. The Shulamite lady clearly made it known to the court ladies that they should not cross the boundary that she had set. She refused to tolerate any unsolicited persuasion from the same or opposite sex.

Even if Satan, the grand master of deception, comes to put pressure on you because of your present state: joblessness, poverty, inability to pay your school fees or your children's school fees, you need to take your stand and refuse all his suggestions like Jesus did when He was tempted (Matthew 4:1-11). You maintain your integrity no matter what may come your way like Job. Temptations and pressures from pals are not sin but falling into it or yielding to it is sin. The bible says *"Resist the devil and he will flee from you."*

*"My son, if sinners entice thee, consent thou not. If they say, Come with us, let us lay wait for blood, let us lurk privily for the innocent without cause: Let us swallow them up alive as the grave; and whole, as those that go down into the pit: We shall find all precious substance, we shall fill our houses with spoil: Cast in thy lot among us; let us all have one purse: My son, walk not thou in the way with them; refrain thy foot from their path: For their feet run to evil, and make haste to shed blood"* (Proverb 1:10-16).

## Proclamation for Revival by the Shulamite Lady Song 2:8-13

1. **Understand His voice**
   *"The voice of my beloved!"* (Song of Solomon 2:8a).

   For genuine revival to come, we must give ourselves to the study of God's word and give proper attention, with active listening, to understand His voice. We cannot know anything about His coming without active listening to the Holy Spirit's voice. Adam and Eve, though they sinned unto God, they could recognise the voice of the Lord walking in the Garden of Eden. Else, they would not have been revived or cried out about their deplorable condition (Genesis 3:8-9). What a great mistake for those who gather to pray for revival without a heart preparation and a readiness to hear His voice.

*"Verily, verily, I say unto you, He that entereth not by the door into the sheepfold, but climbeth up some other way, the same is a thief and a robber. But he that entereth in by the door is the shepherd of the sheep. To him the porter openeth; and the sheep hear his voice: and he calleth his own sheep by name, and leadeth them out. And when he putteth forth his own sheep, he goeth before them, and the sheep follow him: for they know his voice. And a stranger will they not follow, but will flee from him: for they know not the voice of strangers"* (John 10:1-5).

The reason why many are falling into temptation is that they listen to the voice of man or Satan (Genesis 3:17; 16:2). There are many Christians who cannot differentiate the voice of Christ from that of Satan. That's why it is so easy for them to be deceived by Satan, false prophets, and false teachers. We need to look up unto God and wait patiently for Him to grant us the understanding of His voice so that when the enemy comes to imitate His voice, we will be able to detect the gimmick. We must be able to differentiate the voice of Jacob from that of Esau (Genesis 27:22). The ability to hear, detect, and understand His voice will help us take our stand in the times of temptations, knowing for sure that He will come speedily to our aid. The armies of the General that led the US troops heard the sound of his coming to the battlefield with the US flag raised. They were full of joy, knowing that their deliverance and salvation was at hand.

2. **Be assured of His coming and have confidence in His power to subdue mountains**
   *"Behold, he cometh leaping upon the mountains, skipping upon the hills"* (Song of Solomon 2:8b-c).

The assurance of the coming of the Shepherd boy might have been a great encouragement to the Shulamite lady and a wonderful sign that her hour of deliverance was near. Christ, in this way, is very discernible to anyone that is watchful. Christ promised that He will be with us always, and so when it seems that we are alone passing through the fire of temptations, trials, troubles, and turmoil, let's wait for His appearance. He will deliver us. When the three Hebrew children: Shadrach, Meshach, and Abednego were arrayed for capital punishment for not bowing down to an idol, it was like the fourth man, the Son of God, was not there with them neither ready to deliver them. Until they were cast into the fire, He did not visibly appear to the king of Babylon— king Nebuchadnezzar (Daniel 31-25). Brethren, we just need to "hold the fort" when faced with temptations and troubles. Jesus came to set the captives free (both the lawful like Dinah who walked into the place of temptation voluntarily—Genesis 34:1-2; Isaiah 49:24-25 and unlawful captives like the Shulamite lady who did not voluntarily entered into the palace of Solomon). See Him coming with the host of heaven to deliver you from the captivity of Satan. Do not yield to temptations; never give up to fate for He will definitely come to your rescue.

There are mountains that we cannot, by our human strength, subdue but by His grace and strength, we can. *"Then he answered and spake unto me, saying, this is the word of the LORD unto Zerubbabel, saying, Not by might, nor by power, but by my spirit, saith the LORD of hosts. Who art thou, O great mountain? Before Zerubbabel thou shalt become a plain: and he shall bring forth the headstone thereof with shoutings, crying,*

*Grace, grace unto it"* (Zechariah 4:6-7). Jesus Christ has a strength like that of the unicorn to overcome all stumbling blocks and mountains (Numbers 23:22; 24:8) which stand between Him and us, hindering our access to him, and his familiarity with us.

3. **Christ is swift in battle and lovely to own**
   Kindness and love characterised the attitude of Christ just like the young hart—*"My beloved is like a roe or a young hart"* (Song 2:9a). He will come to the aid of His own because he loves them even to the end. His love is the caring type like that of eagles carrying their protégés on their wings to a safe haven. *"The LORD hath appeared of old unto me, saying, Yea, I have loved thee with an everlasting love: therefore with lovingkindness have I drawn thee"* (Jeremiah 31:3). His love will never let Him forsake your cry. *"But Zion said, The LORD hath forsaken me, and my Lord hath forgotten me. Can a woman forget her sucking child, that she should not have compassion on the son of her womb? yea, they may forget, yet will I not forget thee. Behold, I have graven thee upon the palms of my hands; thy walls are continually before me"* (Isa 49:14-16).

   Like a young hart, He will come swiftly without delay to fight the enemies of His children. He will get the captives out of the den of lions. Let it be known unto you that He is stronger than the strongest (Devil).

4. **Christ is closer to us than our cloth, even when we do not realize it**
   *"Behold, he standeth behind our wall, he looketh forth at the windows, shewing himself through the lattice"* (Song of Solomon 2:9b-c).

   This can be compared with God's love for Israel. He often called them by name (Isaiah 50:2), sought them and looked for them (Jer. 7:13; 35:17). He, as the shepherd wooing the Shulamite, stood behind their wall, and even looked through the lattice. But they kept Him outside, not wanting Him to interfere in their daily lives (Matthew 23.37). And once we are His, He regularly calls us and tells us that it is time for love, a time for renewal. But how often do we leave Him standing behind the wall, or looking through the lattice of the window just because we are too busy with other things? And the moment of opportunity passes us by.

5. **The call of the renewal of the genuine love for God**
   *"My beloved spake, and said unto me, Rise up, my love, my fair one, and come away. For, lo, the winter is past, the rain is over and gone; The flowers appear on the earth; the time of the singing of birds is come, and the voice of the turtle is heard in our land; The fig tree putteth forth her green figs, and the vines with the tender grape give a good smell. Arise, my love, my fair one, and come away"* (Song of Solomon 2:10-13).

   Living in Sodom, vexing our righteous spirit every minute is not God's plan for us neither is it a good way to live our victory. Know you not that a little yeast will cause the flour to rise? Therefore, staying for a longer time in the palace of Solomon where temptations and corrupt, dirty words abound can weaken our faith and spiritual strength. Therefore, *"Arise ye, and depart; for this is not your rest: because it is polluted, it shall destroy you, even with a sore destruction"* (Micah 2:10).

   *"Come, and let us return unto the LORD: for he hath torn, and he will heal us; he hath smitten, and he will bind us up. After two days will he revive us: in the third day he will raise us up, and we shall live in his sight. Then shall we know, if we follow on to know the LORD: his going forth is prepared as the morning; and he shall come unto us as the rain, as the latter and former rain unto the earth"* (Hosea 6:1-3). *"Sow to yourselves*

*in righteousness, reap in mercy; break up your fallow ground: for it is time to seek the LORD, till he come and rain righteousness upon you"* (Hosea 10:12).

For the Shulamite lady, the unavoidable and inevitable plea of her beloved Shepherd boy came to her. He told her that it is now spring and the time for love. The winter had gone, the rainy season was over, the flowers were blooming, the birds were singing, and the trees were blossoming and showing signs of fruits.

So "the winter" of estrangement and sin is "past" to the believer (Isaiah 44:22; Jer. 50:20; 2 Cor. 5:17; Eph. 2:1). The rising "Sun of righteousness" dispels the "rain" (2 Samuel 23:4; Psalms 126:5; Malachi 4:2). It is time for their love to blossom as they walk together in the countryside, in the sunshine, enjoying the delights of nature. And how often do the voice of our Beloved Jesus Christ calls to us to leave behind what is past and come aside with Him and looks forward to the future and all the delights that He has in store for us? He calls for the non-Christians to experience the time of rebirth (John 1:12-13; 3:1-6; 2 Cor. 5:17) and for the tempted, weaken, weary souls to enjoy a time of renewal. He wants us to enjoy our lives in His presence and walk with Him in the springtime of our lives, in the time when all is renewed. God has done all the necessary groundwork, and it is now time for us to enter into it. *"Do not be conformed to this world,"* He counsels, 'but be renewed in the spirit of your mind, that you might prove what is that good, acceptable and perfect will of God"* (Romans 12:2). We are being called on to enjoy continual spring times with Him, even when the going is hardest.

## Prayer of the Shulamite Lady

1. **Request for the reality of His existence or closeness to us**
   *"O my dove, that art in the clefts of the rock, in the secret places of the stairs, let me see thy countenance"* (Song of Solomon 2:14).

   We must pray at all time and ask for the reality of His presence with us. Our song and prayer should be that we want Him to be so close to us, more than ever, especially before we enter into temptation and during the temptation. We need to promise Him that we will serve Him to the end without denying Him neither defiling His temple (our body) with adultery. We need to tell Him that we need to feel Him by our side because the world is ever near to snatch us away from Him. Meditate upon the words of the song written by John E. Bode in 1868, titled **"O JESUS, I HAVE PROMISED."**

   1. O Jesus, I have promised to serve Thee to the end;
      Be Thou forever near me, my Master and my Friend;
      I shall not fear the battle if Thou art by my side,
      Nor wander from the pathway if Thou wilt be my Guide.

   2. O let me feel Thee near me! The world is ever near;
      I see the sights that dazzle, the tempting sounds I hear;
      My foes are ever near me, around me and within;
      But Jesus, draw Thou nearer, and shield my soul from sin.

   3. O let me hear Thee speaking in accents clear and still,
      Above the storms of passion, the murmurs of self will.
      O speak to reassure me, to hasten or control;

O speak, and make me listen, Thou Guardian of my soul.

4. Jesus, Thou hast promised to all who follow Thee
That where Thou art in glory there shall Thy servant be.
And Jesus, I have promised to serve Thee to the end;

5. O give me grace to follow, my Master and my Friend.
O let me see Thy footprints, and in them plant mine own;
My hope to follow duly is in Thy strength alone.
O guide me, call me, draw me, uphold me to the end;
And then in Heaven receive me, my Saviour and my Friend.

2. **Request for the removal of the foxes and the little foxes**
*"Take us the foxes, the little foxes, that spoil the vines: for our vines have tender grapes"* (Song of Solomon 2:15).

Every sinful thought and ungodly desire, every pursuit of that which waste our time of devotion to Him and every trifling visit, every small departure from truth and every conformity to the world are some of the little foxes which must be removed. This is a charge to pray fervently so that God will grant us the grace to mortify every sinful appetite and passion that destroys man's relationship with God.

3. **Reaffirmation of His divine ownership over us**
*"My beloved is mine, and I am his: he feedeth among the lilies"* (Song of Solomon 2:16).

The Shulamite lady knew that without being named after her beloved Shepherd boy, her life would be meaningless. So also is the situation with Christians. Without Christ, Christians are nothing. **Christ + IAN =**

**Christian. So without Christ, the "IAN" becomes I Am Nothing.** Therefore, Christ belongs to us and we belong to Him. In Him we live, without Him the Christian's life is meaningless. All that we have belong to Him. Since He feeds among the lilies, we are sure of His divine providence with words of exhortation and grace; our souls will not famish for lack of comfort from Him. Then shall we be good enough to sing **"BLESSED ASSURANCE"** written by Fanny Crosby in 1873:

1.  Blessed assurance, Jesus is mine!
    O what a foretaste of glory divine!
    Heir of salvation, purchase of God,
    Born of His Spirit, washed in His blood.

    *Chorus*
    *This is my story, this is my song,*
    *Praising my Saviour, all the day long;*
    *This is my story, this is my song,*
    *Praising my Saviour, all the day long.*

2.  Perfect submission, perfect delight,
    Visions of rapture now burst on my sight;
    Angels descending bring from above
    Echoes of mercy, whispers of love.

3.  Perfect submission, all is at rest
    I in my Saviour am happy and blest,
    Watching and waiting, looking above,
    Filled with His goodness, lost in His love.

4.  **Request for His full return to our heart—His dwelling place**
    *"Until the day break, and the shadows flee away, turn, my beloved, and be thou like a roe or a young hart upon the mountains of Bether"* (Song of Solomon 2:17).

*James Fabiyi*

A day of comfort will come after a night of desertion. Come over the mountains of Bether (the mountains that divide), looking forward to that day of light and love. Christ will come over every separating mountain to take us home to himself. Are you ready for Him?

# Chapter Nine

## The Little Foxes

*"Take us the foxes, the little foxes, that spoil the vines: for our vines have tender grapes."* (Song of Solomon 2:15)

Foxes are also called Jackals. These animals like to destroy fruits especially the tender ones. She referred to King Solomon here as one of the foxes just like Jesus called Herod (Luke 13:31-32). As Christians, we wonder why many brethren fall from grace to grass. We wonder why the power of God is diminishing in the church and also wonder why Christianity is not as effective as in the good old days. The more we pray for revival, the less of it we see. Our inheritance is turned to strangers. We pay to drink our own water. Our wood is sold to us. We labour but have nothing to show for it. A terrible famine is looming upon us and servants are ruling over us (Lamentation 5:1-10; Ecclesiastes 10:5-7). We see churches supposed to rule communities be the ones that communities are ruling over. People that belong to the heavenly king are the ones serving while the ungodly are ruling over them. Why are all these coming upon us? The major problem we have with God is that we tolerate the little foxes in our lives.

**Identifying the Little Foxes:** Song of Solomon 2:15

The little foxes are the subtle, unperceivable sins that we may be living with or accommodating in our hearts (Psalms 139:23;

145

Jeremiah 17:9-10). We need to identify the little foxes that hinder us from becoming who God wants us to be. God wants us to be giant killers like David and revivalists like the Apostle Paul. When hurricane Katrina passed through New Orleans, Louisiana (USA) in 2005, it left so much damage that generations to come will live to hear the impart of that hurricane whereas many birds had passed through the same land, though noticed for a few seconds, they were soon forgotten. So, God wants us to have such a great impact in this world that from generation to generation, we will be remembered for the good we have done. No wonder the Bible says that the memory of the just shall be blessed, that the just will be remembered after they have gone to the world beyond.

Unfortunately, the little foxes that destroy our vines do not allow us to accomplish the great tasks that are divinely assigned to us. Some of these foxes are:

1. **Little compromise and disobedience to God's word: Exodus 4:18-24; Gen 17:9; 1 Samuel 15:1-23.**
   The account about how God wanted to kill Moses seems to be one of the most gruesome, but it is the most valuable lesson when it comes to teaching about how to serve God with power. The compromise of Moses to the law of circumcision might have resulted from listening to his wife's logical reasoning, which many do tolerate in the Christendom today. Partial obedience to God's instructions cost King Saul his kingship. For, King Saul spared the beautiful animals from the land that was doomed for destruction saying they be used to offer sacrifices unto the Lord. But God sees obedience better than sacrifice. Our jumping up and down in the service of the Lord while disobeying the complete injunction of the Bible is a manifestation of little foxes in our lives.

2.  **Too many activities that hinder us from building our spiritual lives: Song of Sol 1:6.**

    Engaging in too many activities are foxes that do hinder us from keeping and tendering our spiritual life. *"And as the king passed by, he cried unto the king: and he said, Thy servant went out into the midst of the battle; and, behold, a man turned aside, and brought a man unto me, and said, Keep this man: if by any means he be missing, then shall thy life be for his life, or else thou shalt pay a talent of silver. And as thy servant was busy here and there, he was gone"* (1 Kings 20:39-40). The complaint here is that *thy servant was busy here and there*. So, he could not pay proper attention to the assignment committed to his hands. Many a time we play into the hands of Satan, allowing him take advantage of us because we are too busy here and there. Satan can take advantage of that which you know how to do best. For example, if you love to counsel people, Satan can manipulate you to the point that there will be thousands of people on the queue for you to counsel in a day. He is using that to keep you so busy that you will have less time to fellowship with God in your personal bible reading and prayer.

3.  **Little sleep**

    Most of the times, a little sleep causes us to neglect our spirituality. I am not saying that you should over sleep, sleep for six to eight hours a day, but do not over sleep. *"By much slothfulness the building decayeth; and through idleness of the hands the house droppeth through."* (Ecclesiastes 10:18). Excessive sleep is bad for Christians because it robs them of the quiet time in the morning. When you sleep late and wake up late, the problem you will face is that there will be no time to fellowship with God because you have to rush out to your workplace. Too much sleep robbed King Saul of his sword and cruse of water.

4. **Unchecked association with the ungodly**
   *"Ephraim, he hath mixed himself among the people; Ephraim is a cake not turned. Strangers have devoured his strength, and he knoweth it not: yea, gray hairs are here and there upon him, yet he knoweth not."* (Hosea 7:8-11).

   For Ephraim, strange doctrines and philosophic ideas are coming into his life but he detects it not. Dear readers, sharing of pulpit with ungodly preachers and politicians for the sake of the ecumenical movement and fund raising is a little fox that is raging in our churches today. The danger of mingling ourselves with the ungodly is that they will teach us their evil works. The Israelites mingled with the heathen and learned their works (Psalms 106:35). Evil association corrupts good manner. Apostle Peter denied his Master and Friend because he warmed himself up in the camp of the ungodly. Most Christian sisters have turned away from the faith and become prostitutes as a result of the counsel they received from their ungodly friends. Peer pressures could be very deadly too. The Bible says that he that walks with the wise shall be wise. Sometimes you may be pressed to take a negative decision but the probability of following it through may depend on the type of friends you are keeping. Godly friends will counsel you not to r take such a decision but the ungodly will encourage you to do it quickly and even suggest the easiest way to accomplish it.

1. **Little accommodation of erroneous doctrines**
   There are some attitudes and lifestyles that seem to be Christianly acceptable but when fully matured, are satanic and poisonous. Such attitudes have a similitude of godliness but deny the power thereof.

   *"Another parable put he forth unto them, saying, The kingdom of heaven is likened unto a man which sowed good seed in his field: But while men slept, his enemy*

*came and sowed tares among the wheat, and went his way. But when the blade was sprung up, and brought forth fruit, then appeared the tares also."* (Matthew 13:24-26).

False prophets are likened to foxes because of their craftiness and lying in wait to deceive the Lord's people (Ezekiel 13:4, 10). False prophets are likened to foxes in the deserts because they prey, hurt and destroy the Lord's people. Dear readers, allowing false prophets into your life signifies that you are accommodating their lifestyles and false doctrines. Listen to what the Holy Spirit is saying about the false prophets and teachers in 2 Peter 2:1-3:

*"But there were false prophets also among the people, even as there shall be false teachers among you, who privily shall bring in damnable heresies, even denying the Lord that bought them, and bring upon themselves swift destruction. And many shall follow their pernicious ways; by reason of whom the way of truth shall be evil spoken of. And through covetousness shall they with feigned words make merchandise of you: whose judgment now of a long time lingereth not, and their damnation slumbereth not."*

Erroneous doctrines are referred to as the leaven of the Pharisees. These are teachings that seem to be in accordance to the truth but when we read between the lines; we could detect the inclusion of human opinions that sap the very foundational pillars of Christ's doctrine. The doctrines the Pharisees taught were the commandments and inventions of men: the traditions of the elders.

Today, there are many doctrines concerning tithes and offerings that people invented, which are a twist to the Scriptures. For example, when pastors want to collect tithes or offerings in the church, they will usually quote the Bible to coerce people into giving satisfactorily. One of the things they do say is "do not appear before the Lord empty handed."

But Let us examine the Bible passage that they are alluding to in Deuteronomy 16:16-17: *"Three times in a year shall all thy males appear before the LORD thy God in the place which he shall choose; in the feast of unleavened bread, and in the feast of weeks, and in the feast of tabernacles: and they shall not appear before the LORD empty: Every man shall give as he is able, according to the blessing of the LORD thy God which he hath given thee."*

Brethren, it is not three times a week (as we do have Sunday Worship Service, Bible, and Prayer meeting programmes) that the male children of Israel appeared before the Lord but just three times a year. So, to quote the same scripture to coerce people to donate money is unbiblical, dubious, and deceptive. It is good to give to God for the furtherance of the gospel but not with coercive efforts from the pastors. It is a free will offering. How will an unemployed brother not come to the church empty handed? If you have joined this group of money-milking machine in the church, note that you have at least a little fox in your life. This destroys your effectiveness in ministry.

Other false doctrines include match-making of people for marriage, eternal security—once saved, saved for ever even when you continue to sin—and liberty in Christ with emphasis on the loose relationship between the opposite sex, thereby encouraging sexual immorality and sex before marriage. Oversimplifying law and grace whereby they teach that we are no longer under the law but grace, forgetting that we are to work out our salvation with trembling and fear. They also forget that the whole Bible is referred to as the Law or God's word.

Introduction or accommodation of harlot's dress is another deceptive doctrine of the devils that rocks the church today and destroys it like the tsunamis and hurricane Katrina (hurricane that killed hundreds of people in New Orleans, USA in 2006).

*"And to the angel of the church in Pergamos write; These things saith he which hath the sharp sword with two edges; I know thy works, and where thou dwellest, even where Satan's seat is: and thou holdest fast my name, and hast not denied my faith, even in those days wherein Antipas was my faithful martyr, who was slain among you, where Satan dwelleth. But I have a few things against thee, because thou hast there them that hold the doctrine of Balaam, who taught Balack to cast a stumblingblock before the children of Israel, to eat things sacrificed unto idols, and to commit fornication. So hast thou also them that hold the doctrine of the Nicolaitans, which thing I hate. Repent; or else I will come unto thee quickly, and will fight against them with the sword of my mouth."* (Revelation 2:12-16)

There are some liberal and modern pastors who teach that fornication (sexual intercourse between unmarried brother and sister) is no sin. Worse still, there are some in developing countries who call themselves prophets but encourage people to do some sacrifices by asking them to bring to them a new Bible, coconut, new soap, new sponge for bath in exchange of a promise to carry out prophet's work on these items after which they will become prosperous or find a lifetime partner. What a great erroneous doctrine!

2. **Loves of pleasures and cares for the things of this world**

The channels through which sin or spiritual destroyers come into many Christians' life are the love of pleasures and the cares for the things of this world. One day in the Garden of Eden, Eve was doing some things when Satan approached her and tempted her through one of these channels (love of pleasure).

*"And when the woman saw that the tree was good for food, and that it was pleasant to the eyes, and a tree to be desired to make one wise, she took of the fruit thereof, and did eat, and gave also unto her husband with her; and he did eat."*

As a Christian, it is not everything that is pleasant to the eyes that we should go after; there could be a death in the pot. Comfort is one of the functions that the Holy Spirit gives to Christians. However, we must understand that this comfort is not synonymous to love of pleasure but relief and, comfort in times of difficulties. Indulging oneself in merriment all year round, pampering one's body at the expense of one's spiritual commitment, not able to accommodate little inconveniences indicate that love of pleasure reigns in your life. In the letter of Theanus to Eubulus, he wrote *"What can be done with that boy, who, if he has no food when and as he pleases, bursts out into weeping; and, if he eats, must have dainties and sweetmeats? If the weather be hot he complains of fatigue; if it be cold, he trembles; if he be reproved, he scolds; if everything be not provided for him according to his wish, he is enraged. If he eats not, he breaks out into fits of anger. He basely indulges himself in pleasure; and in every respect acts voluptuously and effeminately. Knowing then, O friend, that boys living thus voluptuously, when they grow up are wont to become slaves; take away, therefore, such pleasures from them."* This quotation can be simply summarised as love for luxurious living. Many so-called Christians cannot tolerate praying earnestly with fasting for just a single day because they cannot deny their appetite for food. *"Woe to thee, O land, when thy king is a child, and thy princes eat in the morning!"* (Ecclesiastes 10:16). It is very easy for foxes to come and destroy church members and a ministry when lazy, pleasure-loving pastors who cannot engage in a prayer-and-fasting lifestyle lead our churches. Apostle Paul mentioned fasting often.

Unfortunately, this appetite drives its victims to falling into the sin of immorality and corruption for monetary gain. Our beloved brother Esau, the twin brother of Jacob (in the Bible) sold his birthright just because of the evil appetite for food. This account is written in Genesis 25:29-34:

*"And Jacob sod pottage: and Esau came from the field, and he was faint: And Esau said to Jacob, Feed me, I pray thee, with that same red pottage; for I am faint: therefore was his name called Edom. And Jacob said, Sell me this day thy birthright. And Esau said, Behold, I am at the point to die: and what profit shall this birthright do to me? And Jacob said, Swear to me this day; and he sware unto him: and he sold his birthright unto Jacob. Then Jacob gave Esau bread and pottage of lentiles; and he did eat and drink, and rose up, and went his way: thus Esau despised his birthright."*

It must be noted that a day's hunger cannot kill Esau but because of his craving for the red pottage of another man, he became restless, wanting to eat this food by all means. Even if he was fainting because of hunger, mere drinking of water or fruit juice at such a time would have still given him the strength needed to prepare his own food. The love of pleasure to satisfy his appetite NOW made him despise his birthright which had a lot of benefits attached to it. The dignity and honour of many

Christian sisters and brothers as well as pastors have been destroyed because of their appetite for money and worldly comfort. Birthright of virginity, holiness, spiritual power, and spiritual gifts are sold to meet the present needs. Esau said, *Behold, I am at the point to die: and what profit shall this birthright do to me?* We must all learn how to deny ourselves, taking our cross, and following Jesus.

*"And when he had called the people unto him with his disciples also, he said unto them, Whosoever will come after me, let him deny himself, and take up his cross, and follow me. For whosoever will save his life shall lose it; but whosoever shall lose his life for my sake and the gospel's, the same shall save it. For what shall it profit a man, if he shall gain the whole world, and lose his own soul? Or what shall a man give in exchange for his soul?"* (Mark 8:34-36)

3. **Little bitterness**
The life of Esau was illustrated as a pleasure-loving man. What a pity? After selling his birthright, his eyes of understanding opened but his dignity had been sold. He pursued his brother Jacob with the intention of killing him, which aggravated to bitterness in his heart (Hebrew 12:14-15). Bitterness can spring up in our hearts because of the disappointment we experienced from a so trusted brother or sister. If care is not taken and we do not quickly pray it off our minds, this little fox will destroy our relationship with God and man. Accommodation of a little anger and resentment between close friends, husband and wife are little foxes that hinder most Christians from growing to a higher level in God. Many miracles of healing, breakthrough, and deliverance are hindered because of these foxes. My wife and I have a principle which I normally tell newly wedded Christian couples. My wife or I must not sleep with resentment in the heart against each other. We are to speak out and

forgive each other if necessary before we sleep. This is because we do not want to lose our peace of mind, miss the rapture of the saints in case Christ comes in the night while we are sleeping with anger or resentment in our hearts, or even death may come. Many Christian' homes are in chaos and at the verge of divorce because of this little fox that crept into their relationship. Many churches are not growing spiritually and numerically because of the little fox of bitterness in the hearts of church members against one another or the pastor. Remember, *"be ye angry, and sin not: let not the sun go down upon your wrath: Neither give place to the devil."* Ephesians 4:26-27

4. **Little grumbling and fault finding**
Little grumbling and fault finding here and there about an activity or the other could be very destructive to our tender vine. Christians should be very careful about political and church affairs. There are many reasons why we grumble. Miriam and Aaron complained about the marriage of Moses to a strange woman, Zipporah. They faulted his ministry.

*"And Miriam and Aaron spake against Moses because of the Ethiopian woman whom he had married: for he had married an Ethiopian woman. And they said, Hath the LORD indeed spoken only by Moses? hath he not spoken also by us? And the LORD heard it. (Now the man Moses was very meek, above all the men which were upon the face of the earth.) And the LORD spake suddenly unto Moses, and unto Aaron, and unto Miriam, Come out ye three unto the tabernacle of the congregation. And they three came out. And the LORD came down in the pillar of the cloud, and stood in the door of the tabernacle, and called Aaron and Miriam: and they both came forth. And he said, Hear now my words: If there be a prophet among you, I the LORD will make myself known unto him in a vision, and will speak unto him in a dream. My*

*servant Moses is not so, who is faithful in all mine house. With him will I speak mouth to mouth, even apparently, and not in dark speeches; and the similitude of the LORD shall he behold: wherefore then were ye not afraid to speak against my servant Moses? And the anger of the LORD was kindled against them; and he departed. And the cloud departed from off the tabernacle; and, behold, Miriam became leprous, white as snow: and Aaron looked upon Miriam, and, behold, she was leprous."* (Numbers 12:1-10)

Like Miriam and Aaron, there are many brethren that are busy bodies, fault finders against others, and grumbling about other people's life and ministry, doctrine of holiness, righteousness, and so on. If you are one of these people, it is a sign that little foxes are right in your vineyard.

5. **Unforgiving spirit**
There are many people who run from pillars to poles and vice versa seeking for solutions to the problems that are devastating their lives, yet without solution. Jesus dedicated quantity time to teach about Christians' forgiveness and the impending danger of unforgiveness.

*"Therefore if thou bring thy gift to the altar, and there rememberest that thy brother hath ought against thee; Leave there thy gift before the altar, and go thy way; first be reconciled to thy brother, and then come and offer thy gift. Agree with thine adversary quickly, whiles thou art in the way with him; lest at any time the adversary deliver thee to the judge, and the judge deliver thee to the officer, and thou be cast into prison. Verily I say unto thee, Thou shalt by no means come out thence, till thou hast paid the uttermost farthing"* (Matthew 5:23-26)

From this Bible reference, we can see that an unforgiving spirit will make your offering, service, and labour in His vineyard to be unacceptable before God. If anybody offends you, you need to forgive them or else all your contributions to the growth of the work of God will be in vain, un-noticed, and unacceptable. So it is like a little fox that destroys your labour in His vineyard.

Another consequence of unforgiving spirit is being locked in the prison yard of Satan. To be realistic, not all afflictions, sicknesses, diseases, or problems need deliverance prayer or fasting and prayer. The way out of some of these problems may just be that you forgive the person that has offended you. Jesus said that *"Agree with thine adversary quickly, whiles thou art in the way with him; lest at any time the adversary deliver thee to the judge, and the judge deliver thee to the officer, and thou be cast into prison."* You can remain in the prison where various problems abound just because you have not agreed with your enemy quickly. Dear reader, please stop for a while and think deeply, ponder upon it and ask yourself that you have been praying for breakthrough, pastors and deliverance ministers have prayed for your breakthrough, nothing is forthcoming. An unforgiving spirit may be the yoke that you have to break and decide to pay the price of forgiveness to get your breakthrough. When you release the person you have imprisoned in your heart through forgiveness, you shall also be released from the prison of Satan. Most Christians find it difficult to forgive their fathers or mothers who refused to sponsor them during their schooling days, to forgive Christian brothers or sisters, relative or unbeliever who lied against you or block your progress or promotion. Remember, Christ taught us to forgive even our enemies. It is difficult for un-regenerated man to forgive but a regenerated and sanctified soul finds it possible to forgive. Therefore, you need the mind of Christ to forgive your enemy.

*"And when they were come to the place, which is called Calvary, there they crucified him, and the malefactors, one on the right hand, and the other on the left. Then said Jesus, Father, forgive them; for they know not what they do"* (Luke 23:33-34).

Let me quickly talk about how God has been helping me to forgive people who have offended me. Immediately, when someone offends me, the first that always come to my mind is that it may not be intentional. There are lots of circumstances that might have surrounded his or her action. If she or he is married, I used to think that maybe he has a problem at home with his or her spouse and unleashed the carry over on me. If he or she is not married, I think that may be someone has hurt him or her, which might have caused his or her action. Another thought that always come is that may be Satan is using him or her to make me angry and possess unforgiving spirit in order for him to take advantage of that against me to imprison me. I guess that if you are thinking like these, you will not count any offence against you as a weighty matter and will always find it possible and easy to forgive.

**Importance of Being Mindful of Little Foxes:** Song of Sol 2:15
The question is, why should we be mindful of the little foxes?

1. *Sin is sin*
   One of the reasons for being mindful of these little foxes is that sin is sin. Accommodation of just a little sin in our lives or church differs not from accommodating same sex marriage or murder. Sin of disobedience is as weighty as that of witchcraft.

2. *Sin separates us from God*
   Whether little or great sin, its consequence is the erection of a wall of partition and separation between man and God.

*"Behold, the LORD'S hand is not shortened, that it cannot save; neither his ear heavy, that it cannot hear: But your iniquities have separated between you and your God, and your sins have hid his face from you, that he will not hear. For your hands are defiled with blood, and your fingers with iniquity; your lips have spoken lies, your tongue hath muttered perverseness."* (Isaiah 59:1-3)

*"If I regard iniquity in my heart, the Lord will not hear me"* (Psalm 66:18). There are lots of prayers that were denied or unanswered because of the committed secret and presumptuous sin.

3. *Sin causes spiritual poverty*
   *"Though a sinner do evil an hundred times, and his days be prolonged, yet surely I know that it shall be well with them that fear God, which fear before him: <u>But it shall not be well with the wicked, neither shall he prolong his days</u>, which are as a shadow; because he feareth not before God."* (Ecclesiastes 8:13)

   *"There is no peace, saith the LORD, unto the wicked."* (Isaiah 48:22; 57:21)

   Bible makes it clear that sin which is wickedness brings spiritual poverty, premature death and lack of peace. Once you accommodate any little fox to nest on your head, spiritual problems and disasters will take over your life.

4. *Sin incapacitates man*
   Sin enslaves man into a perpetual babyhood, demonic bondage, calamities, and catastrophes. *"Jesus answered them, Verily, verily, I say unto you, Whosoever committeth sin is the servant of sin"* (John 8:34). *"Know ye not, that to whom ye yield yourselves servants to obey, his servants ye are to whom ye obey; whether of sin unto death . . . ?"* (Romans 6:16)

So if you yield yourself to sin, it becomes your lord and master; thereby having power to control and manipulate your life and passion. The only way to escape its slavery is to accept Jesus Christ as your Lord and Master and then obey the word of God.

5.   *Sin destroys man*
     The eternal destiny of all unrepented sinners is hell fire (lake of fire). The wages of sin is death.

     *Know ye not that the unrighteous shall not inherit the kingdom of God? Be not deceived: neither fornicators, nor idolaters, nor adulterers, nor effeminate, nor abusers of themselves with mankind, Nor thieves, nor covetous, nor drunkards, nor revilers, nor extortioners, shall inherit the kingdom of God." (1 Corinthians 6:9-10)*

## Impending Dangers of Little Foxes

1.   Little foxes cause us to fall into sin
     Remember, *a little leaven leaveneth the whole lump* (1 Corinthians 5:6). The sin of adultery committed by King David caused him to falsely withdrew Uriah from the battlefield, intoxicating him with wine until he becomes drunk, forced Uriah to live a life of pleasure at a wrong time, set up and sentence Uriah to death. It really became a spider web on him. One leads to the others. The enjoyment of a night of sexual immorality with your boss and the gain of some amount of money from it can wind you up into becoming an expert in prostitution.

2.   Little foxes weaken our relationship with God thereby diminishing our spiritual power or limit our effectiveness in service to God. Once the foundation of your salvation and relationship with God is destroyed by any of these little foxes, your entire spiritual life and ministry are in jeopardy. The love of pleasure and women by Samson

caused him a loss of power in the hands of Delilah. How is your spiritual life faring since you fell into the hands of that young lady among your church choirs? Or since you removed a large amount of money from the tithes and offering in your church purse anybody without allowing to know about it?

3.  Little foxes corrupt wisdom and honour
    One single act of sin, may injure the character of a wise and honourable man, and greatly expose him to shame and contempt, and cause him to stink in the nostrils of men and to be reproached by men. *"Dead flies cause the ointment of the apothecary to send forth a stinking savour: so doth a little folly him that is in reputation for wisdom and honour."* (Ecclesiastes 10:1)

    Believers are commanded to mortify their sinful appetites and passions, which are the little foxes that destroy their graces and comforts, and crush good beginnings. We must not underestimate the destructive power of the little foxes. We must understand that little foxes come in different shapes, sizes, and colours, and if we really want God's power to follow us through, we must pray like David and the Shulamite girl (Psalms 139:23; Song of Sol 2:15). The problem that we have today is not because we do not pray or study our Bible, indeed, we pray a lot for revival but little or no revival evolved from it. The problem that we have is because we accommodate the little foxes. We do substitute sacrifices for obeying the entire words of God.

## YIELD NOT TO TEMPTATION

1.  Yield not to temptation, For yielding is sin,
    Each vict'ry will help you, Some other to win;
    Fight manfully onward, Dark passions subdue,
    Look ever to Jesus, He will carry you through.

*Chorus*
*Ask the Saviour to help you,*
*Comfort, strengthen, and keep you,*
*He is will to aid you,*
*He will carry you through.*

2. Shun evil companions, Bad language disdain,
   God's name hold in rev'rence, Nor take it in vain;
   Be thoughtful and earnest, Kind hearted and true,
   Look ever to Jesus, He will carry you through.

3. To him that o'er cometh God giveth a crown,
   Through faith we shall conquer, Though often cast down,
   He who is our Saviour, Our strength will renew.
   Look ever to Jesus, He will carry you through.

# Chapter Ten

## The Pain of Separation

"*By night on my bed I sought him whom my soul loveth: I sought him, but I found him not. I will rise now, and go about the city in the streets, and in the broad ways I will seek him whom my soul loveth: I sought him, but I found him not. The watchmen that go about the city found me: to whom I said, Saw ye him whom my soul loveth? It was but a little that I passed from them, but I found him whom my soul loveth: I held him, and would not let him go, until I had brought him into my mother's house, and into the chamber of her that conceived me. I charge you, O ye daughters of Jerusalem, by the roes, and by the hinds of the field, that ye stir not up, nor awake my love, till he please.*" (Song of Solomon 3:1-5)

"*I sleep, but my heart waketh: it is the voice of my beloved that knocketh, saying, Open to me, my sister, my love, my dove, my undefiled: for my head is filled with dew, and my locks with the drops of the night. I have put off my coat; how shall I put it on? I have washed my feet; how shall I defile them? My beloved put in his hand by the hole of the door, and my bowels were moved for him. I rose up to open to my beloved; and my hands dropped with myrrh, and my fingers with sweet smelling myrrh, upon the handles*

> *of the lock. I opened to my beloved; but my beloved had withdrawn himself, and was gone: my soul failed when he spake: I sought him, but I could not find him; I called him, but he gave me no answer. The watchmen that went about the city found me, they smote me, they wounded me; the keepers of the walls took away my veil from me. I charge you, O daughters of Jerusalem, if ye find my beloved, that ye tell him, that I am sick of love."* (Song of Solomon 5:2-8)

The Shulamite's nightmare is considered in this chapter. She narrated an experience she had "on her bed," (Song of Solomon 3:1; 5:2). She dreamed that she could not find her lover, the Shepherd boy, even though she searched everywhere for him. However, after much distress, she found him and then took him to the most secure and intimate place she knew—her mother's bedroom.

**Causes of Separation** Song 3:1; 5:2-3.

In our text, there are only three reasons for separation that could be deduced: love of sleep, lack of communication, and lack of commitment that results in giving untenable excuses. In addition, from Song of Solomon chapter one, the number one reason why the Shulamite lady was initially separated from her lover boy was because King Solomon lusted after her beauty and abused his power as the king by kidnapping her against her consent to force her into marrying him. However, it is worth noticing that there are many reasons why husbands and wives separate all over the world. Therefore, we shall try to cover only few reasons.

1. **Love for too much sleep**
   During one of my counselling sessions, a husband complained about not having much time to spend with his wife because every day when she returned from work, she would just sleep. As a result, they had a poor sexual life. According to his wife, the husband never

helped her with housework. So, by the time she finished cooking, doing the dishes, taking care of their daughter or doing the laundry, and preparing for the next day's activities, she would always be extremely tired. Both of them are physically together under the same roof but they live like roommates. My counsel to the husband was to help his spouse in the house, which would enable them to always be on the same page either tired or strengthened. I also explained to the wife how important it was for her marriage not to always reject her husband when he demands for sexual intimacy.

Many homes are broken and families separated because either the wife or the husband sleeps too much. Sleep could be the consequence of deeper problem like chronic laziness, decrease of love, "fell out" of love, finances issue or simply some types of depression. The Bible says, *"woe to them that are at ease in Zion"* (Amos 6:1). *"Rise up, ye women that are at ease; hear my voice, ye careless daughters; give ear unto my speech. Many days and years shall ye be troubled, ye careless women: for the vintage shall fail, the gathering shall not come. Tremble, ye women that are at ease; be troubled, ye careless ones: strip you, and make you bare, and gird sackcloth upon your loins."* (Isaiah 32:9-11).

Understand that sleeping is a not a criminal act but a blessing from God which is designed to help the body to recuperate from fatigue experienced during the day and the brain to function properly. However, too much sleep which sensualises the soul is a thief of time and causes dullness of mind. A little sleep, a little slumber, a little folding of hands to sleep, so shall your poverty come. It will be too bad if too much sleep causes your husband to abscond from you for another woman who can satisfy his sexual desire. If you engage in sleeping business, you may end up in a troubled and broken home. Learn to be a virtuous woman. *"She riseth also while it is yet night, and giveth meat to her household, and a portion to her maidens"* (Proverbs 31:15). Be prepared to give your body to your husband while it is yet night.

*"Drink waters out of thine own cistern, and running waters out of thine own well. Let thy fountains be dispersed abroad, and rivers of waters in the streets. Let them be only thine own, and not strangers' with thee. Let thy fountain be blessed: and rejoice with the wife of thy youth. Let her be as the loving hind and pleasant roe; let her breasts satisfy thee at all times; and be thou ravished always with her love."* (Proverbs 5:15-19)

One of the best ways to prevent strange women from your husband is to satisfy him at all times (night or day, not talking of a 24 hours affair) with your mutual and sexual love. The husbands should do likewise with their wives. Love is reciprocal. This counsel is not for unmarried people who are only in courtship. Their bed must be undefiled and honourable.

Remember, the relationship between husbands and wives is compared to that which exists between Christ and the church. When the church oversleeps, it can cause a separation between her and her bridegroom, Jesus Christ. Sometimes the Holy Spirit wakes us up in the night to pray or study the word of God, but we ignore him and therefore do not yield to his call. But we do not realize sometimes that a continuous disobedience to the Holy Spirit can grieve Him and cause His withdrawal. Do not let Him give you over to a reprobate mind and let you do things as you wish. Careless soul, oh heed the warning, be prepared to obey the Holy Spirit when He wakes you up in the night to pray. Lots of dangers, troubles, and attacks can be averted if you would yield to such a call because the Holy Spirit is a very good, dynamic and effective watchman. Pastors or spiritual leaders are the watchmen to whom God has given the ministry of looking and taking care of the sheep and to alert the sheep when dangers loom on their ways. Unfortunately, *"they are all ignorant, they are all dumb dogs, they cannot bark; sleeping, lying down, loving to slumber"* (Isaiah 56:10). No wonder, most Christian marriages suffer attacks from the enemy and divorce prevails in the church under their watch. Sleeping in the night prayer meeting (known as vigil) while others are praying, binding and loosing is very disastrous and deadly because the cast out demons from another person can find it easy to attack you.

David decided that he would not sleep comfortably and quietly until he had found a place for God to rest or worship God in the land of Israel.

*"LORD, remember David, and all his afflictions: How he sware unto the LORD, and vowed unto the mighty God of Jacob; Surely I will not come into the tabernacle of my house, nor go up into my bed; I will not give sleep to mine eyes, or slumber to mine eyelids, Until I find out a place for the LORD, an habitation for the mighty God of Jacob."* (Psalm 132:1-5)

We too must not give sleep to our eyes or go to bed until we have found a place, a rest, a satisfaction in our relationship with God and with our spouse.

The Shulamite lady said that she slept but her heart was still awakened. This is different from insomnia. A Clear revelation to the meaning of her problem is given by the event that took place during the prayer at the garden of Gethsemane. The spirit of the disciples was willing to watch and pray but the exhausted flesh was not ready to cooperate with the spirit. They loved to pray but did not want to deprive themselves of sleep.

*"And he (Jesus) took with him Peter and the two sons of Zebedee, and began to be sorrowful and very heavy. Then saith he unto them, My soul is exceeding sorrowful, even unto death: tarry ye here, and watch with me. And he went a little further, and fell on his face, and prayed, saying, O my Father, if it be possible, let this cup pass from me: nevertheless not as I will, but as thou wilt. And he cometh unto the disciples, and findeth them asleep, and saith unto Peter, What, could ye not watch with me one hour? Watch and pray, that ye enter not into temptation: the spirit indeed is willing, but the flesh is weak. He went away again the second time, and prayed, saying, O my Father, if this cup may not pass away from me, except I drink it, thy will be done. And he came and found them asleep again: for their eyes were heavy. And he left them, and went away again, and prayed the third time, saying the same words. Then cometh he to his disciples, and saith unto them, Sleep on now, and take your rest: behold, the hour is at hand, and the Son of man is betrayed into the hands of sinners."* (Matthew 26:37-45)

Note that natural sleep dulls the external senses so also does spiritual sleep. Most Christian couples are so insensitive to the impairment in their family that until the relationship breaks down completely, they cannot see it. Don't be pleased when you find out that your disposition to the things of God is not right.

*"But ye, brethren, are not in darkness, that that day should overtake you as a thief. Ye are all the children of light, and the children of the day: we are not of the night, nor of darkness. Therefore let us not sleep, as do others; but let us watch and be sober. For they that sleep sleep in the night; and they that be drunken are drunken in the night. But let us, who are of the day, be sober, putting on the breastplate of faith and love; and for an helmet, the hope of salvation."* (1 Thessalonians 5:4-8)

Let your love for your spouse or the Lord compels you to wake up from sleep to do as he needs.

2. **Lack of communication**

   Another problem that causes separation in the family is a lack of effective communication. Communication between two persons helps them to get acquainted, build up a relationship, share information, and express emotion. It helps them build trust and respect. It enhances the spirit of team work and goals accomplishment. Effective communication helps people from different background (social, economic, religion, educational) to understand each other and foster a quick and result-oriented decision making. Effective communication is achieved when there is active listening and clear expression (speaking). A Lack of active listening may cause the receiver to respond abruptly. Lack of communication is not necessarily the absence of talking. The husband may tell the wife to come here or go there and the wife may say yes sir, to this or that but this is still not communicating. She is just like a robot.

   From this, we can deduce that there might have been a lack of communication between Adam and Eve, which Satan used as a tool to destroy their relationship with God. Definitely, Adam was in the Garden of Eden yet Eve did not take counsel from Adam before taking the final decision.

   *"Let the husband render unto the wife due benevolence: and likewise also the wife unto the husband. The wife hath not power of her own body, but the husband: and likewise also the husband hath not power of his own body, but the wife. Defraud ye not one the other, except it be with consent for a time, that ye may give yourselves to fasting and prayer; and come together again, that Satan tempt you not for your incontinency.* (1 Corinthians 7:3-5).

Apostle Paul told the church members at Corinth that if it is the husband that wants to pray and fast for a certain period of time, that is not a problem but he must inform the wife before he starts likewise the wife to the husband. Not communicating such spiritual program to your spouse may lead to suspicion at home. If the wife has already prepared food and the husband does not eat she may begin to suspect that her partner ate outside probably from a strange woman. Or, if the husband comes from his workplace and the wife has not prepared any food for him, the man may begin to suspect that may be his spouse is having a skeleton in her cupboard. Therefore, letting your spouse know that you will be fasting is quite expected for the mutual love between both of you.

3. **Lack of commitment leads to giving untenable excuses:** Song 5:3; Luke 14:18-20; Ruth 1:1-18; Roman 8:35-39.
   *"Then said he unto him, A certain man made a great supper, and bade many: And sent his servant at supper time to say to them that were bidden, Come; for all things are now ready. And they all with one consent began to make excuse. The first said unto him, I have bought a piece of ground, and I must needs go and see it: I pray thee have me excused. And another said, I have bought five yoke of oxen, and I go to prove them: I pray thee have me excused. And another said, I have married a wife, and therefore I cannot come."* (Luke 14:16-20)

There are three main untenable excuses that a man can give to exonerate himself from investing into his marriage. The necessities of life like accommodation, giving hundred percent attentions to business, and marriage are great tools that Satan can use to manipulate us to do contrary to God's will. Sometimes we plead that we are under a "necessity" therefore we cannot pay attention to the affairs of our family or spiritual life. We see the affairs of this world as so important that we tend to neglect our wives or husbands and even our souls.

For a relationship between two parties to be fruitful and flourishing, each of the parties should be fully committed to its well being. A good example of commitment to keep the relationship intact is shown by Ruth to her mother-in-law in Ruth 1:1-18:

*"Now it came to pass in the days when the judges ruled, that there was a famine in the land. And a certain man of Bethlehemjudah went to sojourn in the country of Moab, he, and his wife, and his two sons. And the name of the man was Elimelech, and the name of his wife Naomi, and the name of his two sons Mahlon and Chilion, Ephrathites of Bethlehemjudah. And they came into the country of Moab, and continued there. And Elimelech Naomi's husband died; and she was left, and her two sons. And they took them wives of the women of Moab; the name of the one was Orpah, and the name of the other Ruth: and they dwelled there about ten years. And Mahlon and Chilion died also both of them; and the woman was left of her two sons and her husband. Then she arose with her daughters in law, that she might return from the country of Moab: for she had heard in the country of Moab how that the LORD had visited his people in giving them bread. Wherefore she went forth out of the place where she was, and her two daughters in law with her; and they went on the way to return unto the land of Judah. And Naomi said unto her two daughters in law, Go, return each to her mother's house: the LORD deal kindly with you, as ye have dealt with the dead, and with me. The LORD grant you that ye may find rest, each of you in the house of her husband. Then she kissed them; and they lifted up their voice, and wept. And they said unto her, Surely we will return with thee unto thy people. And Naomi said, Turn again, my*

*daughters: why will ye go with me? are there yet any more sons in my womb, that they may be your husbands? Turn again, my daughters, go your way; for I am too old to have an husband. If I should say, I have hope, if I should have an husband also to night, and should also bear sons; Would ye tarry for them till they were grown? would ye stay for them from having husbands? nay, my daughters; for it grieveth me much for your sakes that the hand of the LORD is gone out against me. And they lifted up their voice, and wept again: and Orpah kissed her mother in law; but Ruth clave unto her. And she said, Behold, thy sister in law is gone back unto her people, and unto her gods: return thou after thy sister in law. And Ruth said, Intreat me not to leave thee, or to return from following after thee: for whither thou goest, I will go; and where thou lodgest, I will lodge: thy people shall be my people, and thy God my God: Where thou diest, will I die, and there will I be buried: the LORD do so to me, and more also, if ought but death part thee and me. When she saw that she was steadfastly minded to go with her, then she left speaking unto her.”*

The logical reasoning that Naomi presented before her daughters-in-law to discourage them from following her to the "house of bread" (Bethlehem Judah) appeared reasonable to Orpah but could not convince Ruth to change her mind from the decision she had already made. Let's quickly consider her strong logical reasoning:

1) "Go, return each to her mother's house." A widow in Moab in those days usually goes back to their mothers' houses where they can be well taken care of.
2) *"The LORD grant you that ye may find rest, each of you in the house of her husband."* She reminded them that they were still young with no child, so they needed to get married and the best thing to do was to marry their own people. It was almost certain

that no Israelite would marry them based on the commandment of the Lord.

3) *"Turn again, my daughters: why will ye go with me? Are there yet any more sons in my womb, that they may be your husbands?"* She dwelt more on getting a husband to marry because she knew the weak spot of Moabite girls. The first mother of Moab wanted to marry a man by all means to the point that she made her father, Lot, drunk so he would lay with her. So marriage is a must for the Moabites, they don't joke with it. In fact, during their time, marriage was a must for women, a sign of success and a sign of stability. So, it was the dream of every woman to be married. Note that man shall be ensnared by his own desire.

The last argument struck Orpah to the bone and marrow, she could not resist it, so she went back to fulfill the lust of the flesh. Orpah deserted Naomi, her mother-in law, after much persuasion from Naomi. Ruth chose to cleave to Naomi irrespective of the hardships, no curdling, probability of having no food and other daily needs, no hope to remarry but to remain probably a widow till death, and no hope of acceptance by the Israelites except Naomi. *"And Ruth said, Intreat me not to leave thee, or to return from following after thee: for whither thou goest, I will go; and where thou lodgest, I will lodge: thy people shall be my people, and thy God my God: Where thou diest, will I die, and there will I be buried: the LORD do so to me, and more also, if ought but death part thee and me."* Most divorces today are due to a lack of forbearance, longsuffering, hope for a better future, and trust. Satan will always make us focus on the night, when we are full of sorrow but he will never point out to us the morning that is full of fruitfulness, refreshment, and gladness. Young brothers and sisters separate themselves from the Lord because of marriage like Orpah, worldly pleasures and prosperity forgetting that there is no crown without a cross, no success without suffering. Money or no money, child or no child, house or no house, you must remain cleaved to your spouse. Many think or have been taught that Christianity is a bed of roses. For your marriage to work and your relationship to the Lord to remain intact, there is a price of commitment that you need to pay. Jesus said that you need to take your cross which means denying your personal and selfish wish to follow Him. If you can stand uprightly, not bending to the left, right, back or front, then stretch your two hands straight. The position you are right now is a cross: your head upward, two hands stretched to the left and right, and the legs downward. Assuming that Jesus is standing in front of you and he is moving forward as you are following Him, still forming the cross, if your cell phone rings in your pocket, you cannot take it or else you break the cross. If you are sweating, don't try to wipe it or else you break the cross. If a mosquito bites you, don't try to kill it or else you break the cross. If a lion roars in the bush either from your left or right hand side, if you decide to run, you need your hands to swing to run faster and escape the threat of that wicked beast, but in doing so, you break the cross. From these analogies, you can see that it takes a great commitment to maintain your cross in order to remain cleaved to Jesus as well as your husband or wife. I would like to let you know that hardship or no hardship; whether things are bad or good, you must not separate or divorce your spouse until death do you part. There are lots of consequences for separation.

## 4. Sin of infidelity

Infidelity is an act of unfaithfulness. From the case of the Shulamite lady, she did not commit immorality with Solomon, so this was not the reason for her separation from her lover. However, many marriages are in chaos because of immorality—adultery that either of the partners has committed. Mary, the mother of Jesus, was to be put away by Joseph who found out that she was with a baby (conceived) while she was just espoused to him. She was been mistakenly accused to have committed immorality with another man.

*"Now the birth of Jesus Christ was on this wise: When as his mother Mary was espoused to Joseph, before they came together, she was found with child of the Holy Ghost. Then Joseph her husband, being a just man, and not willing to make her a publick example, was minded to put her away privily."* (Matthew 1:18-19).

Jesus mentioned this same problem of extra-marital affairs as a reason for divorce in Matthew 19:9: *"And I say unto you, Whosoever shall put away his wife, except it be for fornication, and shall marry another, committeth adultery: and whoso marrieth her which is put away doth commit adultery."*

Sexual intercourse is commanded to be only between husband and wife, nothing more. The Bible commands that *"Drink waters out of thine own cistern, and running waters out of thine own well. Let thy fountains be dispersed abroad, and rivers of waters in the streets. Let them be only thine own, and not strangers' with thee. Let thy fountain be blessed: and rejoice with the wife of thy youth. Let her be as the loving hind and pleasant roe; let her breasts satisfy thee at all times; and be thou ravished always with her love. And why wilt thou, my son, be ravished with a strange woman, and embrace the bosom of a stranger?"* (Proverbs 5:15-20).

## Consequences of Separation

1. Loneliness
   *"By night on my bed I sought him whom my soul loveth: I sought him, but I found him not"* (Song of Solomon 3:1).

It is a tough thing to see a woman who has lived with a husband whom she loved with all her heart, strength, and might go through a separation. I happen to know a woman who has separated from her husband. She usually weeps and complains that she feels lonely on the bed at nights; she needs a man beside her. Whenever she tells me this, it's always with tears. Separated couples experience lower levels of satisfaction with life than the married people because they normally miss the companionship that marriage provides. If you have heard of a divorced husband or wife telling you that he or she does not feel the absence of his or her spouse after the separation, check it out, such an individual is likely to be going out with another woman or man.

2. Restlessness

*"By night on my bed I sought him whom my soul loveth: I sought him, but I found him not. I will rise now, and go about the city in the streets, and in the broad ways I will seek him whom my soul loveth: I sought him, but I found him not. The watchmen that go about the city found me: to whom I said, Saw ye him whom my soul loveth?"* (Song of Solomon 3:1-5)

*"I opened to my beloved; but my beloved had withdrawn himself, and was gone: my soul failed when he spake: I sought him, but I could not find him; I called him, but he gave me no answer."* (Song of Solomon 5:6)

People who come from separated home are most of the time restless, uncoordinated, and unorganised. The reason is that they have wounded hearts and a traumatised life. Like the Shulamite lady, they are everywhere looking for someone who will fill the emptiness in their heart. Some ladies who are separated from their husbands, always try their best to win the attraction of other men. Whenever the man seems to be lukewarm about their newly found relationship, her heart breaks and she becomes restless, not knowing whether the man has found another lover elsewhere. Such people are not physically and psychologically stable.

3.  Depression and diseases
    *"I opened to my beloved; but my beloved had withdrawn himself, and was gone: my soul failed when he spake: I sought him, but I could not find him; I called him, but he gave me no answer."* (Song of Solomon 5:6)

    Another danger of separation is depression. Depression is a psychological breakdown commonly caused by loneliness. When you live alone and there is no one to share the secular, social, and spiritual bottle up challenges and problems with, its accumulation results to depression. It is different from being mentally derailed. It causes you to withdraw into your own shell. Studies have claimed positive correlations between divorce and rates of stroke, cancer, and acute infectious diseases.

    A Christian who is separated from God will have spiritual depression and mind torture.

4.  Public harassment
    *"The watchmen that went about the city found me, they smote me, they wounded me; the keepers of the walls took away my veil from me."* (Song of Solomon 5:7)

    A woman who has her head or husband removed is subject to public harassments and embarrassments. In the olden days, people did not normally respect divorcees, they like to insult her. When a Christian is separated from God, he or she will always receive harassments and embarrassments from Satan and his demons or agents. *"He or she that dwelleth in the secret place of the most High shall abide under the shadow of the Almighty. Surely he shall deliver thee from the snare of the fowler, and from the noisome pestilence. He shall cover thee with his feathers, and under his wings shalt thou trust: his truth shall be thy shield and buckler."* (Psalm 91:11, 13, 14) If you are not under the roof of your husband, men on the street would like to mess up with you.

One of my wife's classmates found herself in the mess of a divorce. She was told by people that she was an unwanted commodity in the society because in her middle age, she was still looking for a job to be able to care for herself and her children. What a great embarrassment and harassment!

5.  Raising of ungodly children
    The children of divorced families face a lot of untold hardships. Due to the fact that both parents are not together to support these children financially and morally, they become wayward. They join bad gangs who influence them wrongly. This leads to an increase rate of unmarried teen pregnancy, juvenile delinquency, school drop-outs and unemployment. Some of these children found it difficult to be committed to a relationship later in life because of the bad legacy laid down by their parents. They think that marriage is not worth it. Mavis Hetherington, a University of Virginia professor, reports that seventy percent of children coming from divorced families consider divorce an adequate answer to marital problems even if children are present. There is a program called *regeneration* (similar to rehabilitation program) in a church that my family attended some time ago. More than ninety percent of the people in that program testified that they were from divorced home. Some of the children from divorced families are being abused by their step-father or stepmother either sexually or physically.

There is always division in the homes of divorced couples. Some children will support their mother while the others may support their father, and a house that divides against itself cannot stand.

6. Financial hardship

   Most women from divorced homes are facing great financial problems. Many of them are into rearing children which debar them from getting a job outside their home. When the father who has been the bread winner of the family becomes absent, it will be a tough experience for them. They may find it difficult to get a job because they lack the experience that it takes.

7. Untimely death

   Many people had met with untimely death because of divorce. Loneliness which can lead to depression and consequently to several diseases or sicknesses may eventually result in untimely death. In addition to that, the step father or mother may not want to have anything to do with the step children. He or she may also not want their new spouse to care for them. So, they try to terminate their lives. Others killed their former spouse because of life-insurance and properties. These lives that had been wasted might have contributed immensely to the advancement of our society.

**Cure for Separation** Song 3:1-4; 5:2-8;

The threats of separation or divorce could be so overwhelming. However, having it at the back of our mind that there is no two parties that exist without a conflict will help us decide to resolve any issue that arise in our marriages. The story of the prodigal son who collected his share of his father's inheritance, separated from his father, squandered his resources, became wretched, and later returned to his father is a very good illustration and example of cure for separation (Luke 15:17-24). The followings are the steps to cure the problem of separation.

1. Resolution to return to the lover

   *"I rose up to open to my beloved."* The Shulamite lady resolved in her heart to rise up in search of her Lover boy just like the prodigal son made up his mind to return to his father. Decision always determines destiny. Your

decision to return to your spouse or remain separated will make or mar your future respectively. The resolution of Ruth to remain with Naomi while Orpah separated from her caused her to be the great-grandmother of our Lord Jesus Christ. Likewise, your resolution to return to God after you have separated from Him will bring glory and gain into your present and future, eternal glory. Resolve never to allow anything whatsoever or any suggestion from friends and extended family to hinder you from returning to your spouse. People may make jest of you if they know that you are planning to go back to your spouse after the separation, don't mind them; go ahead with your plan and publicly confess like Apostle Peter that your spouse is yours and there is no other elsewhere and that you will cleave to him.

*"From that time many of his disciples went back, and walked no more with him. Then said Jesus unto the twelve, Will ye also go away? Then Simon Peter answered him, Lord, to whom shall we go? thou hast the words of eternal life."* (John 6:66-68)

It is only that first husband or wife that has the best plan, best suggestion and counsel, better satisfaction and rest for you. Go back to him or her.

2. Relying on God's promises
   *"And ye shall seek me, and find me, when ye shall search for me with all your heart."* (Jeremiah 29:13)

If you have lost your relationship with God, that is not good but there is hope of Him accepting you back to His fold if you will seek Him with all your heart, with a sincere heart.

*"For there is hope of a tree, if it be cut down, that it will sprout again, and that the tender branch thereof will not cease. Though the root thereof wax old in the*

*earth, and the stock thereof die in the ground; Yet through the scent of water it will bud, and bring forth boughs like a plant."* (Job 14:7-9)

What you only need to do is to take Him by His word or promise. He never fails and will not deny His promise to you.

3. Running after the lover: Song 3:1-3; 5:6.
   It is not just for you to decide to return and be claiming that your spouse will take you back; you are to stand up and run after him or her. Seek him or her where you can. *"If thou seek him, he will be found of thee; but if thou forsake him, he will cast thee off for ever."* Seek him or her when it is convenient or inconvenient, night or day, in season or out of season. Don't hide your love for returning to him or her, make it known publicly. This world or another man or woman has nothing for you; make up your mind to follow your deserted spouse. Run simply implies pursue, not just walking as if you are contented, run to show that you mean the business of returning to your spouse.

4. Request about the lover from the watchmen: Song 3:3; 5:7.
   As you are running after spouse for reconciliation, please don't just ask to the wrong man on the street about your Lover; ask the right people who know him or her. Ask the watchmen who have sharp eyes and a broad vision. The watchmen who are the ministers of God can help you locate the Lover of your soul (Isaiah 62:6; Jeremiah 6:17; Ezekiel 3:17; Hebrews 13:17). They can give instruction and enlightenment that will help you locate your Lover. However, you have to be very careful because we are already in the last days that the Bible talks about. There are many watchmen out there that are not sent by God but by Satan to remove your veil, deflower you, molest you, and add salt to your injury. Listen to the Shulamite

lady, "*The watchmen that went about the city found me, they smote me, they wounded me; the keepers of the walls took away my veil from me.*" These kinds of watchmen are sons of Belial like Hophni and Phinehas who *lay with the women that assembled at the door of the tabernacle of the congregation.* I have heard cases whereby a woman will go to a prophet or herbalist to help pray that an estranged husband will come back home. Unfortunately, the prophet or the herbalist ends up stealing her love by using demonic power to hypnotise her. With fervent prayers, come back to the Bible, study it with full concentration and be ready to do as it commands.

5. Resolving grievances with the lover
   "*It was but a little that I passed from them, but I found him whom my soul loveth: I held him, and would not let him go, until I had brought him into my mother's house, and into the chamber of her that conceived me.*" (Song of Solomon 3:4)

   "*And he arose, and came to his father. But when he was yet a great way off, his father saw him, and had compassion, and ran, and fell on his neck, and kissed him.*

   *And the son said unto him, Father, I have sinned against heaven, and in thy sight, and am no more worthy to be called thy son. But the father said to his servants, Bring forth the best robe, and put it on him; and put a ring on his hand, and shoes on his feet: And bring hither the fatted calf, and kill it; and let us eat, and be merry: For this my son was dead, and is alive again; he was lost, and is found. And they began to be merry.*" (Luke 15:20-24)

   There are many tenable reasons why many couples divorce or separate, but there may be solutions to these problems if a commitment and a vision for the future are present. One of such reasons is that the partner is unfaithful. However, this might have been his attitude before, so the other partner can try to make it work by trying to do what pleases the infidel spouse. Also the report of abuse is great which could be a cogent point for divorce, but we should know that abuse has stages. Peradventure there could be solution if the partner has been sensitive to the first stage which is tension building, re-evaluate his or her behaviour since the tension started and look for a period when the battered will be calmed and then try to talk it over. We should realise that two wrongs cannot make a right.

Moreover, some complain because the spouse doesn't have enough time to spend with the family then the next decision is divorce. Who knows may be it is because of the effort to meet the family needs that is why he or she is working himself to the bone. If there could be a dialogue and compromises probably there can be a way forward.

There could be thousands of reasons for divorce to be contracted, but I am of strong belief that divorce is not good because of its profound effects on our present society and future generations. It must be understood that since a husband and a wife are probably from different social, cultural, academic, economic and family background, conflicts in decision making is bound to occur, but despite all these problems, husbands and wives should always find a way of resolving the conflicts. Marriage should be worked upon through affection to one another, effective communication, no boss, no subordinate relationship, tolerance and forgiveness. Since love is claimed to be the basis of marriage, our world may be a better one if we really practice this love. The Bible says that love endures all things.

6. Reaffirmation of love and commitment to the lover
   As soon as you find your estranged spouse, hold him or her fast like a baby will grasp its mother in the face of danger and as Jacob held the Angel fast and refused to let him go until he blessed him. So hold your spouse, tell him or her that you love him or her and will be committed to your newly reunited relationship. Tell him or her that you are sick of love for him or her. Not only by telling but by acting and showing that you do; surrender yourself to him or her, satisfy him or her with everything needed and required between husband and wife.

7. Rejection of the interference of the outsiders: Song 3:5; 2 Kings 2:3,5.
   Now that you have come back to your spouse, reject, resist, and renounce every intruder or outsiders from ruining your relationship the second time. Let nobody or anything comes in between you again. There are lots of people that Satan may raised up to cause misunderstanding by supplying you with various allegations and suggestions, please, don't give them that chance again. They will come and tell you like the sons of prophets did to Elisha that *"Knowest thou that the LORD will take away thy master from thy head to day?"* They will cook lies and inform you that your spouse goes out with strange woman or man just to mar your relationship and cause separation.

# Chapter Eleven

## Test of Love

"[The Shulamite lady asked] *Who is this that cometh out of the wilderness like pillars of smoke, perfumed with myrrh and frankincense, with all powders of the merchant? [Someone replied] Behold his bed, which is Solomon's; threescore valiant men are about it, of the valiant of Israel. They all hold swords, being expert in war: every man hath his sword upon his thigh because of fear in the night. King Solomon made himself a chariot of the wood of Lebanon. He made the pillars thereof of silver, the bottom thereof of gold, the covering of it of purple, the midst thereof being paved with love, for the daughters of Jerusalem. Go forth, O ye daughters of Zion, and behold king Solomon with the crown wherewith his mother crowned him in the day of his espousals, and in the day of the gladness of his heart.*" (Song of Solomon 3:6-11)

"*Behold, thou art fair, my love; behold, thou art fair; thou hast doves' eyes within thy locks: thy hair is as a flock of goats, that appear from mount Gilead. Thy teeth are like a flock of sheep that are even shorn, which came up from the washing; whereof every one bear twins, and none is barren among them. Thy lips are like a thread of scarlet, and thy speech is comely: thy temples are like a piece of a pomegranate within*

185

James Fabiyi

*thy locks. Thy neck is like the tower of David builded for an armoury, whereon there hang a thousand bucklers, all shields of mighty men. Thy two breasts are like two young roes that are twins, which feed among the lilies. Until the day break, and the shadows flee away, I will get me to the mountain of myrrh, and to the hill of frankincense. Thou art all fair, my love; there is no spot in thee. Come with me from Lebanon, my spouse, with me from Lebanon: look from the top of Amana, from the top of Shenir and Hermon, from the lions' dens, from the mountains of the leopards. Thou hast ravished my heart, my sister, my spouse; thou hast ravished my heart with one of thine eyes, with one chain of thy neck. How fair is thy love, my sister, my spouse! how much better is thy love than wine! and the smell of thine ointments than all spices! Thy lips, O my spouse, drop as the honeycomb: honey and milk are under thy tongue; and the smell of thy garments is like the smell of Lebanon. A garden inclosed is my sister, my spouse; a spring shut up, a fountain sealed. Thy plants are an orchard of pomegranates, with pleasant fruits; camphire, with spikenard, Spikenard and saffron; calamus and cinnamon, with all trees of frankincense; myrrh and aloes, with all the chief spices: A fountain of gardens, a well of living waters, and streams from Lebanon."*
(Song of Solomon 4:1-15)

Solomon and all the people travelling with him are returning to the palace in Jerusalem. The Shulamite lady is probably sitting beside him as the distance is increasing between her and her shepherd lover. At the entry of the city, Jerusalem reveals the extravagance of the worldly rich people who always draws the attention of the crowd. Once in his palace, the king grabs an opportunity to have a conversation with the Shulamite lady; there, he again expresses his desire for her, attracted by her physical appearance. Above all, the Shulamite lady remains uncompromised in her stand and fixes her heart on the real thing.

**Description of Solomon's Procession** Song 3:6-11; 1 John 2:15-17; Ephesians 4:29.

1.  *Pictographic appearance for the eyes to lust after*: Song 3:6; Genesis 3:6; 2 Samuel 11:1-4.
    Gorgeous dressing and extravagant living will always draw attention of passers-by to have a second look on us. Remember that it is easy to fall into the trap of Satan through the lust of the flesh and lust of the eyes. So, people who want attention usually put on a special attire to attract people to them. Jezebel painted her face or eyes to make them look beautiful and tired her head in an elegant manner probably to lure Jehu to adopt her as queen. When rich men who have issues with immorality go out for a special occasion, they love to dress gorgeously and in a manner that will attract young, unmarried or even married women. ". . . *Though thou clothest thyself with crimson, though thou deckest thee with ornaments of gold, though thou rentest thy face with painting, in vain shalt thou make thyself fair; thy lovers will despise thee, they will seek thy life*" (Jeremiah 4:30). "*Moreover the LORD saith, Because the daughters of Zion are haughty, and walk with stretched forth necks and wanton eyes, walking and mincing as they go, and making a tinkling with their feet*" (Isaiah 3:16).

    First of all, it is important to consider the meaning of lust of the eyes, how it affects male and female, and how to avoid it. The dictionary defines lust as having an eager, passionate, and inordinate or strong sinful desire for the gratification of sexual appetite or of covetousness. The flesh and the eyes are the two main channels through which lust can be expressed. A good description of the "lust of the eyes" is expressed in the "Notes on the Bible" by Albert Barnes [1834]. In his words, Barnes explains that ". . . the lust of the eyes is that which is designed merely to gratify the sight. These would include costly clothes, jewels, gorgeous furniture, splendid palaces, pleasure-grounds, etc. The object is to refer to the frivolous vanities of this world, the thing on which the eye delights to rest where there is no higher object of life. It does not, of course, mean that the eye is never to be gratified. It is not sinful to find pleasure in beholding objects of real beauty—for the world, as formed by its Creator, is full of such things. He could not but have intended that pleasure should enter the soul through the eye, or that the beauties which he has shed so lavishly over his works should contribute to the happiness of his creatures. The apostle (John) refers to this when it is the great and leading object of life—when it is sought without any connection with reference to the world to come."

The lust of the eyes usually causes people to fall into various sins. King David fell into immoral act with Bathsheba. For long, preachers have condemned King David by ascribing his fall into adultery with Bathsheba, Uriah's wife, to his decision to stay away from the battlefield and relax at home when the battle was going on. However, occurrences in our days shed more light on the possible explanation that might have also come to play in his problem. Somebody who is trying to trap you normally calculate your steps before doing it. Bathsheba might have planned a long time earlier that one day, she would sleep with David. So, on that devilish day, she decided to take her bath at a place where she could be noticed by the king in case he did not go to war. You can easily be deceived if you have a problem with lust. Remember, Satan took Jesus and showed him the glory of this world in order to lure him to do his command. Make a covenant with your eyes that you will not allow what you see to affect your mind. There is no problem with looking once and erasing the scene on your mind; but looking twice is deadly. The reason why those people who want to destroy your virginity or marriage are using pictographic images is because they know that what man sees gives an enduring impression on the mind.

We must understand that lust is not from God. *"But I say unto you, That whosoever looketh on a woman to lust after her hath committed adultery with her already in his heart"* (Matthew 5:28). *"For all that is in the world, the lust of the flesh, and the lust of the eyes, and the pride of life, is not of the Father, but is of the world"* (1 John 2:16). Lust chokes the word of God

Jesus admonishes us to "take heed and beware of covetousness, for one's life does not consist in the abundance of the things he possesses" (Luke 12:15). Paul instructs us to "put to death your members which are on the earth: fornication, uncleanness, passion, evil desire, and covetousness, which is idolatry" (Colossians. 3:5).

Solomon like the prince of this world, employed all possible means to win the affection of the Shulamite lady. Christians must understand the fact that when Satan failed in one way, he will still employ another means to achieve his goal (Matthew 4:1-11; Genesis 39:2-20). He is never fed up, he never retires. On no occasion should any Christian lady allow any flattering word to allure her into taking an evil decision.

2. *Pleasure for the flesh*
   Solomon surrounded himself with sixty bodyguards. Why will he do this? Is it because he is a king? Of course yes, because as a king, he needed security. However, we must understand that there is no security in this insecure world. *With him is an arm of flesh* which is extremely weak and frail; guided by mortal men that should not at all be feared. For us Christians, *there is the LORD our God to help us, and to fight our battles. Our security comes from God not from man.*

*"Woe to the rebellious children, saith the LORD, that take counsel, but not of me; and that cover with a covering, but not of my spirit, that they may add sin to sin: That walk to go down into Egypt, and have not asked at my mouth; to strengthen themselves in the strength of Pharaoh, and to trust in the shadow of Egypt! Therefore shall the strength of Pharaoh be your shame, and the trust in the shadow of Egypt your confusion."* (Isaiah 30:1-3)

To convince the Shulamite about the pleasure that awaits her in the palace if she agrees to marry Solomon, he started showing her his palace of gold and silver. *"He made the pillars thereof of silver, the bottom thereof of gold, the covering of it of purple."* There are lots of men who lure young women into immorality because of the display of their wealth. You will not easily fall into the trap of these evil men and women who like to parade their wealth to entice their victims if you are settle for godliness, *which* is a great gain.

*"But they that will be rich fall into temptation and a snare, and into many foolish and hurtful lusts, which drown men in destruction and perdition. For the love of money is the root of all evil: which while some coveted after, they have erred from the faith, and pierced themselves through with many sorrows. But thou, O man of God, flee these things; and follow after righteousness, godliness, faith, love, patience, meekness."* (1 Timothy 6:9-11)

The Shulamite lady followed after righteousness, godliness, love and patience. So she refused to be carried away with the display of the fame and the funds of Solomon. It's a pity today that many ladies are going after the glory and gold of rich people! Can you imagine Christian ladies also falling into the same snare? They lack the decorum to maintain their chastity. They sell their birthright for delicious and decorated pottage like Esau. Dear reader, it is not only men that do parade their wealth; women do it too to attract men with their gorgeous and transparent dresses. It was this same Solomon who counselled young men not to fall into the trap of gorgeously dressed women.

In Proverbs 7:7-8, 10-17:

*"And beheld among the simple ones, I discerned among the youths, a young man void of understanding, Passing through the street near her corner; and he went the way to her house, And, behold, there met him a woman with the attire of an harlot, and subtil of heart. So she caught him, and kissed him, and with an impudent face said unto him, I have peace offerings with me; this day have I paid my vows. Therefore came I forth to meet thee, diligently to seek thy face, and I have found thee. I have decked my bed with coverings of tapestry, with carved works, with fine linen of Egypt. I have perfumed my bed with myrrh, aloes, and cinnamon."*

Such women are not prostituting themselves for gain. They are well to do and sufficient housewives. They have a considerable affluence of life; they want nothing from their victims but their companies, the enjoyment and fulfilment of sexual desire. These women always act as "sugar-mummy" to the young men who fell in their trap.

There is a warning to men and women at this point. I have heard from victims and read a story from a Nigeria newspaper in 1997 about a young lady who fell in a trap set to destroy her. One day, her boyfriend asked her to accompany her to a place and she agreed. On getting to the place (an uncompleted building), there were two or three men waiting for them. The lady was scared but was told to calm down. The men who were waiting told her that she should cooperate with them and that they were not planning to kill her. They undress her and one of them inserted his fingers into her private part and began to caress her. They collected the vagina discharge that flow out of her private part due to the caressing. They then informed her that the discharge collected will be used for ritual to make money for her boyfriend and that whatsoever she wanted as per material thing, her boyfriend will provide. However, she was told that the only adverse effect is that she would not be able to give birth to any child in life. Later in her life, she did all she could to have pregnancy but all to no avail.

The stories that I have heard are similar for all the victims. In Africa, in the olden days and even up to today, some people regularly visit the native doctors (satanic agents) in order to get wealth or attain positions of power that they will not be able to gain otherwise. Most of these people, who got their money from the kingdom of darkness, are usually required to make rituals from time to time to renew their vow or wealth. So, just like the story of this lady, one of the things they usually use is sperm from man or vagina discharge (mucous like fluid). The bad part to this story is that such a victim may not be able to give birth to children after marriage because of the ritual his manhood or her womanhood has been used for. The affluent and influence of these predators always bring their victims to slavery; therefore, they command the praise of their subjects (Song of Solomon 3:7-8, 11). If you are a victim of these people, please, do not wait; go for deliverance before it is too late.

## David's Son Pornographic Expression

The pornographic expressions penned down in Song of Solomon 4:1-5 does not depict the character of our Lord Jesus Christ, a Man of purity, a holy God, and a righteous Redeemer. The Bible made it known to us that *"Let no corrupt communication proceed out of your mouth, but that which is good to the use of edifying, that it may minister grace unto the hearers"* (Ephesians 4:29). Corrupt communication means bad, decayed, rotten, offensive and unchaste words. We cannot shy away from the evil that prevail in our days; obscene and dirty conversations prevail everywhere even among the assemblies of the so called Christians. It is worst even in our schools (from elementary to tertiary institutions) to the point that children from godly homes vex their spirit daily with such filthy and defiling conversations. What a pity! Our citadel of knowledge becomes centres of dirty conversations and spirit defilement. Immoral talks prevail among our young men and women; it is not also found wanting among the adults or old people in our society. Corrupt communications that stir up evil desires and lusts should not come out of the mouth of a godly person. It is unimaginable that a pure God will speak a word that sensitises immoral thought. Out of the abundance of the heart, the mouth speaks.

Jesus himself clearly declared that *"O generation of vipers, how can ye, being evil, speak good things? For out of the abundance of the heart the mouth speaketh"* (Matthew 12:34).

*"A good man out of the good treasure of his heart bringeth forth that which is good; and an evil man out of the evil treasure of his heart bringeth forth that which is evil: for of the abundance of the heart his mouth speaketh"* (Luke 6:45).

What Jesus is saying is that your speech betrays what is in your heart and who you are. *How can you, being evil, speak good things?*

A Christian should be pure in his conversations because our Master, heavenly Father, and heaven where the Godhead dwells are pure. Never should any Christian indulge in a jest that stirs up lust in the heart of the hearers. The word of God rightly counsels us that *"Be ye therefore followers of God, as dear children; And walk in love, as Christ also hath loved us, and hath given himself for us an offering and a sacrifice to God for a sweet smelling savour. But fornication, and all uncleanness, or covetousness, let it not be once named among you, as becometh saints; Neither filthiness, nor foolish talking, nor jesting, which are not convenient: but rather giving of thanks"* (Ephesians 5:1-4).

In addition, Christians should never even listen to songs that promote filthiness, immoral and dirty character. We are to abstain from every form of evil. We are to jettison every association or gathering where immoral discussions exist. Let everyone that is named after the Lord departs from it. Our conversations should be seasoned with grace.

## Expression of physical beauty

Solomon knew the weakness of women. He knew that singing their praises, especially about their beauty relax them and cause them to submit to their predators. Probably, he succeeded in marrying many wives and getting many concubines using this same approach. It is worth mentioning that this same technique is what many men use to gain the attention of ladies in our days. Such men talk about their prey's body, thereby describing the body structure and sensitive parts of their prey as the best they have ever seen. That is just a lie; they are trying to entice you so you will give them what they want. When people begin to comment that they admire you not because of your spiritual life but because of your dress, beauty, and body structure, you have to run away from such person.

There are lots of separations and divorces today because many couples got married not because of their spouse spiritual gems but because of their beauty. What they failed to understand is that beauty fails after sometimes, especially after a long period of familiarisation.

*"And it came to pass after this, that Absalom the son of David had a fair sister, whose name was Tamar; and Amnon the son of David loved her. And Amnon was so vexed, that he fell sick for his sister Tamar; for she was a virgin; and Amnon thought it hard for him to do any thing to her. But Amnon had a friend, whose name was Jonadab, the son of Shimeah David's brother: and Jonadab was a very subtil man. And he said unto him, Why art thou, being the king's son, lean from day to day? wilt thou not tell me? And Amnon said unto him, I love Tamar, my brother Absalom's sister. And Jonadab said unto him, Lay thee down on thy bed, and make thyself sick: and when thy father cometh to see thee, say unto him, I pray thee, let my sister Tamar come, and give me meat, and dress the meat in my sight, that I may see it, and eat it at her hand. So Tamar went to her brother Amnon's house; and he was laid down. And she took flour, and kneaded it, and made cakes in his sight, and did bake the cakes. And she took a pan, and poured them out before him; but he refused to eat. And Amnon said, Have out all men from me. And they went out every man from him. And Amnon said unto Tamar, Bring the meat into the chamber, that I may eat of thine hand. And Tamar took the cakes which she had made, and brought them into the chamber to Amnon her brother. And when she had brought them unto him to eat, he took hold of her, and said unto her, Come lie with me, my sister. And she answered him, Nay, my brother, do not force me; for no such thing ought to be*

*done in Israel: do not thou this folly. And I, whither shall I cause my shame to go? and as for thee, thou shalt be as one of the fools in Israel. Now therefore, I pray thee, speak unto the king; for he will not withhold me from thee. Howbeit he would not hearken unto her voice: but, being stronger than she, forced her, and lay with her. Then Amnon hated her exceedingly; so that the hatred wherewith he hated her was greater than the love wherewith he had loved her. And Amnon said unto her, Arise, be gone"* (2 Samuel 13:1-5, 8-15)

Amnon's love for his half sister was just a lust for her beauty. Immediately after the evil desire and passion was satisfied, the Bible says that he hated her much more than before. So likewise, most people married their spouses for their beauty. When that beauty fades away with time, they begin to look for other beautiful women outside. They forget that beauty is vain (Proverbs 31:30).

The main purpose for the description given by Solomon was to arouse and sensitise the sexual emotion of the Shulamite lady. Thanks be to God for her strong determination to remain faithful to her beloved Shepherd boy. She did not fall into the hand of Solomon in spite of the displayed glory and gold.

**Determination of Shulamite Lady** Song 4:6

1. *Picture of liberation or escape envisaged*
   *"Until the day break, and the shadows flee away, I will get me to the mountain of myrrh"* (Song of Solomon 4:6a).

   The Shulamite lady envisaged her escape from the palace of Solomon. She believed that the shadow of darkness, sorrow, temptation, trial, and trouble would soon pass away and the light would come. What a great encouragement! Instead of her to succumb to the hand of her tempter, she was only seeing herself getting out of the snare. She saw the deliverance ahead of time. She saw a wonderful wedding and a great reward that her mother's children had promised her if she would be faithful to the end. She had faith of her escape from the dirty game played by Solomon. For faith is the substance of things hoped for, the evidence or (conviction) of things not seen.

*"By faith Abraham, when he was called to go out into a place which he should after receive for an inheritance, obeyed; and he went out, not knowing whither he went. By faith he sojourned in the land of promise, as in a strange country, dwelling in tabernacles with Isaac and Jacob, the heirs with him of the same promise: For he looked for a city which hath foundations, whose builder and maker is God. For they that say such things declare plainly that they seek a country. And truly, if they had been mindful of that country from whence they came out, they might have had opportunity to have returned. But now they desire a better country, that is, an heavenly: wherefore God is not ashamed to be called their God: for he hath prepared for them a city"* (Hebrews 11:8-10, 15-16)

Men and women of faith always see the glory that lies ahead of them, so they do not allow the pleasure of sin for a moment to destroy their ultimate reward of eternal glory and life. They believe that this world has nothing for them, so they *declare plainly that they seek a country*. They know that as good soldiers of the Lord they needed to endure hardness and refused to entangle themselves with the affairs of this life (2 Timothy 2:3-4). Those who are mindful of the things that the world can offer them are the types of people that can easily be enticed with the worldly glory, gold, girls and guys.

Men of faith always look up and see with the eyes of the Deliverer that their salvation is nearer than before. In the time of trouble, *"Joseph took an oath of the children of Israel, saying, God will surely visit you, and ye shall carry up my bones from hence."* (Genesis 50:25). Brethren, you need to know that God will not forsake us forever; He will come to your rescue whatever the situation of life that you are passing through. David already saw that Christ's soul would not be left in hell or His body see corruption in the grave. *"He seeing this before spake of the resurrection of Christ, that his soul was not left in hell, neither his flesh did see corruption"* (Acts 2:31). Since you belong to Christ, you too should see with the eyes of faith that your soul will not suffer in hell, a place of troubles, temptations, trials, and tragedy. Please, do not fall into the trench of Satan. Do not give up to your sorrow. Do not quit the race; *for now is our salvation nearer than when we believed.* See the victory ahead, hold the forth.

1. Ho, my comrades! See the signal
   Waving in the sky!
   Reinforcements now appearing,
   Victory is night.

   Chorus
   Hold the forth, for I am coming,
   Jesus signals still;
   Wave the answer back to heaven,
   By Thy grace we will.

2. See the mighty host advancing,
   Satan leading on:
   Mighty men around us falling,
   Courage almost gone!

3. See the glorious banner waving!
   Hear the trumpet blow!
   In our Leader's name we'll triumph
   Over every foe!

4. Fierce and long the battle rages,
   But our help is near:
   Onward comes our great Commander,
   Cheer, my comrades, cheer!

2. *Promise of returning to the place where the first lover was met*
   *"I will get me to the mountain of myrrh, and to the hill of frankincense"* (Song of Solomon 4:6b).

She envisaged that after her deliverance from the captivity of Solomon, she would return to the mountain of myrrh and hill of frankincense. The church is this mountain of myrrh and hill of frankincense (Isaiah 2:2; Micah 4:1-2). She needed to return to the place where she first met her lover for purification and rededication because she had heard a lot of polluted words that corrupt the soul. She needed to pray those filthy and unchaste words off her mind lest they negatively affect her future living. God already promised in Isaiah 1:25: *"And I will turn my hand upon thee, and purely purge away thy dross, and take away all thy tin."* All the dross and dust that clog the mind during temptations are to be cleansed. Allowing them to lodge in our minds is like covering up leprosy; it will spread over time. Like Prophet Isaiah, dwelling among the sexually corrupt and morally decayed people vex our mind. So, coming to the temple or church of God for refining is very much important.

*"Woe is me! for I am undone; because I am a man of unclean lips, and I dwell in the midst of a people of unclean lips: for mine eyes have seen the King, the LORD of hosts.*

*Then flew one of the seraphims unto me, having a live coal in his hand, which he had taken with the tongs from off the altar: And he laid it upon my mouth, and said,*

*Lo, this hath touched thy lips; and thine iniquity is taken away, and thy sin purged.*" (Isaiah 6:5-7)

Isaiah was not cleansed until he saw God on His throne in the temple of heaven. In the Leviticus order, the priests are the only licensed persons that declare a leper free or not free. Thank God, Jesus is a High Priest. Coming to Him will not only guarantee our discovering of the problem of our dusty and defiled minds, but total cleansing will also be offered. Read about how the plague of leprosy was been handled in the Old Testament as recorded in Leviticus 13:1-28:

*"And the LORD spake unto Moses and Aaron, saying, When a man shall have in the skin of his flesh a rising, a scab, or bright spot, and it be in the skin of his flesh like the plague of leprosy; then he shall be brought unto Aaron the priest, or unto one of his sons the priests: And the priest shall look on the plague in the skin of the flesh: and when the hair in the plague is turned white, and the plague in sight be deeper than the skin of his flesh, it is a plague of leprosy: and the priest shall look on him, and pronounce him unclean. If the bright spot be white in the skin of his flesh, and in sight be not deeper than the skin, and the hair thereof be not turned white; then the priest shall shut up him that hath the plague seven days: And the priest shall look on him the seventh day: and, behold, if the plague in his sight be at a stay, and the plague spread not in the skin; then the priest shall shut him up seven days more: And the priest shall look on him again the seventh day: and, behold, if the plague be somewhat dark, and the plague spread not in the skin, the priest shall pronounce him clean: it is but a scab: and he shall wash his clothes, and be clean. But if the scab spread much abroad in the skin, after that he hath been seen of the priest for his cleansing, he shall be seen of the priest again: And if the priest see that, behold, the scab spreadeth in the skin, then*

*the priest shall pronounce him unclean: it is a leprosy. When the plague of leprosy is in a man, then he shall be brought unto the priest; And the priest shall see him: and, behold, if the rising be white in the skin, and it have turned the hair white, and there be quick raw flesh in the rising; It is an old leprosy in the skin of his flesh, and the priest shall pronounce him unclean, and shall not shut him up: for he is unclean. And if a leprosy break out abroad in the skin, and the leprosy cover all the skin of him that hath the plague from his head even to his foot, wheresoever the priest looketh; Then the priest shall consider: and, behold, if the leprosy have covered all his flesh, he shall pronounce him clean that hath the plague: it is all turned white: he is clean. But when raw flesh appeareth in him, he shall be unclean. And the priest shall see the raw flesh, and pronounce him to be unclean: for the raw flesh is unclean: it is a leprosy. Or if the raw flesh turn again, and be changed unto white, he shall come unto the priest; And the priest shall see him: and, behold, if the plague be turned into white; then the priest shall pronounce him clean that hath the plague: he is clean. The flesh also, in which, even in the skin thereof, was a boil, and is healed, And in the place of the boil there be a white rising, or a bright spot, white, and somewhat reddish, and it be shewed to the priest; And if, when the priest seeth it, behold, it be in sight lower than the skin, and the hair thereof be turned white; the priest shall pronounce him unclean: it is a plague of leprosy broken out of the boil. But if the priest look on it, and, behold, there be no white hairs therein, and if it be not lower than the skin, but be somewhat dark; then the priest shall shut him up seven days: And if it spread much abroad in the skin, then the priest shall pronounce him unclean: it is a plague. But if the bright spot stay in his place, and spread not, it is a burning boil; and the priest shall pronounce him clean. Or if there be any flesh, in the skin whereof there is a hot burning, and the quick flesh that burneth have a white bright spot, somewhat reddish, or white; Then the priest shall look upon it: and, behold, if the hair in the bright spot be turned white, and it be in sight deeper than the skin; it is a leprosy broken out of the burning: wherefore the priest shall pronounce him unclean: it is the plague of leprosy. But if the priest look on it, and, behold, there be no white hair in the bright spot, and it be no lower than the other skin, but be somewhat dark; then the priest shall shut him up seven days: And the priest shall look upon him the seventh day: and if it be spread much abroad in the skin, then the priest shall pronounce him unclean: it is the plague of leprosy. And if the bright spot stay in his place, and spread not in the skin, but it be somewhat dark; it is a rising of the burning, and the priest shall pronounce him clean: for it is an inflammation of the burning."*

Therefore, when we find ourselves in troubles and temptations, we should not accommodate any negative thought but begin to envisage our deliverance and returning to the congregation of the saints; sharing testimony on how we escaped from the prison of our desire, then offering prayers for cleansing and praises for our deliverance as incense unto the Lord. The Apostles did that after their release from the hands of the council in Acts 4:21-31:

*"So when they had further threatened them, they let them go, finding nothing how they might punish them, because of the people: for all men glorified God for that which was done. For the man was above forty years old, on whom this miracle of healing was shewed. And being let go, they went to their own company, and reported all that the chief priests and elders had said unto them. And when they heard that, they lifted up their voice to God with one accord, and said, Lord, thou art God, which hast made heaven, and earth, and the sea, and all that in them is: Who by the mouth of thy servant*

*David hast said, Why did the heathen rage, and the people imagine vain things? The kings of the earth stood up, and the rulers were gathered together against the Lord, and against his Christ. For of a truth against thy holy child Jesus, whom thou hast anointed, both Herod, and Pontius Pilate, with the Gentiles, and the people of Israel, were gathered together, For to do whatsoever thy hand and thy counsel determined before to be done. And now, Lord, behold their threatenings: and grant unto thy servants, that with all boldness they may speak thy word, By stretching forth thine hand to heal; and that signs and wonders may be done by the name of thy holy child Jesus. And when they had prayed, the place was shaken where they were assembled together; and they were all filled with the Holy Ghost, and they spake the word of God with boldness."*

When the brethren come together, there is always encouragement, exhortation, and boldness to fight on and stay in the battle.

Are you falling away? You need to come back. Apostle Peter denied Christ three times but when he returned through repentance, he was accepted back to the fold. A song (Lord, I'm Coming Home) composed by William J. Kirkpatrick was published 1892 and it goes thus:

1. I've wandered far away from God,
   Now I'm coming home;
   The paths of sin too long I've trod,
   Lord, I'm coming home.

   Chorus:
   *Coming home, coming home,*
   *Nevermore to roam;*
   *Open wide Thine arms of love,*
   *Lord, I'm coming home.*

2. I've wasted many precious years,
   Now I'm coming home;
   I now repent with bitter tears,
   Lord, I'm coming home.

3. I'm tired of sin and straying, Lord,
   Now I'm coming home;
   I'll trust Thy love, believe Thy word,
   Lord, I'm coming home.

4. My soul is sick, my heart is sore,
   Now I'm coming home;
   My strength renew, my home restore,
   Lord, I'm coming home.

5. My only hope, my only plea,
   Now I'm coming home;
   That Jesus died, and died for me,
   Lord, I'm coming home.

6. I need His cleansing blood I know,
   Now I'm coming home;
   Oh, wash me whiter than the snow,
   Lord, I'm coming home.

The prodigal son repented and returned to his father, he was received with joy and a great party was thrown for him. Have you been to the den of lion or city of Sodom, stained or not stained? Just make up your mind to come to the Saviour, He will not cast you away, He will take you back. There is a perfect rest with Him (Matthew 11:28-30).

## Disciplinary Life of Shulamite Lady Commended Song 4:7-15

1. *Purity of life commended*
   *"Thou art all fair, my love; there is no spot in thee"*
   (Song of Solomon 4:7).

The Shepherd boy commended the Shulamite lady that there is no spot in her. What a great commendation! Spot is synonymous to blemish, dot, mark, stain, and speck. Hence, an object without spot is an object without blemish, dot, mark, stain, and speck. There are many Bible characters that have this same title of being spotless.

The first that came to mind is Job. *"There was a man in the land of Uz, whose name was Job; and that man was perfect and upright, and one that feared God, and eschewed evil. And the LORD said unto Satan, Hast thou considered my servant Job, that there is none like him in the earth, a perfect and an upright man, one that feareth God, and escheweth evil"* (Job 1:1, 8)? There was no spot or blame in his life that any of his community dwellers could point an accusing finger on.

Apostle Paul is a New Testament saint that was bold enough to publicly declare that *"Ye are witnesses, and God also, how holily and justly and unblameably we behaved ourselves among you that believe"* (1 Thessalonians 2:10). He and his companions lived a pure life and maintained their integrity in their community and beyond.

Our Lord Jesus Christ is a Lamb of God without spot or wrinkle; *"He who through the eternal Spirit offered himself without spot to God"* (Hebrew 9:14). In addition, He publicly mentioned that both His public and private life are without spot. *"Hereafter I will not talk much with you: for the prince of this world cometh, and hath nothing in me."* (John 14:30). There was nothing, no mark or spot in Him. He was free from any accusation and allegation of Satan.

We are to offer unto God ourselves as a sacrifice without spot or wrinkle. *"I beseech you therefore, brethren, by the mercies of God, that ye present your bodies a living sacrifice, holy, acceptable unto God, which is your reasonable service"* (Romans 12:1). Our bodies, in connection with our hearts, must be offered unto God without spot. In the Old Testament, the Israelites were to offer unto God a red heifer without spot (Number 19:2) and lambs without spot (Numbers 28:3, 11). So, we are to offer our lives as a living sacrifice unto the Lord without blemish. Many so-called Christians are like leopards (Jeremiah 13:23). They are corrupted, polluted, and perverted. Sins of fornication, adultery, bribery, corruption, forgery, cheating in the examination hall, backbiting, gossip, malice, envy, covetousness, jealousy, abortion, and deception have spotted or stained their white garment. Do not forget that we are warned by Apostle Peter that *"wherefore, beloved, seeing that ye look for such things, be diligent that ye may be found of him in peace, without spot, and blameless"* (2Peter 3:14). We are privileged to be without spots and that is what Christ is doing in us. *"Even as Christ also loved the church, and gave himself for it; That he might sanctify and cleanse it with the washing of water by the word, That he might present it to himself a glorious church, not having spot, or wrinkle, or any such thing; but that it should be holy and without blemish"* (Ephesians 5:25-27). Therefore, it is our responsibility to remain without spot by His grace. *"Wherefore come out from among them, and be ye separate, saith the Lord, and touch not the unclean thing; and I will receive you"* (2 Corinthians6:17). *"Pure religion and undefiled before God and the Father is this, To visit the fatherless and widows in their affliction, and to keep himself unspotted from the world"* (James 1:27).

Will your garment still be white in the face of tribulations, temptations, and trials of this life? Will your garment still be white when you are positioned in the seat of power, in the land of prosperity, or in the city of

Sodom and Gomorrah (city of immorality)? *"But Daniel purposed in his heart that he would not defile himself with the portion of the king's meat, nor with the wine which he drank: therefore he requested of the prince of the eunuchs that he might not defile himself"* (Daniel 1:8). The Shulamite lady was commended that despite the fact that she had been to the lions' dens and the mountains of the leopards, she remained spotless, so she had the privilege of coming up with her Lover (Song of Solomon 4:8). She was commanded to come with her lover; she was to quit the dens of lions and mountains of leopards. We are not to stay comfortable in the city of corruption and immorality. Get out of it in order to maintain the whiteness of your garment. Only those that have their garments white in spite of all these temptations will have the privilege of making heaven. For no unclean person shall enter there. *"And I said unto him, Sir, thou knowest. And he said to me, These are they which came out of great tribulation, and have washed their robes, and made them white in the blood of the Lamb"* (Revelation 7:14). The right question to ask you is what Elisha A. Hoffman penned down in the wording of a song written in 1878:

## ARE YOU WASHED IN THE BLOOD?

1. Have you been to Jesus for the cleansing power?
   Are you washed in the blood of the Lamb?
   Are you fully trusting in His grace this hour?
   Are you washed in the blood of the Lamb?

   *Chorus*
   *Are you washed (are you washed) in the blood*
   *(in the blood),*
   *In the soul cleansing blood of the Lamb?*
   *Are your garments spotless? Are they white as snow?*
   *Are you washed in the blood of the Lamb*

2. Are you walking daily by the Saviour's side?
   Are you washed in the blood of the Lamb?
   Do you rest each moment in the Crucified?
   Are you washed in the blood of the Lamb?

3. When the Bridegroom cometh will your robes be white?
   Are you washed in the blood of the Lamb?
   Will your soul be ready for the mansions bright,
   And be washed in the blood of the Lamb?

4. Lay aside the garments that are stained with sin,
   And be washed in the blood of the Lamb;
   There's a fountain flowing for the soul unclean,
   O be washed in the blood of the Lamb!

2. *Singleness of purpose*
   *"Thou hast ravished my heart, my sister, my spouse; thou hast ravished my heart with one of thine eyes, with one chain of thy neck."* (Song of Solomon 4:9).

   The Bible tells us that our eyes must be single (Matthew 6:22). Understand that the eye regulates the motion of the body, so if you have two eyes, you are likely to be confused on what way to take. Having one eye connotes singleness of purpose. *"Let thine eyes look right on, and let thine eyelids look straight before thee"* (Proverbs 4:25). We must be people of a single purpose (serving Christ), vision (making heaven), and goal (remaining holy unto His coming, 1 John 3:1-3). Apostle Paul's purpose was that he may win Christ, be found in Christ, know Christ and the power of His resurrection as well as the fellowship of his sufferings, and being made conformable unto his death (Philippians 3:7-10). So he counted all pleasures and privileges as lost for that. No wonder he affirmed that nothing in this world would separate him from the love of Christ, not tribulation, or distress, or persecution, or famine, or nakedness, or peril, or sword, or death, or life, or angels, or principalities, or powers, or things present, or things to come, or height, or depth, or any other creature (Romans 8:35-39). So also, not King Solomon's palace, prosperity or pleasure would separate the Shulamite lady from the lover of her soul, the Shepherd boy. Please, be a man or woman of single purpose and determination; then nothing shall separate you from the love of Christ. Remember, decision determines destiny.

3.  *Genuine love better than wine or worldly pleasure*
    *"How fair is thy love, my sister, my spouse! how much better is thy love than wine! and the smell of thine ointments than all spices!"* (Song of Solomon 4:10).

    Indeed, wine rejoices the heart but genuine love supersedes it. Worldly pleasure is a weapon that Satan uses to draw many souls to hell. Listen to this *"stolen waters are sweet, and bread eaten in secret is pleasant. But he knoweth not that the dead are there; and that her guests are in the depths of hell"* (Proverbs 9:17-18). It is an ironical statement that stolen waters from neighbour's wells and fountains are sweeter than your own. In addition, all prohibited unlawful lusts and pleasures are desirable to men, and sweet in the enjoyment of them than what they have with their spouses. The promises of worldly pleasure make them so desirable. The truth is worldly pleasure endures but for a moment, however, genuine love endures forever. It suffers long in time of persecution and temptation. It does not behave itself unseemly, seeks not her own, thinks no evil; bears all things, believeth all things, hopes for better future, and it never fail (1 Corinthians 13:4-8).

4.  *Lips filled with refreshing words of encouragement and strength*
    *"Thy lips, O my spouse, drop as the honeycomb: honey and milk are under thy tongue;"* (Song of Solomon 4:11).

The words that were coming out of the Shulamite lady contained words of assurance and encouragement that nothing would come in between their relationship as husband and wife. She was saying that she was not going to yield to the tempter. She would remain a close door, a virgin for her Shepherd boy (Song of Solomon 8:10). I think that the Shepherd boy might have been so worried about her safety and chastity but those words came from her to him that she had not defiled herself with the tempter. She informed her lover that she remained faithful in spite of all hurdles of life. Jesus Christ asked, *"when the Son of man cometh, shall he find faith on the earth?"* (Luke 18:8). This question was not answered by any of His disciples. But the question is now laid before us. What is your answer as related to your spiritual life and faithfulness to Christ? Will your public and private life serve as refreshing words of encouragement and strength to both believers and Christ?

Christians' words are to be seasonable, prudent, and edifying. Let your words be seasoned with grace. Job said that his words dropped on his hearers (Job 27:22) while Moses said that his doctrine shall drop as the rain (Deuteronomy 31:2). Know for sure that the "the lips of the wise feed many" (Proverbs 10:21). A good counsellor is the one that has his words drop as the rain, seasoned with grace. As a nurse or medical doctor, you are to see your patients as clients and then accord them with respect and courtesy. It is not a Christian's character to be rude to your clients. The unbelievers and demonic healthcare practitioners may be rude and arrogant but not the Christians. Your lips should drop as the honeycomb; honey and milk should be under your tongue. The same goes to most of the Nigeria Universities lecturers who speak to their students as to servants and nonentities.

5. *Life covers with spiritual garments*
   *"the smell of thy garments is like the smell of Lebanon"*
   (Song of Solomon 4:11c).

   The origin of clothing was traced to the time that Adam and Eve sinned; they were looking for leaves to cover their nakedness. So garments are to cover our nakedness. For the brides of Christ, righteousness should cloth them (Job 29:19). *"And to her was granted that she should be arrayed in fine linen, clean and white: for the fine linen is the righteousness of saints"* (Revelations 19:8). Therefore, the practice of holiness is hereby commended, which is compared to garments. Apostle Peter admonished women to put on the garments of inward holiness which influences outward holiness. *"Whose adorning let it not be that outward adorning of plaiting the hair, and of wearing of gold, or of putting on of apparel; But let it be the hidden man of the heart, in that which is not corruptible, even the ornament of a meek and quiet spirit, which is in the sight of God of great price"* (1 Peter 3:3-4). It is not enough to dress to cover our nakedness as Christians; we are to also clothe our character with righteousness and holiness. The Bible talked about Jacob's garments which smelled to his father, so our holiness is very savoury to our heavenly father and should be to our neighbours. Where there is true holiness within, it will appear in the fruits of holiness without.

6. *Maintenance of her virginity was a great testimony and admiration.*
   *"A garden inclosed is my sister, my spouse; a spring shut up, a fountain sealed"* (Song of Solomon 4:12).

   A garden is usually a small but fenced farm behind the house. So fence, wall or locked door is for protection, preservation, and safety. People without wall are always exposed to the attack and ridicule of their enemies.

*"Thus saith the Lord GOD; It shall also come to pass, that at the same time shall things come into thy mind, and thou shalt think an evil thought: And thou shalt say, I will go up to the land of unwalled villages; I will go to them that are at rest, that dwell safely, all of them dwelling without walls, and having neither bars nor gates, To take a spoil, and to take a prey; to turn thine hand upon the desolate places that are now inhabited, and upon the people that are gathered out of the nations, which have gotten cattle and goods, that dwell in the midst of the land"* (Ezekiel 38:9-12).

*"Arise, get you up unto the wealthy nation, that dwelleth without care, saith the LORD, which have neither gates nor bars, which dwell alone. And their camels shall be a booty, and the multitude of their cattle a spoil: and I will scatter into all winds them that are in the utmost corners; and I will bring their calamity from all sides thereof, saith the LORD"* (Jeremiah 49:31-32).

As Christians, your doors must be locked; fully enclosed and your testimony intact as relating to virginity. The Shulamite lady kept herself enclosed as a wall, a virgin for the man she would marry. She refused to sell her virginity unlike Esau. What a good challenge to our young, unmarried men and women today! They are to keep themselves pure. Marriage is honourable with undefiled beds. Recently, I was told of a Christian couple who professed that they saw God's will to each other and the lady was even a pastor's daughter. But they had defiled their bed before the wedding day yet they stood on the altar as innocent, virgin, and undefiled. They forget that *"He that covereth his sins shall not prosper: but whoso confesseth and forsaketh them shall have mercy"* (Proverbs 28:13). *"Marriage is honourable in all, and the bed undefiled: but whoremongers and adulterers God will judge"* (Hebrew 13:4). Unfortunately, most weddings in our churches today are comprised of couples who defiled themselves with each other or with another man or woman even after they have professed to be Christians. This is an abomination. It is the responsibility of our pastors and parents to counsel our spinsters and bachelors to remain undefiled and to wait after the wedding ceremony before consummating the marriage (sexual relationship).

*"Nevertheless the foundation of God standeth sure, having this seal, The Lord knoweth them that are his. And, Let every one that nameth the name of Christ depart from iniquity."* (2 Timothy 2:19)

7.  *She was like a garden full of beautiful and pleasant plants that was now open to her lover* (Song 4:13-15).
    These spices, fruits, and flowers probably represent her whole person (spirit, soul, and body) rather than her individual parts of her body. Though she had kept her most intimate parts from others in the past, they were now open to her lover, and he experienced full satisfaction with her genuine love and uncompromising standard to hold the forth. We do not see the flavour of a tea bag until it is put in hot water. So also, the dedication, commitment, and faithfulness of the Shulamite lady to the Shepherd boy were not revealed until she was tried by fire and worldly glory in a palace full of gold.

If Christ comes or you die today, will you be able to stand pure, chaste, undefiled before Him with garment white as snow? Whenever Jesus comes, will you still remain in the faith?

# Chapter Twelve

## Greatest Invitation Made by Man

*"Awake, O north wind; and come, thou south; blow upon my garden, that the spices thereof may flow out. Let my beloved come into his garden, and eat his pleasant fruits. I am come into my garden, my sister, my spouse: I have gathered my myrrh with my spice; I have eaten my honeycomb with my honey; I have drunk my wine with my milk: eat, O friends; drink, yea, drink abundantly, O beloved."* (Song of Solomon 4:16; 5:1)

One of the greatest invitations a man can make is inviting the Lord Jesus into his life (Acts 16:14,15; Acts 2:22-23, 38). By doing that, he is actually responding to the call of the Saviour to every human being (Matthew 11:28; Rev. 22:17). The Shulamite lady in our text invited the north and the south wind to come and blow on her garden in order to release the fragrances that were going to bring her lover to her. So, the two winds helped her to find her man and invite him into her garden.

Sometimes, we can be trapped as Christians. We want Christ to be part of our lives but the sin we are involved in or the strongholds the enemy is using to keep us bound prevent us from inviting the Son of God into our lives and hearts. Opening the door of our heart give the Lord the opportunity to come in and dine with us. The Shulamite invited her spouse to take her completely. She called on the winds to carry the scents to which her beloved spouse had pleasure so that he would find full satisfaction (Song 4:13-14).

## Prayer for Liberation from Stronghold Song 4:16a.

❖ Everyone must realise that Man is bound by chains and fetters of sin which do hinder a full revelation of one's glory and flavour. The Shulamite realised that her glory is covered and imprisoned in a stronghold which hinders it from shining and being enjoyed by her spouse. Therefore, she requested through a heartfelt and sincere prayer for her deliverance. She cried out saying "awake," "come," and "blow" O winds upon my garden. For a believer to be delivered from satanic stronghold there is always the need to stir up divine visitation by moving the Spirit of God. In the beginning, the earth was visited and brooded upon by the Spirit of God and its formlessness, invalidity, and darkness were transformed (Genesis 1:2-3).

The main goal why Satan and his agents hold God's children in bondage or stronghold is to hinder them from fulfilling God's purpose for their lives. A new Pharaoh in Egypt knew that the children of Israel were becoming fruitful, multiplying, and waxing exceedingly mighty, so he hated them and put them in bondage in order to tame them.

*"And the children of Israel were fruitful, and increased abundantly, and multiplied, and waxed exceeding mighty; and the land was filled with them. Now there arose up a new king over Egypt, which knew not Joseph. And he said unto his people, Behold, the people of the children of Israel are more and mightier than we: Come on, let us deal wisely with them; lest they multiply, and it come to pass, that, when there falleth out any war, they join also unto our enemies, and*

*fight against us, and so get them up out of the land. Therefore they did set over them taskmasters to afflict them with their burdens. And they built for Pharaoh treasure cities, Pithom and Raamses. But the more they afflicted them, the more they multiplied and grew. And they were grieved because of the children of Israel. And the Egyptians made the children of Israel to serve with rigour: And they made their lives bitter with hard bondage, in morter, and in brick, and in all manner of service in the field: all their service, wherein they made them serve, was with rigour"* (Exodus 1:7-14).

Satan binds men, holds them tight and refuses to let them go free until they are weakened and dance to the tune of Satan.

*"They that see thee shall narrowly look upon thee, and consider thee, saying, Is this the man that made the earth to tremble, that did shake kingdoms; That made the world as a wilderness, and destroyed the cities thereof; <u>that opened not the house of his prisoners?</u>"* (Isaiah 14:16-17).

Because he opens not the house of his prisoners, man needs a stronger hand than Satan to set him free. No wonder, Jesus Christ, the Redeemer of Jacob, the Stronger than Satan came to this world to set the captives free. He came to set you and I free from the shackles of sin, trials, temptations, and troubles.

*"And there was delivered unto him (Jesus) the book of the prophet Esaias. And when he had opened the book, he found the place where it was written, The Spirit of the Lord is upon me, because he hath anointed me to preach the gospel to the poor; he hath sent me to heal the brokenhearted, to preach deliverance to the captives, and recovering of sight to the blind, to set at liberty them that are bruised"* (Luke 4:17-18).

*"For the LORD hath redeemed Jacob, and ransomed him from the hand of him that was stronger than he. Therefore they shall come and sing in the height of Zion, and shall flow together to the goodness of the LORD, for wheat, and for wine, and for oil, and for the young of the flock and of the herd: and their soul shall be as a watered garden; and they shall not sorrow any more at all. Then shall the virgin rejoice in the dance, both young men and old together: for I will turn their mourning into joy, and will comfort them, and make them rejoice from their sorrow"* (Jeremiah 31:11-13).

*"Thus saith the LORD of hosts; The children of Israel and the children of Judah were oppressed together: and all that took them captives held them fast; they refused to let them go. Their Redeemer is strong; the LORD of hosts is his name: he shall throughly plead their cause, that he may give rest to the land, and disquiet the inhabitants of Babylon"* (Jeremiah 31:33-34).

*"But if I (Jesus) with the finger of God cast out devils, no doubt the kingdom of God is come upon you. When a strong man armed keepeth his palace, his goods are in peace: But when a stronger than he shall come upon him, and overcome him, he taketh from him all his armour wherein he trusted, and divideth his spoils"* (Luke 11:20-22).

No matter what type of strongholds you are locked in, no matter how strong the pressure on you to deny Christ and do contrary to His will is, even if you mistakenly walked into the palace of Solomon (Satan) willingly before facing the temptation, if you will realise the danger that you are in and call upon the Lord, you will be safely delivered. Prophet Isaiah 49:24-25 read thus:

*"Shall the prey be taken from the mighty, or the lawful captive delivered? But thus saith the LORD, Even the*

> captives of the mighty shall be taken away, and the
> prey of the terrible shall be delivered: for I will contend
> with him that contendeth with thee, and I will save thy
> children"

- ❖ **Every Christian must request for the release of his or
  her flavour and potentials** (Song of Solomon 4:16a).
  When realising that she (the Shulamite lady) was in
  bondage, she called upon the north wind and the south
  wind to awake and come blow upon her garden in order
  to help *the spices thereof flow out*. The wind refreshes
  living organisms and cleanses the air from every polluant
  to enhance fruitfulness. She requested that both north
  and south winds, which are contrary to each other blow
  upon her garden. The North wind is cold, and moist;
  hence comes the comforting and suitable environment
  for growth and fruitfulness of life. On the other hand,
  the south wind is hot, dry, and troublesome (Job 37:17;
  Luke 12:55; Acts 27:13). A careful meditation reveals that
  both winds are contrary to each other. That was the
  right prayer to make for the Shulamite in order to be
  delivered from the stronghold of Satan who was enticing
  her to submit to defilement. The warmth of the south
  wind brings serenity and enhances showers of rain that
  make plants fruitful.

Winds in the Bible are frequently understood as the
Spirit of God in his mighty operations and manifestations
(Ezekiel 37:3, 14). Likewise, the wind is compared to
the special work and operation of the Spirit because of
its purifying power and nature, cooling and comforting
power and efficacy, and its fruitfulness-enhancing virtue
on trees and gardens.

She prayed for the coming of the Spirit of God to make
her garden fragrant. Note that sanctified souls are
the gardens of the Lord and that graces in the soul
are as spices in the garden. The flowing forth of the

spices, the flavour of grace in a Christian's life depends upon the blow of the wind of the Spirit. In times of temptations, we need the operation of the Spirit to meditate, understand and obey God's word. In order to maintain our integrity and flee from the hands of the Potiphar's wife of this age like Joseph (Genesis 39:1-13), we need the Spirit of God to strengthen our spiritual stamina. When we are so weak and dry, almost falling into temptation, we need the Spirit to blow upon our heart and faith to resist Satan and rising up victoriously (Ezekiel 37:1-14).

## Proposition to the Lover Shepherd

She pressed on with her request, saying *"let my beloved come into his garden and eat his pleasant fruits"* (Song of Solomon 4:16b). We ought to always pray unto Christ to come and abide in us and even sup with us in times of temptation and trials of our faith. If we allow Him to be in our boat, we can be very assured of our safety and peace in the time of storming seas, for He will rise and command *"Peace, be still"* (Mark 4:36-39).

The Shulamite lady called unto her Lover to come and take charge of her life. She referred to the garden as "his garden." A sincere Christian will completely devote whatever he or she has to Christ and desire it to be used for his glory alone. Likewise, dear brothers and sisters, your body is solely for your spouse, not for a stranger.

*"Marriage is honourable in all, and the bed undefiled: but whoremongers and adulterers God will judge"* (Hebrews 13:4).

Your bed must not be polluted by admitting others into it, or by acts of fornication and adultery. There must be fidelity to your marriage vow no matter how strong the temptations to do contrary to it are and no matter what situation and circumstance of life you find yourself in. You need to reassure your spouse that this *garden* of yours belongs to him or her only and not for another person. Learn to always invite him or her to come and eat the pleasant fruits of your body.

## IN TIMES LIKE THESE

Words and music: Ruth Caye Jones. 1944
1.  In times like these you need a Saviour
    In times like these you need an anchor;
    Be very sure, be very sure
    Your anchor holds and grips the Solid Rock!

    *Chorus*
    *This Rock is Jesus, Yes, He's the One;*
    *This Rock is Jesus, the only One!*
    *Be very sure, be very sure*
    *Your anchor holds and grips the Solid Rock!*

2.  In times like these you need the Bible,
    In times like these O be not idle;
    Be very sure, be very sure
    Your anchor holds and grips the Solid Rock!

3.  In times like these I have a Saviour,
    In times like these I have an anchor;
    I'm very sure, I'm very sure
    My anchor holds and grips the Solid Rock!

## Prompt Answer by the Loving Saviour

*"I am come into my garden, my sister, my spouse: I have gathered my myrrh with my spice; I have eaten my honeycomb with my honey; I have drunk my wine with my milk: eat, O friends; drink, yea, drink abundantly, O beloved"* (Song of Solomon 5:1).

There are vital lessons that we can draw from the response of the Shepherd boy to the Shulamite lady as to the relationship between Christ and the church as well as husband and wife.

a. **Readiness of God to hear our prayer and readiness of Christ to accept our invitations**
It is not surprising that without delay, God answers when we call upon Him in times of trouble. He told Jeremiah to call unto Him and that He would answer.

*"Moreover the word of the LORD came unto Jeremiah the second time, while he was yet shut up in the court of the prison, saying, Thus saith the LORD the maker thereof, the LORD that formed it, to establish it; the LORD is his name; Call unto me, and I will answer thee, and shew thee great and mighty things, which thou knowest not"* (Jeremiah 33:1-3).

*"Then shalt thou call, and the LORD shall answer; thou shalt cry, and he shall say, Here I am. If thou take away from the midst of thee the yoke, the putting forth of the finger, and speaking vanity"* (Isaiah 58:9).

*"He shall call upon me, and I will answer him: I will be with him in trouble; I will deliver him, and honour him* (Psalm 91:15).

When a great boisterous storm came, disturbing the boat of the disciples of Jesus, they went to Him for assistance. He rose up and rebuked the storm on their behalf (Mark 4:36-39). So, He is always ready to honour our invitation to come to our rescue. We must understand that Jesus Christ is ready to come in to them that throw open the door of their souls to him.

Husbands or wives must not be callous to the call of their spouses whenever they are passing through temptation to sin, trials of faith, and troubles of life. Every husband or wife must be a sound psychologist having the ability to study his or her spouse's moods and read into his or her mind especially when troubled with some uncalled circumstances. Examples of such circumstances are temptations coming from the boss in his or her office, colleagues, business partner, neighbour or even outsiders. We must act fast and help our spouses to stand uncompromisingly in the faith in such a time.

b. **Readiness of Christ to call us His own:** Song 5:1a.
Christ says *"Ye are my friends, if ye do whatsoever I command you. Henceforth I call you not servants; for the servant knoweth not what his lord doeth: but I have called you friends; for all things that I have heard of my Father I have made known unto you"* (John 15:14-15).

At another time He called his followers His *mother, brother, and sister. "While he yet talked to the people, behold, his mother and his brethren stood without, desiring to speak with him. Then one said unto him, Behold, thy mother and thy brethren stand without, desiring to speak with thee. But he answered and said unto him that told him, Who is my mother? and who are my brethren? And he stretched forth his hand toward his disciples, and said, Behold my mother and my brethren! For whosoever shall do the will of my Father which is in heaven, the same is my brother, and sister, and mother"* (Matthew 12:46-50).

As long as we remain faithful to Him in the time of temptations and trials, living for His holiness and glory, He will be pleased with us. Temptations cannot cause Him to depart from us but sin does. When the children of Israel sinned, God was displeased with them and referred to them as Moses' people—"they are thy people" (Exodus 32:7). Likewise, He called the appointed feasts of the Lord their appointed feasts (Isaiah 1:14). However, if we are doing His will and not succumb to temptations and the pursuit of pleasure of prosperity of this world, we will enjoy His favour and our garden will be His own.

Husbands and wives must always associate themselves to their spouses when life is easy and pleasurable or tough and unbearable. Let it be known to you that you cannot have two biological fathers or mothers; so take your husband or wife as your father or mother as the case may be. Therefore, do not try to submit your body to another man or woman out there because your husband or wife is the only and dearest earthly father or mother that God has given you.

c. **Christ's willingness to gather our potentials that Satan has scattered or negatively influenced.** All the negative thoughts that might pass through our mind during our exposure to corrupt and polluted environments, Christ is willing to erase them from our mind. He will always gather all the gracious habits and faith in us and cause them to manifest in us and through us. Instead of frustrating the effort of your spouse to overcome temptation, you need to help him or her gather her thoughts right, discover the great potentials that he or she has been endowed with, and encourage him or her to press forward toward the mark of his or her high calling of God.

d. **Christ's delight to sup with us**
*"And while they yet believed not for joy, and wondered, he said unto them, Have ye here any meat? And they gave him a piece of a broiled fish, and of an honeycomb.*

*And he took it, and did eat before them"* (Luke 24:41-43).

*"Behold, I stand at the door, and knock: if any man hear my voice, and open the door, I will come in to him, and will sup with him, and he with me"* (Revelation 3:20).

223

Whenever God comes into the garden of His people, He brings blessings along with Him (Exodus 20:24). Christ does not only come into our life and for our deliverance whenever we invite Him, neither does He only come to eat the sacrifice that we offer (fruits of the garden) but also come with something more than what we offered. Examples of the blessings that He brings are honey, and wine, and milk, which produce a significant nourishment. The doctrine of Christ is likened to the honey, which is so sweet and comforting to the weary hearts. The best time to be closer to your spouse is during tough and temptation times. Let your words to him or her be seasoned with grace and life. Let him or her feel special by bringing special gifts or presents to him or her. It is a token of love and care. For a faithful and timely gift gladdens the heart.

e. **Christ's pleasure to invite other to enjoy His blessings in our lives**

We have already considered it, that those who do the will of God are the friends of Jesus. He will invite them to come and enjoy the blessings that fill His garden in you. He will invite His friends and the host of heaven to come and listen to the story of how you overcame temptations and likewise tap wisdom from you too. When the battle is over, we shall share testimonies how we overcame and were rewarded with an overcomer's crown.

# Chapter Thirteen

# A Courageous and Contagious Christian

"[The court ladies asked the Shulamite lady] *What is thy beloved more than another beloved, O thou fairest among women? what is thy beloved more than another beloved, that thou dost so charge us? [She said] My beloved is white and ruddy, the chiefest among ten thousand. His head is as the most fine gold, his locks are bushy, and black as a raven. His eyes are as the eyes of doves by the rivers of waters, washed with milk, and fitly set. His cheeks are as a bed of spices, as sweet flowers: his lips like lilies, dropping sweet smelling myrrh. His hands are as gold rings set with the beryl: his belly is as bright ivory overlaid with sapphires. His legs are as pillars of marble, set upon sockets of fine gold: his countenance is as Lebanon, excellent as the cedars. His mouth is most sweet: yea, he is altogether lovely. This is my beloved, and this is my friend, O daughters of Jerusalem.*" (Song of Solomon 5:9-16)

"*1 Where has your beloved gone, O you fairest among women? [Again the ladies showed their interest in the remarkable person whom the Shulammite had championed with such unstinted praise; they too wanted to know him, they insisted.] Where is your beloved hiding himself? For we would seek him with you. ² [She replied] My beloved has gone down to his garden, to the beds of spices, to feed in the gardens and to gather lilies. ³ I am my beloved's [garden] and my beloved is mine! He feeds among the lilies [which grow there]."* (Song of Solomon 6:1-3, AMP)

What is it in your beloved that our king, Solomon or other men do not have? Why is it that all that Solomon had presented to entice you could not prevail over you? In Song 5:9, the daughters of Jerusalem came up to ask those questions because of the impact of the charge that the Shulamite lady had upon them. It surprised and astonished them to see a person so convincingly approvable in her life, so taken up with that which the most part of the world count unimportant. This made them think that he whom she asked for, must be a person beyond ordinary. The questions they asked her were not spoken out of disdain, but out of their desire to know her lover. The question was proposed by way of comparison, 'What is thy Beloved more than another beloved?' Good enough, the conversation ended very well (Song 6:1). The same thing happened after the Pentecost, when Apostle Peter preached. His listeners were puzzled and touched by his words *"when they heard this, they were pricked in their heart, and said unto Peter and to the rest of the apostles, Men and brethren, what shall we do?"* (Acts 2:37). So, he sized that opportunity to show them the way to Christ—REPENTANCE. This is always the outcome of a dynamic preaching. John the Baptist is another perfect example of how Christians or gospel ministers should live their life to point people to Christ.

*"John answered them, saying, I baptize with water: but there standeth one among you, whom ye know not; He it is, who coming after me is preferred before me, whose shoe's latchet I am not worthy to unloose. These things were done in Bethabara beyond Jordan, where John was baptizing. The next day John seeth Jesus coming unto him, and saith, Behold the Lamb of God, which taketh away the sin of the world. This is he of whom I said, after me cometh a man which is preferred before me:*

*for he was before me. And I knew him not: but that he should be made manifest to Israel, therefore am I come baptizing with water. And John bare record, saying, I saw the Spirit descending from heaven like a dove, and it abode upon him. And I knew him not: but he that sent me to baptize with water, the same said unto me, upon whom thou shalt see the Spirit descending, and remaining on him, the same is he which baptizeth with the Holy Ghost. And I saw, and bare record that this is the Son of God. <u>Again the next day after John stood, and two of his disciples; And looking upon Jesus as he walked, he saith, Behold the Lamb of God! And the two disciples heard him speak, and they followed Jesus</u>"* (John 1:26-37).

John the Baptist was not boasting about his ministry but humbled himself to the point of letting people know that he was just a forerunner of the Lamb of God, Jesus Christ. His pointing to Christ convinced two of his disciples to follow Jesus. In your ministry, are you pointing people to Christ? In your workplace or classroom, does your life and conduct point people to Christ? In 1988-1989, it happened that I lived with a Muslim young man as a co-tenant in a house. Unfortunately, I did not preach to him but he was challenged by the way I lived. One day, he told my aunt that he would like to follow me to church because he had observed simplicity, honesty, humility, and righteousness in my life. When I heard that, I was happy and took him to my church. By the end of 1989, I left that town. I was surprised to meet him in a pastors' conference in 1998. The challenge is that we should all live a courageous and contagious Christian life. Let your belief influence your behaviour; practice what you preach, then shall your neighbour be attracted to your Saviour.

## Inquisitiveness of People about of Saviour and Shepherd

*"What is thy beloved more than another beloved, O thou fairest among women? what is thy beloved more than another beloved, that thou dost so charge us? "Whither is thy beloved gone, O*

*thou fairest among women? whither is thy beloved turned aside? that we may seek him with thee"* (Song of Solomon 5:9; 6:1).

The followings are the lessons we can derived from this questions.

a. **The Shulamite lady was given a titled as the "*fairest among women.*"** This does not speak about her physical beauty but her spiritual beauty because she had been tried and tempted, yet she sinned not. The court ladies could not hide their feeling and assessment of her, so they spoke out what was in their mind. They told her that she was different from other young ladies who easily give in to sexual immorality because of money, prestige, power, and position. The court ladies were wondering why the Shulamite was so attached to her shepherd boy when she had a king begging for her love? They did not understand that kind of love but the behaviour of the Shulamite pushed them to want to know more about her lover. This is also the way unbelievers should react when they see us Christians. They should be amazed at our character so much that they would seek to know the Jesus we adore." Ideally and practically, every Christian is expected to live a life that is highly convincing and commendable before others. Moreover, every Christian must have a good report from them which are unbelievers. Your life should be fairest among them. Your spiritual beauty must be very conspicuous as a shining light in a dark place. In Proverbs 14:34, the Bible says that righteousness exalts a nation. So, men who have little knowledge of your Saviour should be able to highly esteem and respectfully deal with you as a result of your Christ-modelled life. Elisha was called a holy man of God by the shulamite woman who accommodated him in her house because she knew that he had a good character. He did not bring a reproach to the name of the Lord.

The sin of adultery that King David committed with Bathsheba was regarded as a deed that *"has given great occasion to the enemies of the LORD to blaspheme"* (1 Samuel 12:14). There are many rich people and politicians who find it difficult to give their lives to Jesus Christ because of the calibre of women that patronise them for sexual satisfaction. These women often consider themselves Christians. They are the chameleons who put on a Christian dress during the day but put on a harlot dress in the night. Are you one of them?

*"Finally, brethren, whatsoever things are true, whatsoever things are honest, whatsoever things are just, whatsoever things are pure, whatsoever things are lovely, whatsoever things are of good report; if there be any virtue, and if there be any praise, think on these things"* (Philippians 4:8).

*"Let no man despise thy youth; but be thou an example of the believers, in word, in conversation, in charity, in spirit, in faith, in purity"* (1 Timothy 4:12).

b.  **The court ladies compared the Shepherd boy, the beloved of the Shulamite lady with other men by saying** *"what is thy beloved more than another beloved."* Likewise, unbelievers do sometimes compare the living God to false gods when the gospel of Christ is being preached to them (Isaiah 36:18, 20; Acts 19:26-28). They even magnify and exalt these false gods to the detriment of their own souls. However, there are some hearers who become so curious and more desirous to know further about the living God. They want to be well informed about the truth and know the difference between Christ and the false gods, false worship, false ordinances, traditions of men, etc. These two sides of the coin happened when Apostle Paul preached about the unknown God.

James Fabiyi

*"Now while Paul waited for them at Athens, his spirit was stirred in him, when he saw the city wholly given to idolatry. Therefore disputed he in the synagogue with the Jews, and with the devout persons, and in the market daily with them that met with him. Then certain philosophers of the Epicureans, and of the Stoicks, encountered him. And some said, what will this babbler say? other some, He seemeth to be a setter forth of strange gods: because he preached unto them Jesus, and the resurrection. And they took him, and brought him unto Areopagus, saying, May we know what this new doctrine, whereof thou speakest, is? For thou bringest certain strange things to our ears: we would know therefore what these things mean. (For all the Athenians and strangers which were there spent their time in nothing else, but either to tell, or to hear some new thing.) Then Paul stood in the midst of Mars' hill, and said, Ye men of Athens, I perceive that in all things ye are too superstitious. For as I passed by, and beheld your devotions, I found an altar with this inscription, TO THE UNKNOWN GOD. Whom therefore ye ignorantly worship, him declare I unto you. God that made the world and all things therein, seeing that he is Lord of heaven and earth, dwelleth not in temples made with hands; Neither is worshipped with men's hands, as though he needed anything, seeing he giveth to all life, and breath, and all things; And hath made of one blood all nations of men for to dwell on all the face of the earth, and hath determined the times before appointed, and the bounds of their habitation; That they should seek the Lord, if haply they might feel after him, and find him, though he be not far from every one of us: For in him we live, and move, and have our being; as certain also of your own poets have said, For we are also his offspring. Forasmuch then as we are the offspring of God, we ought not to think that the Godhead is like unto gold, or silver, or stone, graven by art and man's device. And the times of this ignorance God winked at; but now commandeth*

230

*all men every where to repent: Because he hath
appointed a day, in the which he will judge the world
in righteousness by that man whom he hath ordained;
whereof he hath given assurance unto all men, in that he
hath raised him from the dead. And when they heard of
the resurrection of the dead, some mocked: and others
said, We will hear thee again of this matter. So Paul
departed from among them. Howbeit certain men clave
unto him, and believed: among the which was Dionysius
the Areopagite, and a woman named Damaris, and
others with them.*" (Acts 17:16-34)

Our love and passion to stand for the truth and sincerely
seek our loving Saviour will always cause people around
us to ask questions about His life, ministry, supremacy,
and whereabouts.

People around us will be stirred up in their desire to know
where our Saviour dwells and they will seek Him depending on
our truthful and enthusiastic presentation of Him to them with
the help and power of the Holy Spirit. This statement was true
for the Shulamite lady as the court ladies asked for her lover's
whereabouts. It was also true for the Apostle Peter on the day
of Pentecost. Every nonchalant attitude towards our seeking
the Lover of our souls should be changed or else we become a
stumbling-block for the salvation of others.

The shulamite lady was not ashamed to talk about the
supremacy of her beloved Shepherd boy while she was still in
the palace of Solomon. So we ought not to be ashamed of telling
other about Jesus' warning and commandment in the present
of the tempter. Jesus said that "*whosoever therefore shall be
ashamed of me and of my words in this adulterous and sinful
generation; of him also shall the Son of man be ashamed, when
he cometh in the glory of his Father with the holy angels*"
(Mark 8:38). Brethren, the world is pleading with us to shed
more light and explain why we so much love our beloved Jesus.
This is a challenge to describe and declare Christ to the dying

231

generation. Therefore, we should be ready to tell the world about our beloved Jesus.

## *I'LL TELL THE WORLD THAT I'M A CHRISTIAN*

1. *"I'll tell the world that I'm a Christian,*
   *I'm not ashamed, His name to bear.*
   *I'll tell the world that I'm a Christian,*
   *and take it with me everywhere."*

2. *"I'll tell the world that He's my Saviour,*
   *No other one could love me so,*
   *My life, my all, is His forever,*
   *and where He leads me, I will go."*

3. *"I'll tell the world how Jesus saved me*
   *and how he gave me a life brand new.*
   *And I know that if you trust Him*
   *that all he gave me, he'll give to you."*

4. *"I'll tell the world that He is coming.*
   *It may be near, or far away.*
   *But we must live as if his coming*
   *would be tomorrow or today.*
   *For when he comes and life is over,*
   *for those who love him there's more to be.*
   *Eyes have never seen the wonder that*
   *He's preparing for you and me."*

5. *"Oh tell the world that you're a Christian,*
   *Be not ashamed His name to bear,*
   *Oh tell the world that you're a Christian*
   *and take it with you everywhere."*

**Illustration and Portray of the Sincere Shepherd** Song 5:10-16.

She expanded on the attributes of her beloved with a mixture of descriptions. The church should describe her beloved in His beauty, so as to stir up herself and her listeners' affection for Him in order to draw after Him. If you truly are a Christian and you love Christ with all your heart, there will be a willingness to speak about Him, and commending Him of His attributes. Carefully ponder on the description that the Shulamite gave to her beloved who is a type of Christ.

a. White: This indeed describes Christ in His innocent, spotless, and sinless life despite the fact that he was counted as sinner because of the sin of the whole world that he took upon Himself (2 Corinthians 5:21; Isaiah 53:5). His whiteness talks about His transparent holy life (Daniel 7:9; Matthew 17:2). His whiteness represents His openness, justice, righteousness, mercy and grace to the believers as related to His administration.

b. Ruddy: His ruddiness could be referred to as His blood that He shed on Calvary for the cleansing of man's sin. Administratively, His redness represents His judgment to punish the wicked (Isaiah 63:1-3; Rev 19:11-16).

c. The chiefest among ten thousand: He is the one to be desired most above all other persons, powers, and principalities. *"And he hath on his vesture and on his thigh a name written, KING OF KINGS, AND LORD OF LORDS"* (Revelation 19:16). He is above all Old Testament and New Testament prophets.

d. The glory of His headship and everlasting kingdom: His head is as the finest gold having the emblem of the divine approval of the God of holiness.

*"Which he wrought in Christ, when he raised him from the dead, and set him at his own right hand in the*

*heavenly places, far above all principality, and power, and might, and dominion, and every name that is named, not only in this world, but also in that which is to come: And hath put all things under his feet, and gave him to be the head over all things to the church"* (Ephesians 1:20-20).

*"For unto us a child is born, unto us a son is given: and the government shall be upon his shoulder: and his name shall be called Wonderful, Counsellor, The mighty God, The everlasting Father, The Prince of Peace. Of the increase of his government and peace there shall be no end, upon the throne of David, and upon his kingdom, to order it, and to establish it with judgment and with justice from henceforth even forever. The zeal of the LORD of hosts will perform this"* (Isaiah 9:6-7)

e. Bushy locks: this presents Him as a nazarite of God.

f. The locks of his head are black: This refers to being young, fresh (Isaiah 42:4; Psalm 102:27) as opposite to the grey/white hair which is a sign of decay—weakness and loss of strength (Hosea 7:9). Remember, loveliness and desirableness are in a man when he is in his youth.

g. Eyes of doves: speaks about fair and clear, knows all things—the Lord is omniscience. Eyes are used to discern external objects. The eyes of the Lord are everywhere (Proverbs 15:3; 5:21; 2 Chronicles 16:9; Revelation 2:18, 23; John 21:17; Jeremiah 16:17; Psalm 90:8; 11:4; Habakkuk 1:13). His eyes are "as doves' eyes," meaning quick and lovely. They are as doves' eyes 'by the rivers of water,' where doves are most lovely after bathing themselves at riversides. They are washed 'with milk,' that is, most clean, white and pure. They are 'fitly set,' like the stones in Aaron's breastplate (Exodus 39:10). The eyes of the Lord are upon His people for good

(Deuteronomy 11:12; Psalm 34:15) but upon the wicked for judgment (Psalm 34:16).

h. <u>Refreshment in Him</u>: It speaks about the proportionate height of His sweetness because cheeks are in the face, and as beds are higher than the rest of the ground. It also speaks about the preciousness and sweetness of spirit-refreshing savour. His lip is full of gracious word (Luke 4:22; John 7:45-47; Isaiah 50:4).

i. <u>Lips like lilies</u>: sweet and pleasant to teach and expound the scripture to human understanding and comprehension.

j. <u>His belly is as bright ivory</u>: denotes His tender compassion and affection for His bride.

k. <u>Excellence of His power</u>: The hands and legs are the instruments of action, as the lips are of speaking. The hands of the Lord bring help to His people (Psalm 109:27; Luke 24:19; Revelation 15:4; 1 Chronicles 29:2).

l. <u>His mouth is sweet</u>: His word is comforting.

*"How sweet are thy words unto my taste! yea, sweeter than honey to my mouth!"* (Psalm 119:103).

The doctrines of grace that give assurance of sustenance in the time of temptations and trials, the truths of the Gospel are delightful and pleasant to the Christians like unadulterated milk to the babes, like good food and honey to those that are grown up and always sweet to Christians. In times of temptations and troubles, He gives assurance of victory: *"These things I have spoken unto you, that in me ye might have peace. In the world ye shall have tribulation: but be of good cheer; I have overcome the world"* (John 16:33).

Though the Shulamite lady was enduring difficulties in the palace of Solomon where she was being tempted to commit sexual immorality and forsake her true lover, she was bold enough to give a vivid description of her beloved Shepherd boy without fear of her subjugator. She did it so persuasively to the point that the court ladies sought the Shepherd boy too. A significant lesson from her contagious life is that though she was in trouble, she still pointed others to where her beloved dwelt. So, as the sinners ask where they can find Christ it is our responsibility, if we truly belong to Christ, to point them to Him not to the false gods, false security, or any pastor or place.

**Intimacy in Partnership with the Sweetheart-Saviour** Song 6:2-3.

There is a strong relationship between Christ and the church and both cannot be separated. Therefore, no pressure can be put upon us to separate us from Him. He is our only beloved. We don't belong to the camp of Satan but God's. We cannot compromise our relationship with Him by submitting our body unto the tempter manifesting in the form of our boss or co-workers, lecturers in our school, or rich people in our communities. Our relationship with Him is mutual, and the knot is tied, which cannot be loosed. We cannot defile the temple where He resides. Therefore, give your body (your entire person) to no other than you beloved Bridegroom or earthly husband.

> *"I beseech you therefore, brethren, by the mercies of God, that ye present your bodies a living sacrifice, holy, acceptable unto God, which is your reasonable service.*
>
> *And be not conformed to this world: but be ye transformed by the renewing of your mind, that ye may prove what is that good, and acceptable, and perfect, will of God"* (Romans 12:1-2).

In his commentary, Adam Clarke described giving the body as a living sacrifice by saying that it is "a metaphor taken from bringing sacrifices to the altar of God. The person offering picked out the choicest of his flock, brought it to the altar, and presented it there as an atonement for his sin. They are exhorted to give themselves up in the spirit of sacrifice; to be as wholly the Lord's property as the whole burnt-offering was, no part being devoted to any other use."

Dear reader, **LET OTHERS SEE JESUS IN YOU.**

1. While passing thro' this world of sin,
   And others your life shall view,
   Be clean and pure without, within,
   Let others see Jesus in you.

   *Chorus*
   *Let others see Jesus in you, . . .*
   *Let others see Jesus in you, . . .*
   *Keep telling the story, be faithful and true,*
   *Let others see Jesus in you.*

2. Your life's a book before their eyes,
   They're reading it thro' and thro';
   Say, does it point them to the skies,
   Do others see Jesus in you?

3. What joy 'twill be at set of sun,
   In mansions beyond the blue,
   To find some souls that you have won;
   Let others see Jesus in you.

4. Then live for Christ both day and night,
   Be faithful, be brave and true,
   And lead the lost to life and light;
   Let others see Jesus in you.

# Chapter Fourteen

## Man without God's Grace

*"Thou art beautiful, O my love, as Tirzah, comely as Jerusalem, terrible as an army with banners. Turn away thine eyes from me, for they have overcome me: thy hair is as a flock of goats that appear from Gilead. Thy teeth are as a flock of sheep which go up from the washing, whereof every one beareth twins, and there is not one barren among them. As a piece of a pomegranate are thy temples within thy locks. There are threescore queens, and fourscore concubines, and virgins without number. My dove, my undefiled is but one; she is the only one of her mother, she is the choice one of her that bare her. The daughters saw her, and blessed her; yea, the queens and the concubines, and they praised her. Who is she that looketh forth as the morning, fair as the moon, clear as the sun, and terrible as an army with banners? I went down into the garden of nuts to see the fruits of the valley, and to see whether the vine flourished, and the pomegranates budded. Or ever I was aware, my soul made me like the chariots of Amminadib. Return, return, O Shulamite; return, return, that we may look upon thee. What will ye see in the Shulamite? As it were the company of two armies."*
(Song of Solomon 6:4-13)

> *"How beautiful are thy feet with shoes, O prince's daughter! the joints of thy thighs are like jewels, the work of the hands of a cunning workman. Thy navel is like a round goblet, which wanteth not liquor: thy belly is like an heap of wheat set about with lilies. Thy two breasts are like two young roes that are twins. Thy neck is as a tower of ivory; thine eyes like the fishpools in Heshbon, by the gate of Bathrabbim: thy nose is as the tower of Lebanon which looketh toward Damascus. Thine head upon thee is like Carmel, and the hair of thine head like purple; the king is held in the galleries. How fair and how pleasant art thou, O love, for delights! This thy stature is like to a palm tree, and thy breasts to clusters of grapes. I said, I will go up to the palm tree, I will take hold of the boughs thereof: now also thy breasts shall be as clusters of the vine, and the smell of thy nose like apples; And the roof of thy mouth like the best wine for my beloved, that goeth down sweetly, causing the lips of those that are asleep to speak."* (Song of Solomon 7:1-9)

King Solomon was the wisest man who ever lived in the history of man (1 Kings 3:12). However, he ignored wisdom from God and chose instead to be ruled by his undisciplined and untamed sexual desire (Proverb 6:20-28). He allowed "the lust of the flesh, the lust of the eyes, and the pride of life" to dominate his thinking and he acted by surrounding himself with beautiful women (Ecclesiastes 2:10; Gen 3:6). The exact time that Solomon wrote this song is unknown. However, some think that he wrote it after his recovery from backsliding along with the book of Ecclesiastes as a proof of his repentance from the strongholds of lust for women and worship of idols. This book hereby reveals his decayed, deplorable, depraved, and disaffection conditions as a backslider. Hence, most of the words that were coming out of his mouth vividly describe the state of a man without God's grace in his life.

**The Flatteries of Lustful Solomon** Song 6:4-10; 7:1-9.

The followings are the enticing words that Solomon used to persuade and lure the Shulamite lady to succumb to his sexual desire and proposal.

  a. **Song 6:4—Beautiful as Tirzah.** Tirzah, which means beautiful, acceptable or delightful, was a city in the tribe of Ephraim (Joshua 12:24). **Comely as Jerusalem—** Jerusalem was called the perfection of beauty because it was strongly fortified by nature and art during Solomon's time (Psalm 48:2, 3; 50:2). So, he compared the beauty of the Shulamite lady to the two finest places in the land of Palestine, and the capitals of the two kingdoms of Israel and Judah. He also described the Shulamite as strong and fearful as an army—**"terrible as an army with banners."** These are strong words that Solomon used to describe the Shulamite lady. A worldly-minded person, if likened to them, would be filled with pride. But, in spite of these words, the shepherd's lady rejected the mighty king.

  *"And Herod was highly displeased with them of Tyre and Sidon: but they came with one accord to him, and, having made Blastus the king's chamberlain their friend, desired peace; because their country was nourished by the king's country. And upon a set day Herod, arrayed in royal apparel, sat upon his throne, and made an oration unto them. And the people gave a shout, saying, It is the voice of a god, and not of a man"* (Acts 12:20-22).

  Some ladies always become so weak and ready to do whatever a man requests from them when he praises them. Solomon used his wisdom to steal the love of the Shulamite lady. Therefore, you have to be careful when a brother in your church begins to admire your beauty and always speak out to compare it to the beauty of a queen. When they tell you that you are the sugar in their tea, the most beautiful flower they've ever seen, the smoothest body they've ever touched, the loveliest and most caring person they've ever met, the most delightful person they've ever known, the wisest person they've ever interacted with on earth, then you have to be very careful and prayerful to discern the motive in their hearts, lest you fall into their flattery words.

b. **Son 6:5—Turn away thine eyes**—because her eyes had made a conquest of his heart. If Solomon was a type of Christ, he would not have told his bride or church to turn away her eyes from Him. If a man is truly a child of God, Christ will always want to see him gazing into his eyes and putting all his attention on Him but will not command him to turn away his eyes from him. The Bible says, look and live. One song writer wrote that *"Take time to behold Him, speak often with the Lord."* So, Solomon was truly a man without God's grace upon his life at that time. Hear what he had to say about his fall in Ecclesiastes 2:10-11:

*"And whatsoever mine eyes desired I kept not from them, I withheld not my heart from any joy; for my heart rejoiced in all my labour: and this was my portion of all my labour. Then I looked on all the works that my hands had wrought, and on the labour that I had laboured to do: and, behold, all was vanity and vexation of spirit, and there was no profit under the sun."*

There are some men who lose concentration on the vehicle's steering wheel because they lust after half-dressed women. Just like them, Solomon could not turn his eyes away from women. His life was contrary to Job's life who determined in his heart not to look at women other than his wife—*"I made a covenant with mine eyes; why then should I think upon a maid?"*(Job 31:1). All unbridled lusts proved to be nothing but vanity when they were all fulfilled.

Note that this phrase has been twisted and differently rendered by the advocates of Solomon (those who see Solomon as a good person) as a type of Christ. They reword this verse by saying, "turn away thine eyes over against me, they have strengthened me." They portray Solomon as saying that the gazing of the Shulamite lady at him strengthened him.

c. **Son 6:6—Thy teeth are as a flock of sheep which go up from the washing.** It implies in figure, order, and structure, as well as small and white; neatly set. It indicates that no one is missing, none rotten, nor fallen out, look very beautiful. **"Whereof everyone bear twins, and none is barren among them"** could be because of the convincing words of her mouth as it already turned the hearts of the Court ladies to seek her true beloved (Song 5:9; 6:1). Solomon, in verse 6, was referring to the lifestyle of the Shulamite Lady when he said that her teeth were bony, solid, firm, and strong, sharp to cut and to oppose gainsayers, able to withstand Solomon/ Satan's temptations, and remain firm and unmoveable in her piety, sharp to rebuke such who were corrupt in their morals such like Solomon and the court ladies who were trying their best to arouse her love for Solomon, their king. Remember, a degenerate man can also speak the truth of life. There is truth in unrighteous vessels as stated in Romans 1:18: *"For the wrath of God is revealed from heaven against all ungodliness and unrighteousness of men, **who hold the truth in unrighteousness**"*

d. **Son 6:7—As a piece of a pomegranate are thy temples within thy locks.** Pomegranate—is a lovely mixture of red and white. That is, her temples are decorated with a beautiful, multi-coloured artistic work.

e. **Son 6:8-10**—these words are a pure deception from Satan for her to see herself as the most beautiful and likeable person among hundreds of women already in the palace. This could be likened to the temptation that our Lord Jesus faced in Matthew 4:8-9. Such flattery from a king would have been enough to turn the heart of most women, but would not work on the Shulamite lady.

f. **Song 7:1—How beautiful are thy feet with shoes, O prince's daughter!** The Shulamite was not related to any king, but Solomon used this adjective (prince's daughter) to steal her soul. He was willing to accept her as a princess if she would accept his love. **How beautiful are thy feet with shoes**—here, he speaks about the way she walked. It was beautiful or delightful. I have heard of men talking about the way women walk as something so special to admire. No wonder when some ladies want to entice men, they can change the way they walk. Prophet Isaiah described such walk in Isaiah 3:16, "Moreover the LORD saith, Because the daughters of Zion are haughty, and walk with stretched forth necks and wanton eyes, walking and mincing as they go, and making a tinkling with their feet:." They decorate themselves with ankle rings to make a tinkling and the noise is to attract attention of the passers-by.

g. **Song 7:3—Thy two breasts are like two young roes that are twins.** Likening her two breasts as two young roes that are twins implies that Solomon was praising her breasts for having the same size and shape. None of them was larger than the other, which would have been a sign of deformity if that was the case. It also speaks about their small size as young roes. Most men do not see big ones as a beautiful structure. That is one of the reasons for their going after young ladies who have such breasts, forgetting that they might be small and firm today, but they will lose their firmness after giving birth to children. Remember, beauty is deceitful. Brethren, don't look at the size and shape of the physical butts but a woman's faith in God and love for God should be your desire.

h. Song 7:5—**The hair of thine head like purple**. It is most known that hair adds much to the beauty of a person. More than a decade ago, there were about five brothers who said that they saw God's will in marriage to a single sister. I was puzzled when I heard that. However, a critical investigation revealed that not all of them really saw God's will in marriage but were taken away by her hair. The sister happened to have very long and smooth hair. It was the hair that they saw and fell in lust after. No wonder, most spinsters spend a lot of money styling their hair for beauty contests. These women know what they are doing. The men without God's grace upon his life will see their hair and lust after them.

i. **Son 7:7-8:** Solomon used corrupt and disgusting words here to express how he would enjoy caressing and having sexual relationship with her. He was talking about the roundness, fullness, softness, and succulence of her breast, like the berries of the vine tree, the grapes that grow in clusters on it.

The followings are the lessons that we can derived from these.

i. Note that some of these descriptions in 6:3b and 7 are already mentioned by Solomon in 4:1-3. The point is that Satan does not have any new tactics but still uses the old tricks though in a modified and beautified way. Satan asked Eve "*Yea, hath God said*" the same way he asked Jesus Christ "*If thou be the Son of God.*" It should not surprise us too that men who prey after our beloved Christian sisters have done a thorough job in memorising some Bible verses to lure them into an immoral and corrupt lifestyle.

ii. The king is likely to be repeating a well-rehearsed speech which he has spoken before to other pretty girls. He asked the Shulamite to turn her eyes away from him at one point probably because the look in her eyes was distracting him from quoting his "romantic" speech. These words are basically the same speech he used earlier to convince her. This suggests that he had learned that most women would be turned on by these particular flattering statements. He probably believed that he had finally found that unique body who is the perfect match for his body. One preacher says that "amazingly, many of the wives listening to his praises to the Shulamite's body had probably heard him say the exact same thing about them once."

iii. Spiritually denigrated and weak minds most of the time fall into the trap of harlots. In Proverbs 6:13, it is well outlined that some women use some parts of their body to allure or entice men. The movement of their eyes is one of the ways to deceive men and push them in their trap. Read Proverbs 6:13:

> *"He winketh with his eyes,*
> *He speaketh with his feet,*
> *He teacheth with his fingers"*

iv. There is no satisfaction in the mind of a man without God's grace. There are lots of men who can shower strange lovers or women with luxury and flattering words, but cannot give any woman the kind of love that exist between a godly husband and a wife. Despite the many wives and concubines that Solomon had, he was not yet satisfied. therefore, he or she that seeks to find the perfect sexual adventure with the perfect sexual partner will never find the kind of happiness that only occurs in married couples who keep themselves faithful to each other (Proverb 5:15-20; Hebrew 13:4). Solomon was never satisfied drinking out of his own cistern. So, whenever you see a married person who is still commenting about you as the sweetest and most caring, loveliest person he or she has ever met, please, take a step backward and begin to withdraw from such.

**The Firmness and Labour of the Shulamite** Song 6:11-12.

After Solomon had flattered her, she simply but firmly replied to him that she did not have any urge within her or love for him; telling him that their meeting in the wilderness was by chance, not that she had any plan for it. She was just at her duty post and never thought that she would meet a lustful man. The lady was very firm and told Solomon to his face that she did not position herself to be seen by Solomon. She clearly told him that she was not an harlot who hunt after rich people on the high way.

The followings are the lessons that we can derived from her statements:

a. What we don't plan for can easily come our way. The Shulamite lady was carrying out her normal daily duties, there the tempter came. Remember, Jesus had just finished his forty days and nights fasting when Satan came to tempt Him. Dinah, a daughter of Jacob, just visited her friends when Shechem saw her, took her, and lay with her, and defiled her (Genesis 34:1-2). Always have it at the back of your mind that the temptation you don't plan for can come your way. Actually, most of the temptations that come your ways, you don't expect them

b. Temptations come not only at the point of your idleness but also at the point of dutifulness. It does not matter; temptation may come to you when you are physically weak but spiritually strong. For example, Jesus was physically weak but spiritually strong during His forty days and forty nights of fasting and prayer. Even though he had spent a beautiful time with the Lord, His human body was tired and craving for food which is suitable for Satan to act. Temptation may also come to you when you are spiritually weak.

c. We should be prepared to face challenges and ready to oppose any distraction and corruption that want to hinder us from doing what is right (2 Kings 2:1-11). Generally, nobody expects temptation to come but we should at all times get ready to resist every form of evil suggestions to sin and every seductive touch should be strongly resisted.

d. Be ready to flee all youthful lust (Song 6:13a; Gen 39:7-13; 2 Tim. 2:22).

In 1988, I was living with my uncle in a town where we were co-tenant with other people. One day, after everybody in the house had gone to work and the students gone to school, I was left alone in my room at the backyard of the main building. I was reading my book as I was preparing for an entrance examination to the tertiary institution. Then, there was a married woman who was also living in the same house (in the main building) who was preparing to go out. She just took her bath, wrapped herself with a towel, came to my room and asked if I had any type of body lotion. I said yes ma and I gave it to her. One surprising thing happened that I cannot forget. She collected it and dropped it on my reading table. I thought that it was not a big deal for her to use it there and go. But she did more than just using it there. She removed her towel and dropped it on the table too. She naked herself in my presence, with no third party around except the omniscient God. Immediately, I remembered the story of Joseph before Potiphar's wife, so I turned to the other side and took to my feet, I ran away and sat at the open space in the front of the house where people were going on with their daily businesses. After she finished whatever she was doing in my room, she came out to meet me and told me that I was an impotent guy.

## The Flaw and Laxity of a Perverted Soul Song 6:13.

As the Shulamite lady was ready to go out of Solomon's sight, he began to plead with her to return, wanting to turn her into a sex toy or show her beauty to the court ladies and servants. Have you not noticed that many men associate with young ladies not because they really love them or the condition warrants it but for the pride and pleasure they derive from it?

The followings are the lessons we can derived from this.

a. Strong persuasion to yield to worldly pleasures. Satan used it to deceive Eve, Joseph, and Jesus. Only Eve among these three could not resist the pressure, she fell into it, falling headlong, she burst asunder in the midst, and all her bowels decayed.

b. Nudity of a perverted generation is to entice men. When you see ladies in the church dressing half-naked, note that what they are doing is that they are selling their body right in the sanctuary of God. In fact, nudity prevails nowadays in our churches more than outside the church. No woman from other religions (Islam for example) can dress like our women are dressing today. Therefore, it is the responsibility of heavenly-minded and God-sent pastors to cry aloud, declare unto the church attendees their transgressions, and to nude or half-naked dressed women their sins (Micah 3:8). I believe that we can get rid of this evil of satanic dresses if pastors can pray and preach against it. Unfortunately, most pastors will not do that because they are not after the eternal salvation of their church members, they are only after their presence in the church, crowd and offerings.

c. People enjoy demonic satisfaction in seeing nudity or pornographic pictures.

About three years ago, I went for a men encounter program in one of the Western countries. During the sectional meeting, two mid-aged men shared with my group about their sexual perversion problem. One of them said that God had been faithful to him in his ministry but he had been having problems with pornography. He said that anytime his wife denied him of sex whenever he demanded for it, he always stood up from his bed and logged on to the Internet and satisfied himself with pornographic pictures. I was so blunt in my counsel to him. I told him that the problem he was having was based on the fact that he never had the conversion (heart changed) experience or had backslidden. I counselled him to go back to his wife and tell the woman that this was the dilemma he always faced whenever she denied him sexual relationship. The comment he made shocked me greatly. He said that the woman knew about it and that she always told him that pornographic pictures were made and posted on the web for men, so there was no big deal if he looked at them. Does this surprise you too? Dear readers, this couple was not only been referred to as church members but also as Christian workers in a Pentecostal church. What a great surprise!

I read in one of the Nigeria national newspapers that there were some joint spots where the operators used women for business; the ladies would be naked and dance in the presence of their men customers. A friend told me that one of the cheapest ways to become a celebrity in the country is by dancing nakedly while singing music. The strippers are gaining more popularity even in the United States of America. Many commercial advertisements that are aired on public and cable television are filled with naked women. The appearance of a nude woman may not be connected with the advert at all, but they do it because that is what will appeal to men. There are some so-called Christian movies that a genuine child of God cannot watch because they are filled with clips of both naked and half-naked men and women. There were some respectable movie stars in our nation who were not putting on provocative dressing even when they were acting to represent a worldly or prostitute girl. Unfortunately, the story has changed, some of them are not only dressing with jelweries and provocative dresses in the movie, but they are doing so now on our streets. What a crooked and perverted generation we are in!

# Chapter Fifteen

## Modest or Enticing Dress?

*"Behold, thou art fair, my love; behold, thou art fair; thou hast doves' eyes within thy locks: thy hair is as a flock of goats that appear from mount Gilead. Thy teeth are like a flock of sheep that are even shorn, which came up from the washing; whereof every one bear twins, and none is barren among them. Thy lips are like a thread of scarlet, and thy speech is comely: thy temples are like a piece of a pomegranate within thy locks. Thy neck is like the tower of David builded for an armoury, whereon there hang a thousand bucklers, all shields of mighty men. Thy two breasts are like two young roes that are twins, which feed among the lilies."* (Song of Solomon 4:1-5)

*"Thou art beautiful, O my love, as Tirzah, comely as Jerusalem, terrible as an army with banners. Turn away thine eyes from me, for they have overcome me: thy hair is as a flock of goats that appear from Gilead. Thy teeth are as a flock of sheep which go up from the washing, whereof every one beareth twins, and there is not one barren among them. As a piece of a pomegranate are thy temples within thy locks. There are threescore queens, and fourscore concubines, and virgins without number. My dove, my undefiled is but one; she is the only one of her mother, she is*

*the choice one of her that bare her. The daughters saw her, and blessed her; yea, the queens and the concubines, and they praised her. Who is she that looketh forth as the morning, fair as the moon, clear as the sun, and terrible as an army with banners? I went down into the garden of nuts to see the fruits of the valley, and to see whether the vine flourished, and the pomegranates budded. Or ever I was aware, my soul made me like the chariots of Amminadib. Return, return, O Shulamite; return, return, that we may look upon thee. What will ye see in the Shulamite? As it were the company of two armies."*
(Song of Solomon 6:4-13)

So far in our study on the book of the Song of Solomon, you will notice that we have pointed out by the revelation of God's word that Solomon was morally weak at this time and his evil concupiscence was right before his face. However, it will be unfair to overlook the object that led to the scene we are studying in this book. One of the thoughts that come to mind while thinking about the possible reason why Solomon was able to describe the sensitive body-parts of the Shulamite lady was that, may be her dressing did not completely cover her body. The more we study this book (Song of Solomon), the clearer it becomes that the dressing of the Shulamite lady might have posed a red sign to her onlooker (Proverbs 7:6-10). It must be confessed that preaching against immodest dress is a no-go area in our present world, it is offensive to many people even the so-called Christians. Pastors and teachers of God's word are shying away from teaching about God's view on Christian modest dressing.

It is clear that there is a code of dress for Christians—putting on modest, moderate garments. In one of the articles (titled Modesty, 2001) written by Evangelist Harold Vaughan, the founder of Christ Life Ministry, "One Christian Organization defined modest apparel as long, loose, and lots. By contrast, immodest garments are those which are abbreviated, revealing, or seductive. Immodesty could be defined as: dress that draws attention to the body; dress that leaves more uncovered than covered; or dress that personified pornography".

The question is, does God care about what any Christian wear? Is it not the heart of man that God looks at while man looks at the outside appearance? Are we not like those preachers who say that all that matters is our hearts? Is it not salvation of the man's spirit that matters while the soul and body of a man are not saved? It becomes very imperative for us to consider this no-go and controversial area of the modern day Christians. Let me quickly say this. Scientifically, matter is anything that occupies space. If Christians' dressing does not matter, why then does it occupy a space in your heart? Why do you value it so much that you think you cannot change how you dress to portray a virtuous life? This is because it matters to you, right? One renowned pastor said that the heart of a matter is the matter of a heart. Is that not true? Some people may say that Christ said that what goes into your mouth does not pollute or corrupt you but what comes out of your mouth. That's right. But do not forget that out of the abundance of the heart the mouth speaks. It is what is in your mind or heart that reflects on the outside. If you put on immodest dresses, it implies that your heart is corrupt or immodest. Right? Sure, it is what you have that you can give; you do not give what you do not have. Indeed, salvation, which here means conversion when genuine, always results in a transformation. For example, when the wood is pyrolysed without oxygen, it is transformed into charcoal, known as a conversion experiment. The same thing happens to the wood when transformed into paper. However, when water changes to ice, that is just a change of state. Can you notice the difference between changes that occur from wood to paper or charcoal and water to ice? The glaring difference is that paper or charcoal cannot be reversed to wood but ice can be changed to water depending on the environmental temperature. Many Christians are unfortunately like water. It is the environment that dictates the type of person they are—Saints or Sinners. They are like chameleons. However, a truly converted person cannot metamorphose himself from a sinful state to a saint state and vice versa. The environment where they are has no influence on them; they only brighten the corners where they find themselves. More importantly, a converted person, now called a Christian, is transformed in order to be conformed to the image of Christ, a representative of Christ, a servant-friend of Christ. You become a servant-friend of Christ because of your obedience to Him daily, not wrestling with His words. Today, the salvation experience that people do share is how they were healed from sickness, how they prayed for blessing and God answered them. When it comes to salvation, our ministers are being fooled by the large number of people who rose up their hands when the altar called is made. I happened to work as a retreat counsellor many times in my life. I have come to realise that whenever the altar call is made, people come out in large number but when we ask them about their prayer requests, we find out that most of them are only after the blessings of God (healing or financial miracles, marriage partners, etc). They are not out there for a genuine conversion of their spirits. The conclusion is that genuinely converted people do not normally have problems with changing their dressing to portray their newly-found faith in Christ to glorify Him alone, not self through their dressing.

God pretty much cares about what Christians wear because specific instructions were given in the Bible through Moses, Paul, and Peter. Unfortunately, many Christians seem to follow the waves of fashion that the world dictates. Worse still, some pastors pet the lions in their churches and accommodate madam Jezebels to teach and to seduce God's children to commit fornication through their body-structure-revealing dresses (Revelations 2:20). Right from the early church, modest dressing was emphasized in the Christian community. However, in the modern days, civilised preachers deviate from this unique and important Christian conduct in our society. They forget that Christians are to influence or lighten the world and reprove its evil and not vice versa. Nonetheless, it is the vice versa that we are experiencing today.

## Purpose of Dressing

Understanding the reasons for wearing clothes is very much important as we consider this important, crucial but no-go area message. You need to know why you are putting on clothes; this will help you to re-orientate your reasoning faculties and do what is right in the sight of God. The Bible says:

*"Get wisdom, get understanding: forget it not; neither decline from the words of my mouth. Forsake her not, and she shall preserve thee: love her, and she shall keep thee. Wisdom is the principal thing; therefore get wisdom: and with all thy getting get understanding. Exalt her, and she shall promote thee: she shall bring thee to honour, when thou dost embrace her"* (Proverbs 4:5-8).

Honour and applaud will be given to you when you know and do what is right. Dear readers, you might have been aware that clothing mainly serves three purposes which are covering, identification, and protection.

1. **Covering**
   The origin of clothing dates back to the aftermath of the fall of man in Genesis 3. In Genesis 2:25, we read that when God created Adam and Eve, they were both naked but not ashamed of it because 1) they were one flesh, 2) they were not sensitive to it and no reason to cover themselves due to their innocent state, 3) not conscious of any sin which produces shame, and 4) no sin in their nature, no guilt on their consciences. Immediately after they fell into the sin of disobedience, they started looking for covering. They were trying to cover up their guilt and shame. But they used the wrong, immodest, and inappropriate materials for their clothing; they sewed fig leaves together and made themselves aprons. Two things are clear from their act: they sewed fig leaves and made it aprons. Sewing leaves that are oval or oblong in shape can never be made without perforations,

just like perforated cloth. In addition, they made it aprons which can not cover their whole body. So, they might probably have used it to cover only their private parts which mankind has always been hiding from public view. Let me hereby submit a crucial point that the ways that most women dress in our modern day reveals that they are still daughters of the first Adam; they use aprons, body-revealing clothes, and immodest dresses. Our churches are therefore filled with the daughters of the first Adam, the disobedient creature of God.

When God first gave clothes to human beings, it was to cover their nakedness. The desire to hide parts of their body was brought about by the guilt of sin. Remember that men and women respond to each other in particular ways when their nakedness is exposed. In order to prevent sexual perversion, there is therefore a need for modest and proper clothing. God gave cloth to curb sin.

*"Neither shalt thou go up by steps unto mine altar, that thy nakedness be not discovered thereon"* (Exodus 20:26).

*"And thou shalt put them upon Aaron thy brother, and his sons with him; and shalt anoint them, and consecrate them, and sanctify them, that they may minister unto me in the priest's office. And thou shalt make them linen breeches to cover their nakedness; from the loins even unto the thighs they shall reach: And they shall be upon Aaron, and upon his sons, when they come in unto the tabernacle of the congregation, or when they come near unto the altar to minister in the holy place; that they bear not iniquity, and die: it shall be a statute for ever unto him and his seed after him"* (Exodus 28:41-43).

Most of the clothes that are displayed in our shopping malls give a clear indication that they are made for the daughters of the first Adam and that the purpose of clothing in our generation is to reveal parts of the body to excite and entice men. I am aware that many women who wear clothes that reveal their sensitive body-parts do try to exonerate themselves from being seducers of men into immoral acts by giving different reasons for wearing such clothes. Many women will tell you that they are not doing it to attract men but to reveal their God-given beauty. They claim that when you have a beautiful body, why should you hide it? "You should show it," they said. They failed to realise that their beautiful body is only to be shown to their spouses. Apostle Paul declared *"But God forbid that I should glory, save in the cross of our Lord Jesus Christ, by whom the world is crucified unto me, and I unto the world"* (Galatians 6:14). Dearly beloved sisters, why then should you glory in the flesh. Do you forget that all human being are *"fearfully and wonderfully made"* (Psalm 139:14). Another excuse they give for wearing some of the immodest dresses is that of the too hot weather. That is just an untenable excuse. God sewed animal skin to cover Adam and Eve's nakedness.

Examples of clothes that beckon to attention of men are tight shirts, halter tops, tube tops, miniskirts, belly shirts. Listen to the statement made by Harold Vaughan about Mary Quant, the woman who designed and promoted mini-skirt. "After Mary Quant introduced mini-skirt in 1960, she stated that she designed it to announce to the world that she was ready to go to bed with a man, day or night." Proverbs 7:10 made it clear to us that a person's intentions could be deduced from the type or style of clothing she wears. The business card of a harlot is her dress, which is deliberately designed to captivate weak and unwary minds. A polluted, sexually immoral heart will show itself in the immodesty of the dress it wears. Most of the ladies' outward dressing reveals their inwardly rottenness, corruptness, and filthiness. Whether you know it or not, the dresses that we put on speak to other people about us or our intentions. It can be deduced from the dresses most women wear today that: 1) tight-fitting garment and low-cut neckline blouses call the attention of men to look at women breasts, 2) short shirts call attention to look at the navel, 3) tight skirt call attention to look at women bottom, 4) miniskirts call attention to look at the tight when standing and inner wear when sitting down, 5) tube tops call attention to look at the armpits, and 6) transparent and netted clothes call attention to look at a woman nakedness. Remember, the purpose of the attires that the great Babylon wears in Revelation 17:1-5 is to captivate the weak minds and lure them to commit fornication.

*"And the woman was arrayed in purple and scarlet colour, and decked with gold and precious stones and pearls, having a golden cup in her hand full of abominations and filthiness of her fornication: And upon her forehead was a name written, MYSTERY, BABYLON THE GREAT, THE MOTHER OF HARLOTS AND ABOMINATIONS OF THE EARTH"* (Revelation 17:4-5).

Are there not many *MOTHERS OF HARLOTS* in our churches and communities today? Dear lady, are you not one of the *MOTHERS OF HARLOTS* considering the styles of your dress?

One could deduce that the type of cloth that the Shulamite lady wore was either transparent, tight or revealing her body structure based on the way Solomon described her body parts vividly, which was a source of enticement to the Israeli king. We may want to sympathise with her condition by saying that probably she could not afford a modest dress because of poverty or the way that her brethren treated her. We need to realise that we do not need a lot of money to buy a modest, appropriate and proper dress.

At this point, let us quickly clarify the issue of putting on ugly clothes. Our God is a holy God and people say that cleanliness (neatness) is near to godliness, holiness. God does not want us to put on dirty, ugly-looking clothes. Every form of shabby dresses should not be worn by Christians. Looking good is part of what Christ talked about when he said: *"but thou, when thou fastest, anoint thine head, and wash thy face"* (Matthew 6:17). You are not to smell bad; take your bath, put lotion on your body, let you face look neat. Clothes made from fine materials and beautiful colours do not constitute immodest dressing. The decadent designs and styles make it improper. God is not against fine linen and beautiful clothes. In Proverbs 31:21-22, the virtuous woman used fine linen and colourful dresses to clothe her family so they looked great in their community and the Bible praised her for doing that:

*"She is not afraid of the snow for her household: for all her household are clothed with scarlet. She maketh herself coverings of tapestry; her clothing is silk and purple."*

Colour or no colour, we are to just make sure that our clothes are not transparent and the style is not provocative.

2. **Identification**
*"Be ye not unequally yoked together with unbelievers: for what fellowship hath righteousness with unrighteousness? and what communion hath light with darkness? And what concord hath Christ with Belial? or what part hath he that believeth with an infidel? And what agreement hath the temple of God with idols? for ye are the temple of the living God; as God hath said, I will dwell in them, and walk in them; and I will be their God, and they shall be my people. Wherefore come out from among them, and be ye separate, saith the Lord,*

*and touch not the unclean thing; and I will receive you, And will be a Father unto you, and ye shall be my sons and daughters, saith the Lord Almighty"* (2 Corinthians 6:14-18).

From time immemorial, God has always drawn a line of demarcation between His children and the ungodly. First and foremost, God drew a demarcation line between the Israelis and the Egyptians. *"But against any of the children of Israel shall not a dog move his tongue, against man or beast: **that ye may know how that the LORD doth put a difference between the Egyptians and Israel"*** (Exodus 11:7). It was the type and style of dress that Moses wore that made the seven daughters of the priest of Midian mistakenly referred to him as an Egyptian. Moses was not an Egyptian but an Israelite.

*"Now when Pharaoh heard this thing, he sought to slay Moses. But Moses fled from the face of Pharaoh, and dwelt in the land of Midian: and he sat down by a well. Now the priest of Midian had seven daughters: and they came and drew water, and filled the troughs to water their father's flock. And the shepherds came and drove them away: but Moses stood up and helped them, and watered their flock. And when they came to Reuel their father, he said, How is it that ye are come so soon to day? And they said, An Egyptian delivered us out of the hand of the shepherds, and also drew water enough for us, and watered the flock"* (Exodus 2:15-19).

God also drew a demarcation line between the church and the world system. He gave a warning to the church: *"Love not the world, neither the things that are in the world. If any man love the world, the love of the Father is not in him"* (I John 2:15). *"Ye adulterers and adulteresses, know ye not that the friendship of the world is enmity with God? Whosoever therefore will be a friend of the world is the enemy of God"* (James

4:4). Christian women who dress according to the styles and standards of this world are openly identifying with that which is destined to death. As Jesus told one of His would-be disciples, let the dead bury the dead. Identity crisis sets in when Christian women dress like pagan women do.

Dear sisters, if you put on the attire of a harlot, the ungodly passers-by men will take you for a harlot. The Shulamite lady was known for her commitment and faithfulness to one man, her lover, the Shepherd boy and not another. She remained chaste and waited patiently till her wedding day before submitting herself to a man whom she loved. Nevertheless, her dressing misrepresented her and she was taken as a cheap girl on the street. Solomon must have thought that she was there with that immodest attire to entice weak minds and men without God's grace upon his life. Sisters, you are responsible for the way men look at you. Like Moses, you may be a genuine Christian who put on a harlot's attire. In that case, people will mistake you to be a harlot. Unbelievers will find it difficult to approach a typical "good old day" sister (who dress to cover all the parts of her body that need to be hidden from men except her husband) because her dressing speaks of her faith. Kindly read the following story about a girl who misrepresented herself on the streets (written by D. G. Hunt: Dress of women—Christian and un-christian dress):

> A girl became incensed because a man spoke to her disrespectfully. Her mother was disturbed and referred the matter to her husband. Instead of blaming the man, the father talked to the girl reprovingly, as follows:
>
> "Daughter, you are not an immoral girl but let me tell you a few things that may help you look differently at this matter. You are young and

attractive, and your dress is such that it displays your body structure. Your arms are bare almost to the shoulders, your waist is cut so low that a good portion of your shoulders and breast are exposed to view; your skirt is scant and narrow, and the slit in the front, with your bright, short petticoat and your silk stockings, displays your limbs almost to the knees; your dress is so cut that every line of your figure is seen in bold relief. He is a stranger here, and did not know that you were a moral girl, for he would not think so by your appearance. I'm sorry that this has occurred, but daughter, YOU ARE AS MUCH TO BLAME AS HE."

3. **Protection**

It is also clear that another reason for clothing is to protect human being from either cold or warm weather. Irrespective of the weather, women and men are to put on modest clothes to protect the opposite sex from lusting and falling into sin. Richard Baxter, a Puritan Preacher, said to women, "You must not lay a stumbling block in their way, nor blow up the fire of their lust, nor make your ornaments snare but you must walk among sinful persons as you would with a candle among straw or gunpowder, or else you may see a flame which you would not have foreseen when it is too late to quench it." What a timely warning! Christian women must not wear the harlots' attires because it is detrimental to the spiritual well-being of the brothers. A supportive story is written by D. G. Hunt: Dress of women—Christian and un-christian dress:

"A young man and a young woman stood before a Milwaukee Judge (more than six decades ago). The young man was charged with immoral conduct, and the young woman was there to support the charge. The young man pleaded guilty and was asked to say whatsoever he thought would clarify his case. He spoke as follows:

"I would appreciate the privilege, your Honour, of saying I was raised by a wonderful and godly mother. She brought me up to be a good and responsible man. Your Honour, I met this young lady in a lonely, secluded spot on a country lane. She was so immodestly attired that the moment my eyes fell upon her, my lust feasted upon her. Had she not aroused those unholy desires within me, I would have never been guilty of this dastardly deed. I ask the court, ought she not to share my blame? Did she not contribute to my downfall?"

The Judge said to the young man, "Go and sin no more." But, he kept the girl there and gave her a lecture on the way to dress in public.

Are you dressing to protect the men in your church and in your community? Or are you trying to ensnare their mind with the goal of pulling them into the mud of immoral thoughts and acts?

Our society today is prevalent with nude types of clothing and dressing styles. Some guys and girls put on sag jeans so that whenever they sit down, part of their bottom will be clearly seen by every passer-by. This is done to gain the attention of the opposite sex, saying that they are ready for whosoever will be ready to take them to bed.

We must understand that:

a. Devil promotes nudity in our society
   *"And when he went forth to land, there met him out of the city a certain man, which had devils long time, and*

*ware no clothes, neither abode in any house, but in the tombs*" (Luke 8:27).

"*And the man in whom the evil spirit was leaped on them, and overcame them, and prevailed against them, so that they fled out of that house naked and wounded*" (Acts 19:16).

b. It is Satan's plan to turn humanity against God
Satan uses the nudity of women to corrupt and pollute the minds of men. A Careful consideration of the consequences of nudity in our society reveals that the watching of pornographic movies, rape, premarital sex, unwanted pregnancies, and divorce prevail in our days more than they ever did in the history of man. Why? It is because of the evil behind nudity. No person commits any of the listed consequences and at the same time remains in favour with God. It is like the sin committed by the people who conspired together to build the tower of Babel as a sign of not wanting the word and will of God to come to pass.

c. Women do this to draw attention of men to their beauty
Nudity of women is to draw the attention of men to their beauty in order to lure them to commit sexual immorality. Perhaps, King David had seen Bathsheba several times before the fateful day but her nakedness made her to seem more attractive and beautiful to him than ever before. The main problem with men is the lust of the eyes. Once a man sees the nakedness of a mature lady, the sight signal goes to the brain and a certain hormone is released causing him to begin to desire to have a carnal knowledge with the lady. No wonder, Job said that he would not allow his mind to think upon any lady that his eyes have seen (Job 31:1). Jesus Christ said "*that whosoever looketh on a woman to lust after her hath committed adultery with her already in his heart*"

(Matthew 5:28). Appetite to commit sexual immorality is commonly aggravated by the sight-effect.

*"And it came to pass in an eveningtide, that David arose from off his bed, and walked upon the roof of the king's house: and from the roof he saw a woman washing herself; and the woman was very beautiful to look upon"* (2 Samuel 11:2).

Women are deliberately putting on styles of dresses which reveal their nakedness in order to charm men who will be running after them like a sheep to the slaughter.

d.  To make the sin of immorality prevalence in our society
Have you ever asked yourself why every advertisement carries the image of either a naked or half-naked lady may it be the billboard, signboard, postal, or television advert? The answer is not farfetched. It is to gain the attention of more men. The satanic secret objective for this act is to spread or plant seed of corruption of sexual immorality into the mind of men. The germination of this seed is the actual act of sexual immorality. So, it is not surprising to see teenagers also engaging in this heinous sin. It does not stop with the social class of people; adults like the rich and poor people also fall into it. Do you often wonder why pastors and spiritually fervent ministers of God fall into the same sin of sexual immorality? Well, it is because a kind nudity is permitted in our Christian gatherings or assemblies too. These prostitutes are also in our churches to sell their evil, satanic markets. Examples of the pornographic dresses that they wear to destroy our men are shorts, too low necklines blouses, slits above the knee, tight clothing or tight jeans, bra-less clothing, transparent clothing, and so on.

**Proclaiming Decorous** 1 Tim. 2:9; 1 Pet. 3:1-5.

a. Every Christian woman must understand that God created her beautifully and wonderfully (Psalm 139:14). So, they do not need make-up to be beautiful and admired by others. Make up is necessary where there is not enough, where the standard is not reached, where there is a need of extra assignment or work to pass an examination.

b. She must also know that God created her to be a shining light

Every Christian woman is created to reveal and promote the glory of God; not to promote the kingdom of darkness that corrupts the world through nudity or pornographic representation of women's beauty.

*"Even every one that is called by my name: for I have created him for my glory, I have formed him; yea, I have made him. This people have I formed for myself; they shall shew forth my praise"* (Isaiah 43:7, 21).

Christian women are to preserve the moral conduct of our society as salt preserves perishable things from putrefaction and destruction. Their dressing should help preserve the brothers and not pollute their lives with revealing dresses. They are to make our society and church environments a pleasant, satisfying and conducive place to live without the brothers vexing their righteous soul from day to day with their unlawful deeds and nakedness-revealing clothes.

*"Ye are the salt of the earth: but if the salt have lost his savour, wherewith shall it be salted? it is thenceforth good for nothing, but to be cast out, and to be trodden under foot of men. Ye are the light of the world. A city that is set on an hill cannot be hid. Neither do men light*

*a candle, and put it under a bushel, but on a candlestick;
and it giveth light unto all that are in the house. Let
your light so shine before men, that they may see your
good works, and glorify your Father which is in heaven"*
(Matt 5:14-16).

c.  She has no authority over her body

It is a common saying mostly among women that they
are the owner of their body. So, they can do whatever
they want with it and they can use it as they wish and
cover it with whatever style and type of dress that they
like. But this statement is far from the truth. You are not
your own. Your body is the temple of the Holy Spirit. We
do not need to dress like the worldly people before we
can win them to Christ. If we entice them using fashion
parade, they will one day disappear when they come in
contact with more sophisticated and satanic promoted
clothes fashion. If you are married, your body and
nakedness belong solely to your husband while if you are
still single, you are to day by day please the Lord.

*"I beseech you therefore, brethren, by the mercies
of God, that ye present your bodies a living sacrifice,
holy, acceptable unto God, which is your reasonable
service. And be not conformed to this world: but be ye
transformed by the renewing of your mind, that ye may
prove what is that good, and acceptable, and perfect,
will of God"* (Romans 12:1-2).

*"What? Know ye not that your body is the temple of the
Holy Ghost which is in you, which ye have of God, and
ye are not your own? For ye are bought with a price:
therefore glorify God in your body, and in your spirit,
which are God's"* (1 Corinthians 6:19-20).

d.  That doing only what is right in human's eyes may not be
right in God's eyes, so only the Bible should be followed

In Judges 17:6, the Bible says *"in those days there was no king in Israel, but every man did that which was right in his own eyes."* So when people's own impetus, infatuation, and impulse constitute the guiding principle that orders his or her actions, our society will be in a very devastated and decayed state. We can boldly say that this is what we are experiencing in our society today as people wear clothes that seem right in their own eyes without considering whether it is right or not in the eyes of God. This is the age where everyone is strongly attached to his or her own opinions and modes of acting in a morally perverse way (Proverb 14:12).

Christian ladies must resist every suggestion to dress in such a manner that can provoke men to lust for sexual immorality; instead they must learn to please God in their dressing at all times. *"No man that warreth entangleth himself with the affairs of this life; that he may please him who hath chosen him to be a soldier"* (2 Timothy 2:4). Christians are not to be concerned neither influenced by worldly affairs and cares.

e.  No Christian woman should wear the garments that belong to a harlot.

There is no relationship between light and darkness, Christian and prostitute's dress. They do not belong, they are at variance. Christians are to dress in order to express God's purpose for dressing such as covering, identification, and protecting our neighbours from falling into sexual immorality. *"But when ye sin so against the brethren (**cause your brothers to sin**), and wound their weak conscience, ye sin against Christ. Wherefore, if meat (**dressing**) make my brother to offend (**lust and sin**), I will eat no flesh (**I will not wear any cloth that allure them**) while the world standeth, lest I make my brother to offend"* (1 Corinthians 8:12-13).

What should be the basic guiding principles by which Christian ladies should follow in selecting the type and style of dress they would wear? There are four basic questions that can help in deciding how a Christian lady should sew her dress or buy her clothes: 1) will this be appropriate, modest, and proper? 2) Is this distinctively feminine? 3) Will this item attract undue attention of passersby? and 4) Or will this cause my brothers in Christ and other men to fall or be tempted?

Let everyone that nameth the name of Christ depart from iniquity and also abstain from all appearance of evil. Albert Barnes commented on 1 Thessalonians 5:22 that "There are things, where whatever may be our motive, we may be certain that our conduct will be regarded as improper. A great variety of subjects, such as those pertaining to dress, amusements, . . . and various practices in the transaction of business, come under this general class; which, though on the supposition that they cannot be proved to be in themselves positively wrong or forbidden, have much the "appearance" of evil, and will be so interpreted by others. The safe and proper rule is to lean always to the side of virtue. In these instances, it may be certain that there will be no sin committed by abstaining; there may be by indulgence. No command of God, or of propriety, will be violated if we decline complying with these customs; but on the other hand we may wound the cause of religion by yielding to what can be a possible temptation. If you find it difficult to cross a gutter of less than 90 cm or 2 feet because of your tight skirt, or find it difficult to sit down without crossing your feet because of your too-short skirt, it is an evidence that you have a big problem. You need to go and redress. If your blouse reveals excessive cleavage because of its too low neckline, or your jeans clearly outline your genitalia, then you have a serious problem; you need to go and redress.

f.  The sound and undiluted word of God must be preached
    by all God's ministers and children

> *"And they shall teach my people the difference between
> the holy and profane, and cause them to discern
> between the unclean and the clean"* (Ezekiel 44:23).

> *"I charge thee therefore before God, and the Lord Jesus
> Christ, who shall judge the quick and the dead at his
> appearing and his kingdom; Preach the word; be instant
> in season, out of season; reprove, rebuke, exhort with all
> longsuffering and doctrine. For the time will come when
> they will not endure sound doctrine; but after their own
> lusts shall they heap to themselves teachers, having
> itching ears; And they shall turn away their ears from
> the truth, and shall be turned unto fables"* (2 Timothy
> 4:1-4).

> *"Only take heed to thyself, and keep thy soul diligently,
> lest thou forget the things which thine eyes have seen,
> and lest they depart from thy heart all the days of
> thy life: but teach them thy sons, and thy sons' sons;
> Specially the day that thou stoodest before the LORD
> thy God in Horeb, when the LORD said unto me, Gather
> me the people together, and I will make them hear my
> words, that they may learn to fear me all the days that
> they shall live upon the earth, and that they may teach
> their children"* (Deuteronomy 4:9-10).

So, it is the responsibility of our pastors and teachers
to preach it in season and out of season, when the
members are willing to receive it or not, whether people
want to hear or oppose it or not, whether you are the
only one preaching about such a sound and dynamic
message. Let your congregation know that God want our
ladies to wear "apparel" which mean loose (rooming) and
long flowing garment (1 Timothy 2:9). The Bible teaches
us to instruct our women to put on modest apparel. Our

pastors are the watchmen that need to go up onto the roof, over the gate unto the wall, and lift up their eyes to look and watch for impending danger or pollution (2 Samuel 18:24). They are to be sensitive enough to detect the many women that have gone the way of worldly dressing and who find it difficult to come out of its deception (2 Kings 9:18). They are to thoroughly study the word of God and give the church members a warning from God about indecent dresses (Ezekiel 3:17). There is a repercussion for not warning them about the evil of immodest dresses. *"But if the watchman see the sword come, and blow not the trumpet, and the people be not warned; if the sword come, and take any person from among them, he is taken away in his iniquity; but his blood will I require at the watchman's hand"* (Ezekiel 33:6). The failure of the prophets and pastors to follow God's commands will always precipitate a spiritual destitution in our churches and community which will eventually cause spiritual weakness, darkness, and blindness.

Will you chorus it with the heavenly minded believers that **"I'll tell the world that I'm a Christian"**

1.  I'll tell the world that I'm a Christian
    I'm not ashamed His name to bear;
    I'll tell the world that I'm a Christian
    I'll take Him with me anywhere.
    I'll tell the world how Jesus saved me,
    And how He gave me a life brand-new;
    And I know that if you trust Him
    That all He gave me He'll give to you,
    I'll tell the world that He's my Saviour,
    No other one could love me so;
    My life, my all is His forever,
    And where He leads me I will go.

2. I'll tell the world that He is coming
   It may be near or far away;
   But we must live as if His coming
   Would be tomorrow or today.
   For when He comes and life is over,
   For those who love Him there's more to be;
   Eyes have never seen the wonders
   That He's preparing for you and me.
   O tell the world that you're a Christian,
   Be not ashamed His name to bear;
   O tell the world that you're a Christian,
   And take Him with you ev'ry where.

# Chapter Sixteen

## The Final Reunion

*"I am my beloved's, and his desire is toward me. Come, my beloved, let us go forth into the field; let us lodge in the villages. Let us get up early to the vineyards; let us see if the vine flourish, whether the tender grape appear, and the pomegranates bud forth: there will I give thee my loves. The mandrakes give a smell, and at our gates are all manner of pleasant fruits, new and old, which I have laid up for thee, O my beloved."* (Song of Solomon 7:10-13)

*"O that thou wert as my brother, that sucked the breasts of my mother! when I should find thee without, I would kiss thee; yea, I should not be despised. I would lead thee, and bring thee into my mother's house, who would instruct me: I would cause thee to drink of spiced wine of the juice of my pomegranate. His left hand should be under my head, and his right hand should embrace me. I charge you, O daughters of Jerusalem, that ye stir not up, nor awake my love, until he please.*

*Who is this that cometh up from the wilderness, leaning upon her beloved? I raised thee up under the apple tree: there thy mother brought thee forth: there she brought thee forth that bare thee. Set me as a seal upon thine heart, as a seal upon thine arm: for love is strong as death; jealousy is cruel as the grave: the coals thereof are coals of fire, which hath a most vehement flame. Many waters cannot quench love, neither can the floods drown it: if a man would give all the substance of his house for love, it would utterly be contemned."* (Song of Solomon 8:1-7)

As we consider the final reunion of the Shulamite lady and the Shepherd boy, we are brought to the reality of believers' final goal and end: the coming of our Lord Jesus Christ and our final reunion with Him. The reunion of Christians and Christ is referred to as the Rapture of the Saints which is going to be crowned with the Marriage of the Lamb. The rapture is written in 1 Thessalonians 4:13-18:

*"But I would not have you to be ignorant, brethren, concerning them which are asleep, that ye sorrow not, even as others which have no hope. For if we believe that Jesus died and rose again, even so them also which sleep in Jesus will God bring with him. For this we say unto you by the word of the Lord, that we which are alive and remain unto the coming of the Lord shall not prevent them which are asleep. For the Lord himself shall descend from heaven with a shout, with the voice of the archangel, and with the trump of God: and the dead in Christ shall rise first: Then we which are alive and remain shall be caught up together with them in the clouds, to meet the Lord in the air: and so shall we ever be with the Lord. Wherefore comfort one another with these words."*

The marriage of the Lamb is written in Revelation 19:6-9: *"And I heard as it were the voice of a great multitude, and as the voice of many waters, and as the voice of mighty thunderings, saying, Alleluia: for the Lord God omnipotent reigneth. Let us be glad and rejoice, and give honour to him: for the marriage of the Lamb is come, and his wife hath made herself ready. And to her was granted that she should be arrayed in fine linen, clean and white: for the fine linen is the righteousness of saints. And he saith unto me, Write, Blessed are they which are called unto the marriage supper of the Lamb. And he saith unto me, These are the true sayings of God."*

So, the final reunion with Christ is the ultimate goal and desire that should pre-occupy every believer's heart. Be ready and prepare yourself to be holy, waiting for Him.

*"Behold, what manner of love the Father hath bestowed upon us, that we should be called the sons of God: therefore the world knoweth us not, because it knew him not. Beloved, now are we the sons of God, and it doth not yet appear what we shall be: but we know that, when he shall appear, we shall be like him; for we shall see him as he is. And every man that hath this hope in him purifieth himself, even as he is pure."* (1 John 3:1-3)

*"We know that whosoever is born of God sinneth not; but he that is begotten of God keepeth himself, and that wicked one toucheth him not."* (1 John 5:18)

*"Having therefore these promises (**promises of His coming at rapture, marriage of the Lamb with the saints**), dearly beloved, let us cleanse ourselves from all filthiness of the flesh and spirit, perfecting holiness in the fear of God."* (2 Corinthians 7:1)

**Rejection of Flattery and Evil Proposals** Song of Solomon 7:10; 8:1-4.

The Shulamite lady bluntly interrupted the extravagant flattery of Solomon and declared that she belonged to the Shepherd boy and that her desire and affections were toward whom her soul loved. Therefore, she could not give her love to another. We must always remind ourselves that we belong to God and we shall not yield to other gods. She preferred to marry someone with similar values and background; not to a man of power with a polluted life. Today, there are lots of break-ups in marriages because they do not belong or have the same spiritual values and aspirations. Do not marry because of money or social status but because of your submission to the will of God.

   a. Consolation in her beloved—"*I am my beloved's . . .*" What the Shulamite lady is saying is that she belongs to her beloved. Christians are owned by Christ, not by self or the world. No matter what may come any Christian's way, may it be temptations, trials, troubles, traps, dangers, afflictions, persecutions; he can still boldly say "I am my beloved's." We must not let anything or anybody come between us and our Bridegroom. So, she was confident of deliverance from it all (Psalms 119:94). All that she has in Him satisfies her and all belongs to Him, everything is devoted to Him alone. Knowing for sure that we are the Lord's with no other desire beside Him and to remain with Him forever is a great consolation. Every Christian should be able to sing the song written by Fanny Crosby:

   1. I am Thine, O Lord, I have heard Thy voice,
And it told Thy love to me;
But I long to rise in the arms of faith
And be closer drawn to Thee.

   *Chorus*
*Draw me nearer, nearer blessed Lord,*
*To the cross where Thou hast died.*
*Draw me nearer, nearer, nearer blessed Lord,*
*To Thy precious, bleeding side.*

   2. Consecrate me now to Thy service, Lord,
By the power of grace divine;
Let my soul look up with a steadfast hope,
And my will be lost in Thine.

3. O the pure delight of a single hour
   That before Thy throne I spend,
   When I kneel in prayer, and with Thee, my God
   I commune as friend with friend!

4. There are depths of love that I cannot know
   Till I cross the narrow sea;
   There are heights of joy that I may not reach
   Till I rest in peace with Thee.

There are lots of temptations that may come across our ways to deny Christ or be confused about our identity with Christ. At such times, we must remind ourselves that we belong to Him and there is no other person that we can go to, except Christ. *"From that time many of his disciples went back, and walked no more with him. Then said Jesus unto the twelve, Will ye also go away? Then Simon Peter answered him, Lord, to whom shall we go? Thou hast the words of eternal life. And we believe and are sure that thou art that Christ, the Son of the living God"* (John 6:66-69)

b. Clarity of his interest in her. Without any iota of doubt in her heart, she knows for sure that his love is for her, not for another—*"I am my beloved's, and his desire is toward me."* What the Shulamite lady is saying is that she knows that her submission to the word of God in Genesis 3:16: *"thy desire shall be to thy husband, and he shall rule over thee"* is reciprocated by her beloved—*"his desire is toward"* her. As her aspirations, passions, goals, and pursuits shall be presented to her husband for approval or modification—ready to do His will—*"thy will be done on earth as it is in heaven"* so also is her beloved's desire towards her. From the book of Genesis to Revelation we clearly see that God delights in His people, He cares, protects, and provides for them.

*"How precious also are thy thoughts unto me, O God! how great is the sum of them!*

*If I should count them, they are more in number than the sand: when I awake, I am still with thee"* Psalm 139:17-18).

*"And he said unto them, with desire I have desired to eat this passover with you before I suffer"* (Luke 22:15).

*"The LORD hath appeared of old unto me, saying, Yea, I have loved thee with an everlasting love: therefore with loving-kindness have I drawn thee"* (Jeremiah 31:3).

It must be understood that Christ's desire is toward the Christians even before their redemption as He left His glory in heaven to come, suffer, be crucified and die for the sinful man. After redemption, He continues to desire their well-being by comforting, encouraging, guiding, and nourishing them. He keeps on washing them with the Word of God in order to present them unto Himself holy on the last day. Christians' confidence should be in Christ because He has promised the church that he will never leave nor forsake them, so His desire is toward them.

The Shulamite lady was in conformity with her beloved. She was very satisfied with marrying her beloved Shepherd boy irrespective of his status. The fact that she knew that his desire was towards her revived her faith/trust in him. We, Christians, must realise that though sin abounds, the grace of God is much more available unto us.

c. Comparison of her love for Solomon as just a love for a blood relation but not a husband and wife (Song 8:1-3).

She said that *"O that thou wert as my brother"* meaning that Solomon was not her brother, so she could not even kiss him. If he had been her brother—blood relation she would have kissed him without suspicion and without giving offense to any passersby.

d. Charge to the intermediary not to arouse her sexual love for Solomon (Song 8:4).

There must be a continual refusal to yield to temptation and rejection of every compromising suggestion.

**Request and Restoration of the Shulamite Lady** Song 7:11-13; 8:5.

The Shulamite was so sure and excited that her beloved would soon come for her. She expressed her desire to depart from the luxuriousness of the palace and return to the countryside with her Lover shepherd boy. She vividly described that she has stored up for him sexual delights and her willingness to freely share her sexuality with him after they were married.

a. Request for reunion—"*Come, my beloved*" (Song of Solomon 7:11a). Her request for the beloved to come shows that she did not have enough strength to overcome the temptation she faced. She needed the Bridegroom, her Saviour to come for her rescue. It must be our daily prayer for our Saviour, Jesus Christ to come into our hearts, strengthening us to overcome temptations and trials of life, and come to comfort our weary hearts. Indeed, we cannot bear our burdens alone, we need to tell Jesus, for Him alone can help and deliver us. Then, the song written and sang by Elisha A. Hoffman in 1893 became so appropriate in such a time like this.

   1. I must tell Jesus all of my trials;
      I cannot bear these burdens alone;
      In my distress He kindly will help me;
      He ever loves and cares for His own.

*Chorus*
*I must tell Jesus! I must tell Jesus!*
*I cannot bear my burdens alone;*
*I must tell Jesus! I must tell Jesus!*
*Jesus can help me, Jesus alone.*

2.  I must tell Jesus all of my troubles;
    He is a kind, compassionate friend;
    If I but ask Him, He will deliver,
    Make of my troubles quickly an end.

3.  Tempted and tried, I need a great Saviour;
    One Who can help my burdens to bear;
    I must tell Jesus, I must tell Jesus;
    He all my cares and sorrows will share.

4.  Oh how the world to evil allures me!
    Oh how my heart is tempted to sin!
    I must tell Jesus, and He will help me
    Over the world the victory to win.

b.  Request for dwelling together—"*let us lodge in the villages*" (Song of Solomon 7:11c).
    What a lovely request to dwell together with her beloved. We must desire to dwell together with Christ at all times. There is a song that goes like this "dwelling together, how happy we shall be, throughout eternity, for we shall dwell together, my Lord and I." After the resurrection of Jesus Christ, two of His disciples were on their way to a village called Emmaus, which was from Jerusalem *about* threescore furlongs and He joined them in their conversation. When they were near the village, Jesus seemed to want to go further "*but they constrained him, saying, abide with us: for it is toward evening, and the day is far spent. And he went in to tarry with them*" (Luke 24:29).

We must not allow Him to pass us by but importunately invite Him to abide with us. If He abides with us, He will teach, guide, comfort and enrich us to be fruitful. If He abides with us, it means that He lives within us; then we enjoy His divine presence, preservation, productivity and protection over us.

*"Ye are of God, little children, and have overcome them: because greater is he that is in you, than he that is in the world"* (1 John 4:4).

*"He that dwelleth in the secret place of the most High shall abide under the shadow of the Almighty. I will say of the LORD, He is my refuge and my fortress: my God; in him will I trust. Surely he shall deliver thee from the snare of the fowler, and from the noisome pestilence. He shall cover thee with his feathers, and under his wings shalt thou trust: his truth shall be thy shield and buckler. Thou shalt not be afraid for the terror by night; nor for the arrow that flieth by day; Nor for the pestilence that walketh in darkness; nor for the destruction that wasteth at noonday. A thousand shall fall at thy side, and ten thousand at thy right hand; but it shall not come nigh thee. Only with thine eyes shalt thou behold and see the reward of the wicked. Because thou hast made the LORD, which is my refuge, even the most High, thy habitation; There shall no evil befall thee, neither shall any plague come nigh thy dwelling. For he shall give his angels charge over thee, to keep thee in all thy ways. They shall bear thee up in their hands, lest thou dash thy foot against a stone. Thou shalt tread upon the lion and adder: the young lion and the dragon shalt thou trample under feet. Because he hath set his love upon me, therefore will I deliver him: I will set him on high, because he hath known my name"* (Psalms 91:1-14).

c. Request to labour as partners in business—*"let us go forth into the field; . . . Let us get up early to the vineyards; let us see if the vine flourish, whether the tender grape appear, and the pomegranates bud forth: there will I give thee my loves"* (Song of Solomon 7:12a-b).

The more you labour genuinely for Him, the stronger the relationship you built with Him, the more fruitful you become.

d. Reiterating to give her love to her beloved as they were doing all things in common (Song 7:12c-13). All to Jesus I surrender, all to Him I freely give. Christians need to reserve all their affections for Christ.

e. Reunion and return of the Shulamite lady and her beloved Shepherd boy (Song 8:5). As they returned to their country side, they went by the apple tree where they first met and gained affection for each other. At that place, they recalled the memories of the past and then renewed their pledge of love again. God told Jacob, go back to Bethel. We need to go back to the Bible. It is not only when we fall or lose our first love that we return to Calvary; we often need to go back to the Bible and Calvary whenever we feel a little bit weak or feel lonely. Dear readers, I would like to suggest that we need to always and daily go back to God in prayer, rededicating and re-consecrating ourselves to Him because there are lots of evil and immoralities that we vex our spirit with, in this decayed generation.

**Renewal of Vows by the Shulamite Lady and the Shepherd Boy** Song 8:6-7.

*Set me as a seal upon thine heart, as a seal upon thine arm: for love is strong as death; jealousy is cruel as the grave: the coals thereof are coals of fire, which hath a most vehement flame. Many waters cannot quench love, neither can the floods drown it: if a man*

*would give all the substance of his house for love, it*
*would utterly be contemned."* (Song of Solomon 8:6-7)

Having experienced a time of separation, loneliness, and frustration for a long period of time, the Shulamite lady and the one that her soul loved needed a reassurance of their commitment and a consecration to their reunion.

She cried out, *"set me as a seal upon thine heart."*

A seal is a signature and a rope or glue to fasten or close an envelope. The seal, here, then connotes that only her love will dominate her thinking.

a. Renewal of commitment after the deliverance from Satan's trap: Song 8:6a; Eph. 1:13. The church's desire should be that she might be affectionately loved by Christ, that she might be deeply fixed in his heart, be owned and acknowledged by him, and be protected by the arm of his power.

b. Reiterating the power of love: Song 8:6b.

Remember the marriage vow: The pastor asks, "do you accept this man or woman as your wife or husband?"

The new couple normally answers, "I do, for better or worse, in plenty or poverty, health or sickness till death do us part." So, going over it from time to time, and acting on this vow helps to build a stronger and unquenchable love for your spouse.

c. Recounting the little foxes that destroy relationship: (Song 8:6b-c).

She recounted that the little fox of jealousy and envy that Solomon had for her beloved was targeted to destroy their relationship. For the fact that a strange man or woman cherished your beauty and body structure should not drive you crazy to the point of abandoning your spouse. One thing you must know is that whatsoever makes a stranger to love you, when it fades away, the stranger in your life will also fade away with it. So, renounce to every little foxes that wants to destroy your marriage or wedding.

d. Recognition of the characteristics of genuine love (Song 8:7). Genuine love, but not lust, is strong, and quenchless. Neither common nor uncommon adversities, even of the most ruinous nature, can destroy love when it is pure. Our love for Christ should be inextinguishable and inseparable, neither by the many waters and floods of wicked and ungodly men and their flattery and fair promises, nor by their cruel edicts, forces and persecution (Roman 8:35-39; Psalm 88:1-89:2). If it be not excited naturally, no money can purchase it, no property can procure it, no gift can persuade it. How vain is the thought of perverted men, hoping to procure the affections of young women by loading them with presents and wealth! So, when a man bought you with money, know for sure that that man does not love you; he only wants to use and dump you.

Someone said that "true love is as dependable and as certain as death. Sensuous love, such as that offered by King Solomon, depends upon sex for happiness and cannot be trusted since it lacks an emotional bond of commitment."

Dear readers, will you be ready when the Lord shall come to reunite with the Christians at the Rapture of the Saints? Will He find you faithful and ready for Him in an unstained white garment? The Love of money and sexual immorality are the deceptive sins that will hinder many so-called Christian sisters and brothers from making it to the end when the saints will be wedded with Jesus at the final reunion.

During the roll call, in the times of Ezra and Nehemiah, there were priests whose names were not found in the book of records of the genealogy of Israel. *"And of the priests: the children of Habaiah, the children of Koz, the children of Barzillai, which took one of the daughters of Barzillai the Gileadite to wife, and was called after their name. These sought their register among those that were reckoned by genealogy, but it was not found: therefore were they, as polluted, put from the priesthood"* (Nehemiah 7:63-64).

The question is, when the roll will be called yonder, will you be there?

1.  When the trumpet of the Lord shall sound, and time
    shall be no more,
    And the morning breaks, eternal, bright and fair;
    When the saved of earth shall gather over on the other
    shore,
    And the roll is called up yonder, I'll be there.

    *Chorus*
    *When the roll, is called up yonder,*
    *When the roll, is called up yonder,*
    *When the roll, is called up yonder,*
    *When the roll is called up yonder I'll be there.*

2.  On that bright and cloudless morning when the dead
    in Christ shall rise,
    And the glory of His resurrection share;
    When His chosen ones shall gather to their home
    beyond the skies,
    And the roll is called up yonder, I'll be there.

3. Let us labour for the Master from the dawn till setting sun,
   Let us talk of all His wondrous love and care;
   Then when all of life is over, and our work on earth is done,
   And the roll is called up yonder, I'll be there.

# Chapter Seventeen

## The Final Reward

*"We have a little sister, and she hath no breasts: what shall we do for our sister in the day when she shall be spoken for? If she be a wall, we will build upon her a palace of silver: and if she be a door, we will inclose her with boards of cedar. I am a wall, and my breasts like towers: then was I in his eyes as one that found favour. Solomon had a vineyard at Baalhamon; he let out the vineyard unto keepers; every one for the fruit thereof was to bring a thousand pieces of silver. My vineyard, which is mine, is before me: thou, O Solomon, must have a thousand, and those that keep the fruit thereof two hundred."* (Song of Solomon 8:8-12)

In the continuation of our study of the Song of Solomon, we shall be considering the importance of living a holy and acceptable life unto God in this polluted worldly system. Our bible reference gives us a clear and foundational truth about the reason for the disciplinary measures imposed by the brothers of the Shulamite lady. In Song of Solomon 1:6 *"Look not upon me, because I am black, because the sun hath looked upon me:* ***my mother's children were angry with me; they made me the keeper of the vineyards; but mine own vineyard have I not kept,"*** her brethren did not want her to be exposed to the worldly culture of immorality. They wanted her to bring honour to their family on the day of her wedding when she would be met as a virgin. Her brethren played the role of parents in her life. **Parenting** can simply be defined as the practice of promoting and maintaining the physical, emotional, social, spiritual, and intellectual development of a child from infancy to adulthood. It is the responsibility of the parents not only to provide for the physical needs but to also protect them from harm and impart godly or biblical values to their lives. The Bible says in Luke 2:52 that *"Jesus increased in wisdom and stature, and in favour with God and man."* Therefore, there is a great challenge for Christian parents to raise their children in the way they should go so that when they are old; they will not depart from it.

**Purpose of Discipline** Song 8:8.

The followings are the lessons we can derive from rightly viewed and used discipline.

    a.  God encourage Christian's discipline
        *"Withhold not correction from the child: for if thou beatest him with the rod, he shall not die. Thou shalt beat him with the rod, and shalt deliver his soul from hell"* (Proverbs 23: 13-14).

        *"He that spareth his rod hateth his son: but he that loveth him chasteneth him betimes"* (Proverbs 13:24).

        *"For whom the Lord loveth he chasteneth, and scourgeth every son whom he receiveth. If ye endure chastening, God dealeth with you as with sons; for what son is he whom the father chasteneth not?"* (Hebrew 12:6-7).

        God gives the parent to guide, instruct, and train the children in the right way to go. If we spare the rod, we are destroying a nation or the generation to come. An untrained child sells the house that we built. The training the Shulamite lady had received about being undefiled helped her to stand firm during the temptation.

b.  It (discipline) is to teach the right attitude and piety of life rather than punishment for wrong attitude.

When somebody sins and is disciplined, the purpose is not to destroy the person but to remodel and rehabilitate. It is a modelling technique to build, not to destroy character.

> *"Furthermore we have had fathers of our flesh which corrected us, and we gave them reverence: shall we not much rather be in subjection unto the Father of spirits, and live? For they verily for a few days chastened us after their own pleasure* (**principle**)*; but he for our profit, that we might be partakers of his holiness. Now no chastening for the present seemeth to be joyous, but grievous: nevertheless afterward it yieldeth the peaceable fruit of righteousness unto them which are exercised thereby"* (Hebrew 12:11).

The purpose of discipline is not to cause you to run away from the church, but to help you live a holy and righteous life.

In the light of these, every minister of God is encouraged to have a vision and a goal to raise up holy people and cultivate the habit of safeguarding the young believers from getting involved in the corruption and pollution of this worldly system. The Consequences of living a life well-pleasing unto God must be emphasised.

**Promised Rewards for Holy Living** Song 8:8-9.

The brethren of the Shulamite lady were concerned about the type of gifts that they would give to her on the day of her wedding—*"what shall we do for our sister in the day when she shall be spoken for?"* There is always a reward for hardworking and for holy living. During the marriage of the Lamb, there will be a section called "Bema seat" where the believers will be rewarded for the good life they have lived in Christ. We must realize that *"if a man also strive for masteries, yet is he not crowned, except he strive lawfully."* So, running according to the rules of the race will help us to get the prize.

*"The LORD recompense thy work, and a full reward be given thee of the LORD God of Israel, under whose wings thou art come to trust"* (Ruth 2:12).

The Lord will definitely reward every man for his righteousness and faithfulness (1 Sam 26:23). Everyone that sows righteousness shall receive a sure reward (Proverbs 11:18). *"Therefore, my beloved brethren, be ye stedfast, unmoveable, always abounding in the work of the Lord, forasmuch as ye know that your labour is not in vain in the Lord"* (1 Corinthians 15:58). The following are the rewards for living a holy life:

a. Divine exaltation
   The Shulamite lady's brethren promised that *"If she be a wall, we will build upon her a palace of silver"* (Song of Solomon 8:9). This means that if she employs self-restraint against every advance that would like to defile her purity, if she remains a virgin, then she shall be honoured and exalted.

   *"Righteousness exalteth a nation: but sin is a reproach to any people"* (Proverbs 14:34). Piety and holiness always bring promotion. For instance, it is difficult for Christian women to get promotion and enjoy their right at their workplace in some countries around the world because of injustice. Ladies that are ready to mess up their body by getting involved in sexual immorality with their bosses are the ones that are getting promotions and awards for job performance and excellence. It is not because they worth it but because they sell their body to men for promotion. In our University system, those ladies

that are not intellectually sound scores grade A in many subjects or courses because they allow their professors to sleep with them while those that refuse to practice the ungodly act suffer for it—they are being failed by such professors. There are some women cleaners and clerks that dictate to their bosses what they want in the offices just because they have conquered their bosses on the bed. These bosses have exchanged their position and authority for sexual immorality like Judah in Genesis 38:16-18:

*"And he (**Judah**) turned unto her by the way, and said, Go to, I pray thee, let me come in unto thee; (for he knew not that she was his daughter in law.) And she said, What wilt thou give me, that thou mayest come in unto me? And he said, I will send thee a kid from the flock. And she said, **Wilt thou give me a pledge, till thou send it? And he said, What pledge shall I give thee? And she said, Thy signet, and thy bracelets, and thy staff that is in thine hand. And he gave it her**, and came in unto her."*

It is natural for you as a Christian to think that these harlots are prosperous while you are not. That was what the Psalmist thought several thousands years ago in Psalms 73:1-20:

*"Truly God is good to Israel, even to such as are of a clean heart. But as for me, my feet were almost gone; my steps had well nigh slipped. For I was envious at the foolish, when I saw the prosperity of the wicked. For there are no bands in their death: but their strength is firm. They are not in trouble as other men; neither are they plagued like other men. Therefore pride compasseth them about as a chain; violence covereth them as a garment. Their eyes stand out with fatness: they have more than heart could wish. They are corrupt, and speak wickedly concerning oppression: they speak*

*loftily. They set their mouth against the heavens, and their tongue walketh through the earth. Therefore his people return hither: and waters of a full cup are wrung out to them. And they say, How doth God know? and is there knowledge in the most High? Behold, these are the ungodly, who prosper in the world; they increase in riches. Verily I have cleansed my heart in vain, and washed my hands in innocency. For all the day long have I been plagued, and chastened every morning. If I say, I will speak thus; behold, I should offend against the generation of thy children. When I thought to know this, it was too painful for me; Until I went into the sanctuary of God; then understood I their end. Surely thou didst set them in slippery places: thou castedst them down into destruction. How are they brought into desolation, as in a moment! they are utterly consumed with terrors. As a dream when one awaketh; so, O Lord, when thou awakest, thou shalt despise their image."*

Dear Christian ladies, do not let the seeming success of those women (prostitutes) derail you from your righteousness and piety. That promotion that you think they have is nothing. It is only God that promotes people. Righteousness will exalt you—they that trust their God shall not make haste. Wait patiently for Him, He will definitely come to your rescue and promote you. Mind you, the final exaltation is that which is more glorious when the saints will be granted eternal glorious and everlasting kingship.

*"For I reckon that the sufferings of this present time are not worthy to be compared with the glory which shall be revealed in us. For the earnest expectation of the creature waiteth for the manifestation of the sons of God"* (Romans 8:18-19).

Because *"thou lovest righteousness, and hatest wickedness: therefore God, thy God, hath anointed thee with the oil of gladness above thy fellows"* (Psalms 45:7).

b. Deliverance from eternal damnation

*"If she be a wall, we will build upon her a palace of silver: and if she be a door, we will inclose her with boards of cedar"* (Song of Solomon 8:9). The brethren of the Shulamite lady already told her that if she be a door (open herself up to men through sexual immorality—becoming a door), they will kill her and put her in the coffin of cedar wood. If she be a virgin on the day of her visitation or wedding, then she will be delivered from destruction.

Chaste living will deliver you from eternal damnation. *"Riches profit not in the day of wrath: but righteousness delivereth from death. The righteous is delivered out of trouble, and the wicked cometh in his stead"* (Proverbs 11:4, 8). Worldly riches and promotion as the proceeds from sexual immorality will not deliver the perpetrators from the eternal wrath of God.

*"They shall cast their silver in the streets, and their gold shall be removed: their silver and their gold shall not be able to deliver them in the day of the wrath of the LORD: they shall not satisfy their souls, neither fill their bowels: because it is the stumblingblock of their iniquity"* (Ezekiel 7:19).

The sin of sexual immorality—homosexual and lesbian—incurred the rain of fire upon the people of Sodom and Gomorrah (Genesis 18:23-28).

*James Fabiyi*

c. Divine protection

*"If she be a wall, we will build upon her a palace of silver: and if she be a door, we will inclose her with boards of cedar"* (Song of Solomon 8:9). Protection from sexually transmitted diseases like HIV-AIDS, gonorrhoea, syphilis, and others by using condoms may fail you but chaste living will protect you from contracting those diseases and will never fail you.

*"There shall no evil happen to the just: but the wicked shall be filled with mischief"* (Proverbs 12:21).

*"In famine he shall redeem thee from death: and in war from the power of the sword. Thou shalt be hid from the scourge of the tongue: neither shalt thou be afraid of destruction when it cometh. At destruction and famine thou shalt laugh: neither shalt thou be afraid of the beasts of the earth. For thou shalt be in league with the stones of the field: and the beasts of the field shall be at peace with thee. And thou shalt know that thy tabernacle shall be in peace; and thou shalt visit thy habitation, and shalt not sin. Thou shalt know also that thy seed shall be great, and thine offspring as the grass of the earth. Thou shalt come to thy grave in a full age, like as a shock of corn cometh in his season. Lo this, we have searched it, so it is; hear it, and know thou it for thy good"* (Job 5:20-27).

d. The just will be remembered from generation to generation for the good he did: Proverbs 10:7; Ps 112:6.

The chaste life and faithfulness in standing for what is right by the Shulamite lady are recorded in the Bible for our example. A book of the Bible is dedicated unto her; she will ever be remembered for her well-spent life. It was the running away of Joseph from the stranger's offer (sexual immorality) made by Potiphar's wife that landed him in prison but he was remembered in that prison and called to become the Prime Minister, the second-in command of Egypt. The Bible says that *"the memory (remembrance) of the just is blessed: but the name of the wicked shall rot"* (Proverbs 10:7).

Sinners will fade away, but the holy people will be remembered for their good living.

## ONLY REMEMBERED

1. Fading away like the stars in the morning,
   Soaring from earth to its heavenly home,
   Thus should we leave from this world and its toiling,
   Only remembered for what we have done.

   *Chorus*
   *Only remembered, only remembered,*
   *Only remembered for what we have done.*
   *Thus should we leave from this world and its toiling,*
   *Only remembered for what we have done.*

2. Up and away like the dew of the morning,
   Soaring from earth to its heavenly home,
   Thus would I leave from this world and its toiling:
   Only remembered for what I have done.

3. Shall we be missed when others succeed us,
   Reaping the fields we in spring time have sown?
   Nay, for the sower shall pass from his labour,
   Only remembered for what he has done.

4. Only the truth that in life we have spoken,
   Only the seeds that on Earth we have sown,
   These shall pass on ward while we are forgotten,
   Only remembered for what we have done.

Jezebel's life will only be remembered for the evil, adulterous and sexually immoral life she lived. Dear ladies, what will you be remembered for? Sexual immorality or sexual morality?

e. Divine refreshment and nourishment
*"I am a wall, and my breasts like towers: then was I in his eyes as one that found favour"* (Song of Solomon 8:9). When you remain undefiled despite all the pressures and calls from the worldly systems, God will reward you with a divine refreshment and nourishment. Please, dare to be a Daniel who refused to pollute himself with the king's meat. Do not, because of poverty, lack of job and denial of promotion, enter into the satanic business of messing up with men or other types of compromises. One thing is sure, when it is time, your bell will ring and God will grant you rest and restore unto you all the years that you have laboured without results to show for it. As Daniel and his three friends remained holy, refusing to defile themselves with the unholy and idol sacrificed food, the Lord granted them a great accomplishment and refreshment (Daniel 1:8-15). *"And at the end of ten days their (Daniel and his friends) countenances appeared fairer and fatter in flesh than all the children which did eat the portion of the king's meat."*

f. Boldness in prayer
*"I am a wall, and my breasts like towers: then was I in his eyes as one that found favour"* (Song of Solomon 8:9). Because she lived a chaste life, she was very bold to publicly declare that *"I am a wall."* Sin brings shame and a guilty conscience but holiness brings boldness. In Proverbs 28:1, the Bible says that *"the wicked flee when no man pursueth: but the righteous are bold as a lion."*

Your prayer life gets a momentum and becomes so powerful and effective when you live a holy life (James 5:16). The Lord hears the prayer of the righteous

(Proverbs 15:29). A good example of the righteous being bold in prayer is that of Hezekiah in 2 Kings 20:1-6:

*"In those days was Hezekiah sick unto death. And the prophet Isaiah the son of Amoz came to him, and said unto him, Thus saith the LORD, Set thine house in order; for thou shalt die, and not live. Then he turned his face to the wall, and prayed unto the LORD, saying, I beseech thee, O LORD, remember now how I have walked before thee in truth and with a perfect heart, and have done that which is good in thy sight. And Hezekiah wept sore. And it came to pass, afore Isaiah was gone out into the middle court, that the word of the LORD came to him, saying, Turn again, and tell Hezekiah the captain of my people, Thus saith the LORD, the God of David thy father, I have heard thy prayer, I have seen thy tears: behold, I will heal thee: on the third day thou shalt go up unto the house of the LORD. And I will add unto thy days fifteen years; and I will deliver thee and this city out of the hand of the king of Assyria; and I will defend this city for mine own sake, and for my servant David's sake."*

Though there was a prophecy that Hezekiah would die, not just a fake or false prophecy, but one from God—Isaiah, a national prophet—Hezekiah did not panic or became fearful of the pronouncement. He did not argue with the prophet; he only turned his face to the wall and entered into the throne of grace with boldness, telling God that he had walked with a perfect heart and done what was right in the sight of the Lord. So, God could not deny the prayer of the righteous. He added fifteen more years to his age; thereby, averted the warrant of death that hanged on his neck. If you live a chaste life, you will be bold to approach God in prayer to bring a solution to the delay in child bearing, having no condemnations in your heart.

*James Fabiyi*

## Punishment for Unholy Living

*"If she be a wall, we will build upon her a palace of silver: and if she be a door, we will inclose her with boards of cedar"* (Song of Solomon 8:9).

a. Shame
   The sin of immorality brings shame to the sinner's family, and reproach to the name of God. People would despicably say, "But she called herself a Christian!"

   *"Thus saith the LORD of hosts; Behold, I will send upon them the sword, the famine, and the pestilence, and will make them like vile figs, that cannot be eaten, they are so evil. And I will persecute them with the sword, with the famine, and with the pestilence, and will deliver them to be removed to all the kingdoms of the earth, to be a curse, and an astonishment, **and an hissing, and a reproach, among all the nations whither I have driven them**: Because they have not hearkened to my words, saith the LORD, which I sent unto them by my servants the prophets, rising up early and sending them; but ye would not hear, saith the LORD"* (Jeremiah 29:17-19).

   In Israel, it was a shame to the family when one of its members committed immorality—premarital sex or sex outside the matrimonial home. Such people were to be disgraced and stoned to death.

b. Death
   Inclosing her in the coffin made of cedar wood was a terrible capital punishment in Israel (Song 8:9b). Falling into the sin of immorality brings physical and spiritual death. In the Old Testament, whosoever committed fornication was to be stoned to death. Today, such law is outdated but there are many stones that bring death such as HIV and other sexual transmitted diseases. It also leads to eternal death (separation from God).

c. Family problems
The sin of sexual immorality incurs family problems. When a Christian woman or man cheaply sells himself or herself to the hands of Satan through sexual immorality, their bed becomes defiled, destroyed, disastrous, devastated, and family division sets in. Examples of these family problems can be seen in the lives of Hophni and Phinehas (1 Samuel 3:11-14; 4:10-22) and King David (2 Samuel 11:1-4; 12:10-14).

## Procuring the Rewards for Holy Living

*"I am a wall, and my breasts like towers: then was I in his eyes as one that found favour. Solomon had a vineyard at Baalhamon; he let out the vineyard unto keepers; every one for the fruit thereof was to bring a thousand pieces of silver. My vineyard, which is mine, is before me: thou, O Solomon, must have a thousand, and those that keep the fruit thereof two hundred"* (Song of Solomon 8:10-12).

a. Boldness to stand before a crowd of people to declare our good works (Song 8:10; 1 Thess. 2:10).
The lady was so bold to declare that she had lived a good and chaste life. Prophet Samuel was bold enough to call the attention of all the Israelites to testify against him if he had defrauded anyone; they answered him that he had not done so. Jesus said that the prince of this world came to Him and found nothing sinful in Him. Many so-called Christian ladies cannot come out publicly to testify and defend their moral and sexual life. Most of them are doors even after they professed to be Christians. They are either defiled by the pastors, church members, or street men. What a pity! The house of prayer is turned into a house of prostitutes. The temple of the Holy Spirit is turned into the tabernacle of harlot-Sodomites. Many Christians are incurring curses upon their life and family

299

because of the sin of pre-marital sex before coming to the holy altar of God.

b. Boldness to ask for the promised rewards is based on pleasing God who has called us.
The Shulamite lady was bold to ask for her brethren's promised reward because she fulfilled her terms. If you do what God wants you to do, you will be bold to ask for the kingdom's rights and benefits like the daughter of Joshua asked for a well: *"Give me a blessing; for thou hast given me a south land; give me also springs of water. And he gave her the upper springs, and the nether springs"* (Joshua 15:16-19). Hezekiah asked for the promised long life and God granted it to him (2 Kings 20:1-6).

There is a joy and rest that await us if we can endure hardships and overcome temptations and get to the last mile of the way without stain on our white garment. Johnson Oatman, Jr, in 1908, wrote a hymn titled "the last mile of the way."

1. If I walk in the pathway of duty,
If I work till the close of the day;
I shall see the great King in His beauty,
When I've gone the last mile of the way.

*Chorus*
*When I've gone the last mile of the way,*
*I will rest at the close of the day,*
*And I know there are joys that await me,*
*When I've gone the last mile of the way.*

2. If for Christ I proclaim the glad story,
If I seek for His sheep gone astray,
I am sure He will show me His glory,
When I've gone the last mile of the way.

3. Here the dearest of ties we must sever,
   Tears of sorrow are seen ev'ry day;
   But no sickness, no sighing forever,
   When I've gone the last mile of the way.

4. And if here I have earnestly striven,
   And have tried all His will to obey,
   'Twill enhance all the rapture of Heaven,
   When I've gone the last mile of the way.

# Chapter Eighteen

## Secrets of Steadfastness

*"Solomon had a vineyard at Baalhamon; he let out the vineyard unto keepers; every one for the fruit thereof was to bring a thousand pieces of silver. My vineyard, which is mine, is before me: thou, O Solomon, must have a thousand, and those that keep the fruit thereof two hundred. Thou that dwellest in the gardens, the companions hearken to thy voice: cause me to hear it. Make haste, my beloved, and be thou like to a roe or to a young hart upon the mountains of spices."* (Song of Solomon 8:11-14)

Steadfast simply means unchanging, constant, unmovable, and fixed. There are some secrets that we can deduced from the life of the Shulamite lady, which we believe helped her to stand firmly during the times when she was tempted and lured to deny her espoused Shepherd boy by marrying King Solomon. In the times of temptations and trials, we need a Saviour and an anchor.

1. In times like these you need a Saviour
   In times like these you need an anchor;
   Be very sure, be very sure
   Your anchor holds and grips the Solid Rock!

*Chorus*
*This Rock is Jesus, Yes, He's the One;*
*This Rock is Jesus, the only One!*
*Be very sure, be very sure*
*Your anchor holds and grips the Solid Rock!*

2.  In times like these you need the Bible,
    In times like these O be not idle;
    Be very sure, be very sure
    Your anchor holds and grips the Solid Rock!

3.  In times like these I have a Saviour,
    In times like these I have an anchor;
    I'm very sure, I'm very sure
    My anchor holds and grips the Solid Rock!

## Self Identification

For any Christian to remain steadfast in his walk with Christ in the midst of temptations, he needs to know who he is, discover his identity in Christ. The Shulamite lady knew that she belonged to the Shepherd boy, not to King Solomon.

*"While the king sitteth at his table, my spikenard sendeth forth the smell thereof. A bundle of myrrh is my wellbeloved unto me; he shall lie all night betwixt my breasts. My beloved is unto me as a cluster of camphire in the vineyards of Engedi"* (Song of Solomon 1:12-14).

The presence of Solomon in his glory meant nothing to her. That did not drive her to forget her identity. We must understand that no sin of whatever degree should be found among the Christians according to the Bible in Ephesians 5:1-4

*"Be ye therefore followers of God, as dear children; And walk in love, as Christ also hath loved us, and hath given himself for us an offering and a sacrifice to God for a sweet smelling*

*savour. But fornication, and all uncleanness, or covetousness, let it not be once named among you, as becometh saints; Neither filthiness, nor foolish talking, nor jesting, which are not convenient: but rather giving of thanks."*

Every Christian must depart from iniquity, flee youthful lusts and discard sexual immoral thoughts, but present himself or herself as a vessel of honour, having passed through the fire of temptations and trials and coming out more shining than ever.

*"Nevertheless the foundation of God standeth sure, having this seal, The Lord knoweth them that are his. And, Let everyone that nameth the name of Christ depart from iniquity. But in a great house there are not only vessels of gold and of silver, but also of wood and of earth; and some to honour, and some to dishonour. If a man therefore purge himself from these, he shall be a vessel unto honour, sanctified, and meet for the master's use, and prepared unto every good work. Flee also youthful lusts: but follow righteousness, faith, charity, peace, with them that call on the Lord out of a pure heart"* (2 Timothy 2:19-22).

Recognizing your identity in Christ will help you to stay clear from every form of immoral lifestyle. If you do not have a root or identity, you will not be able to know where you belong. When people counsel you to sell your body to get out of poverty and joblessness, you will reject it because of your identity with Christ. The heroes and heroines of faith in the Old Testament remained steadfast and focused, even called themselves strangers and pilgrims on the earth because they knew that they belonged to God and needed to seek the heavenly country.

*"These all died in faith, not having received the promises, but having seen them afar off, and were persuaded of them, and embraced them, and confessed that they were strangers and pilgrims on the earth. For they that say such things declare plainly that they seek a country. And truly, if they had been mindful of that country from whence they came out, they might have had opportunity to have returned. But now they desire*

*a better country, that is, an heavenly: wherefore God is not ashamed to be called their God: for he hath prepared for them a city"* (Hebrews 11:13-16).

Dear readers, it must be well spelt out that Christians are entirely like chalk and cheese from other people on earth. If truly you are born again, then:

a. You belong to Christ (2 Timothy 2:19; Ephesians 5:1-3).
   Whosoever belongs to Christ must be ready to endure temptations and persecutions like Christ. *"Wherefore seeing we also are compassed about with so great a cloud of witnesses, let us lay aside every weight, and the sin which doth so easily beset us, and let us run with patience the race that is set before us, looking unto Jesus the author and finisher of our faith; who for the joy that was set before him endured the cross, despising the shame, and is set down at the right hand of the throne of God"* (Hebrews 12:1-2).

b. You are the light of the world (Matthew 5:13-16).
   Since Christians are the light of the world, they cannot allow that light to be dim with sin or any form of obscurity.

c. You are kings
   Reputable kings are people of honour and decorum; they do not eat in the public, do not dress shabbily, nor do they parade themselves with ladies around the streets. They do not give their strength unto women, nor their ways to that which destroys kings (Prov. 31:1-5). As a Christian, you are a king because Jesus Christ is the King of kings; the word "kings," here, refers to the Christians and not to the earthly kings of villages and towns. If then you know that you are a king, you have to present yourself as a person of honour and not of dishonour, purity and not impurity, chastity and not immoral.

**Satisfaction in Life** 1 Tim. 6:6-10.

The Shulamite was contented with what she had—her beloved, poor Shepherd boy. She said *"my vineyard, which is mine, is before me: thou, O Solomon, must have a thousand, and those that keep the fruit thereof two hundred"* (Song of Solomon 8:12). She was not moved with Solomon's wealth. She was satisfied with the little that her beloved Shepherd boy had. Let what you have satisfies you. The age that we are in is an age of craving for more like the grave that is never satisfied (Proverbs 30:15-16). The Lack of satisfaction makes some men and women to go out with strangers or concubines. Some are not contented with the love, sexual pleasure, properties, profession, and money of their spouses; hence they seek for such outside their matrimonial home. Note that an unmarried Christian should not defile herself for the pleasure and prosperity presented to her by Satan (Matthew 4:1-11).

Contentment with what you have will give you the inner strength to forgo unnecessary passions for more worldly accumulations. Know for sure that:

a. We brought nothing into this world and we shall take nothing out of it (1 Timothy 6:6-10).
b. Worldly pleasure brings spiritual death (1 Timothy 5:6).
c. Contentment with whatever we have in life without greediness is a great gain (Ecclesiastes 2:10-11; 1 Timothy 6:6).

*"Drink waters out of thine own cistern, and running waters out of thine own well. Let thy fountains be dispersed abroad, and rivers of waters in the streets. Let them be only thine own, and not strangers' with thee. Let thy fountain be blessed: and rejoice with the wife of thy youth. Let her be as the loving hind and pleasant roe; let her breasts satisfy thee at all times; and be thou ravished always with her love. And why wilt thou, my*

*son, be ravished with a strange woman, and embrace the bosom of a stranger?"* (Prov. 5:15-20).

The Shulamite lady like Abraham made up her mind that she was not going to be carried away with the seeking of greener pastures. There are some ladies who jump from the frying pan to the fire because of seeking for better men, richer men, men who can carry their responsibilities. It is unfortunate to say that many women, in their bid to go out with rich people, fall into the hands of ritualists and meet their untimely death. Let us read about how Abraham rejected the offer made by a man to make him rich:

*"And the king of Sodom went out to meet him after his return from the slaughter of Chedorlaomer, and of the kings that were with him, at the valley of Shaveh, which is the king's dale. And Melchizedek king of Salem brought forth bread and wine: and he was the priest of the most high God. And he blessed him, and said, blessed be Abram of the most high God, possessor of heaven and earth: And blessed be the most high God, which hath delivered thine enemies into thy hand. And he gave him tithes of all. And the king of Sodom said unto Abram, Give me the persons, and take the goods to thyself. And Abram said to the king of Sodom, I have lift up mine hand unto the LORD, the most high God, the possessor of heaven and earth, That I will not take from a thread even to a shoelatchet, and that I will not take any thing that is thine, lest thou shouldest say, I have made Abram rich"* (Genesis 14:17-23).

Make up your minds that you will not defile your body because of any king's meat; be contented with whatever food your spouse or parents can afford. Be satisfied with the body structure and built-up of your spouse. There is nothing in the body of that strange woman or man that your spouse does not have. It is the same anatomy and

307

the same pleasure that can be derived from it. Do not be deceived! There is no better thing that a strange person can offer you than hell.

**Single Purpose**; 1 Cor. 9:24-26; Prov.; Heb. 11:8-10; Dan. 1:8.

*"My beloved put in his hand by the hole of the door, and my bowels were moved for him. I rose up to open to my beloved; and my hands dropped with myrrh, and my fingers with sweet smelling myrrh, upon the handles of the lock. I opened to my beloved; but my beloved had withdrawn himself, and was gone: my soul failed when he spake: I sought him, but I could not find him; I called him, but he gave me no answer. The watchmen that went about the city found me, they smote me, they wounded me; the keepers of the walls took away my veil from me. I charge you, O daughters of Jerusalem, if ye find my beloved, that ye tell him, that I am sick of love. What is thy beloved more than another beloved, O thou fairest among women? What is thy beloved more than another beloved that thou dost so charge us?"* (Song of Solomon 5:4-9).

She was determined to seek who her soul loves, not for prosperity, power, and prestige but for love sake. Other men may have money and honey but looking at such should not be your goal. Be of single purpose—living for Him alone. Make up your mind not to defile yourself but plan to please Him who has redeemed you from sin and Satan.

a. Be a man/woman of a single eye (Luke 11:34; Proverb 4:20-27).
b. Be a man/woman of a single goal (1 Corinthians 9:24-26; Hebrews 11:8-10).
c. Be ready to do the will of Him that your soul loves (John 9:4).

## Strong Determination

*"I charge you, O ye daughters of Jerusalem, by the roes, and by the hinds of the field, that ye stir not up, nor awake my love, till he please"* (Song of Solomon 2:7).

Christians are to strongly determine not to allow any worldly counsellors to derail them from following Christ. Elisha was not supposed to obtain the anointing of Elijah because he was just a servant not a son of the prophet. His strong determination to get a double portion of the anointing of Elijah helped him not to allow any distraction. A Strong determination to live an uncompromising life helps a man or woman to patiently wait for the gold not the glittering rubbish.

*"Cast not away therefore your confidence, which hath great recompence of reward. For ye have need of patience, that, after ye have done the will of God, ye might receive the promise. For yet a little while, and he that shall come will come, and will not tarry. Now the just shall live by faith: but if any man drawback, my soul shall have no pleasure in him. But we are not of them who draw back unto perdition; but of them that believe to the saving of the soul"* (Hebrews 10:35-39).

Strong determination involves:

 a. Readiness to pay the price of following Christ to the end (Luke 14:28-33)
 b. Refusal to be distracted from achieving your goal (Song of Solomon 2:7; 2 Kings 2:1-15).
 c. Rejection of every form of pleasure of the palace (Daniel 1:8; Hebrews 11:24-27).
 d. Renouncement of every dream killer (Romans 8:35-39).

*James Fabiyi*

## Self Discipline

*"I am a wall, and my breasts like towers: then was I in his eyes as one that found favour"* (Song of Solomon 8:10). She refused to be a door, defiled, dis-virgined lady. She controlled her passion for sexual relationship with a man. Though she decided to marry the Shepherd boy and determined to be only his, she needed to do more than that. Decision and determination without discipline will be fruitless efforts. *"And every man that striveth for the mastery is temperate in all things. Now they do it to obtain a corruptible crown; but we an incorruptible. I therefore so run, not as uncertainly; so fight I, not as one that beateth the air: But I keep under my body, and bring it into subjection: lest that by any means, when I have preached to others, I myself should be a castaway"* (1 Corinthians 9:25-27). Self-control and restraint from worldly pleasures enhance stability and steadfastness during the storms of temptations. It helps our anchor to hold onto the solid rock.

What does it take to be self-disciplined?

   a. Deny self of worldliness and worldly amusement (1 John 2:15-17).
   b. Deprive yourself of some things that may not necessarily be sinful (1 Cor. 9:27).

## Sound Principle

*"My beloved is mine, and I am his: he feedeth among the lilies. Until the day break, and the shadows flee away, turn, my beloved, and be thou like a roe or a young hart upon the mountains of Bether. My beloved is gone down into his garden, to the beds of spices, to feed in the gardens, and to gather lilies. I am my beloved's, and my beloved is mine: he feedeth among the lilies"* (Song 2:16-17; 6:2-3).

The Shulamite lady had a sound principle. She was not going to defile herself for she believed that her husband would soon be with her. The Rechabites stood by the commandment that their forefathers had given them. They plainly told the prophet Jeremiah that nothing in this world would make them renounce to the principle of not drinking wine, nor dwelling in the house, nor plant vineyards.

*"The word which came unto Jeremiah from the LORD in the days of Jehoiakim the son of Josiah king of Judah, saying, Go unto the house of the Rechabites, and speak unto them, and bring them into the house of the LORD, into one of the chambers, and give them wine to drink. Then I took Jaazaniah the son of Jeremiah, the son of Habaziniah, and his brethren, and all his sons, and the whole house of the Rechabites; And I brought them into the house of the LORD, into the chamber of the sons of Hanan, the son of Igdaliah, a man of God, which was by the chamber of the princes, which was above the chamber of Maaseiah the son of Shallum, the keeper of the door: And I set before the sons of the house of the Rechabites pots full of wine, and cups, and I said unto them, Drink ye wine. But they said, We will drink no wine: for Jonadab the son of Rechab our father commanded us, saying, Ye shall drink no wine, neither ye, nor your sons for ever: Neither shall ye build house, nor sow seed, nor plant vineyard, nor have any: but all your days ye shall dwell in tents; that ye may live many days in the land where ye be strangers. Thus have we obeyed the voice of Jonadab the son of Rechab our father in all that he hath charged us, to drink no wine all our days, we, our wives, our sons, nor our daughters; Nor to build houses for us to dwell in: neither have we vineyard, nor field, nor seed: But we have dwelt in tents, and have obeyed, and done according to all that Jonadab our father commanded us."* (Jeremiah 35:1-9)

The mother of King Lemuel instructed him to build up a sound principle of not defiling himself with wine and women (Proverbs 30:1-5). Job's principle was that he would not think upon a maid (Job 31:1). To operate a sound principle, you need to:

a. Draw guidelines that can help you live an uncompromising life (Job 31:1; Daniel 1:8).
b. Depend on the Word of God for daily living (Psalm 119:9-11).

## Sustaining Prayer

*"I am my beloved's, and his desire is toward me. Come, my beloved, let us go forth into the field; let us lodge in the villages"* (Song of Solomon 7:10-11).

The Shulamite lady was praying for divine assistance from her lover. She was praying for sustenance. The Bible says *"Cast thy burden upon the LORD, and he shall sustain thee: he shall never suffer the righteous to be moved"* (Psalm 55:22). When the Disciples of Christ were faced with persecution from their opponents, they went into a place to pray for courage, strength, and sustenance (Acts 4:23-33). By our physical strength shall no man prevail and overcome temptation, so we need to:

a. Pray for the grace to stand firm during temptations (Acts 4:23-33).
b. Pray for the way to escape during temptations (1 Corinthians 10:13).

   1.   Jesus is my Saviour, I shall not be moved;
In His love and favour, I shall not be moved,
Just like a tree that's planted by the waters,
Lord, I shall not be moved.

*Chorus*
*I shall not be, I shall not be moved;*
*I shall not be, I shall not be moved;*
*Just like a tree that's planted by the waters,*
*Lord, I shall not be moved.*

2. In my Christ abiding, I shall not be moved;
   In His love I'm hiding, I shall not be moved,
   Just like a tree that's planted by the waters,
   Lord, I shall not be moved.

3. If I trust Him ever, I shall not be moved;
   He will fail me never, I shall not be moved,
   Just like a tree that's planted by the waters,
   Lord, I shall not be moved.

4. On His word I'm feeding, I shall not be moved;
   He's the One that's leading, I shall not be moved,
   Just like a tree that's planted by the waters,
   Lord, I shall not be moved.

# Bibliography

Ainsworth H. Annotations on the Pentateuch or the Five Books of Moses; the Psalms of David and the Song of Solomon. Vol II. Published by Blackie and Son: Edinburgh, London. MDCCCXLIII.

Barnes A. (1834). Notes on the Bible. Retrieved May 12, 2009 from http://www.studylight.org/com/bnb/view.cgi?book=1jo&chapter=002 with permission from Jeff Garrison of Study Light.

Cole M.S. Song of Solomon. Retrieved May 10, 2009 from http://www.westarkchurchofchrist.org/library/songofsongs.htm with permission.

Constable T. L. (2004). Notes on Song of Solomon. 2004 Edition. 34P

Durham J. (1840). Commentary of the Song of Songs. Retrieved May 10, 2009 from http://www.puritansermons.com/Durham/durindx.htm with permission.

Hunt D. G. Part four: Dress of women Christian and un-christian dress. Retrieved May 10, from 2009 http://ncbible.org/Resources/FWORD04.PDF

Vaughan H. Modesty. Retrieved May 10, 2009 from http://christlifemin.org/publications/Newsletter/newsletter_2001-2/newsletter_2001-2.htm

CPSIA information can be obtained at www.ICGtesting.com
Printed in the USA
LVOW13s0727170114

369742LV00001B/22/P